Beyond Shareholder Wealth Maximisation

The corporate objective, namely, in whose interests a company should be run, is the most important theoretical and practical issue confronting us today, as this core objective animates or should animate every decision a company makes. Despite decades of debate, however, there is no consensus regarding what the corporate objective is or ought to be, but clarity on this issue is necessary in order to explain and guide corporate behaviour, as different objectives could lead to different analyses and solutions to the same corporate governance problem. In addition to the study on the corporate objective in Anglo-American jurisdictions, the discussion of this topic in the context of China is also very important on the grounds that China has become the second largest economy in the world and is playing an increasingly significant role in global affairs. Though a socialist state, China has also been relying heavily on the corporate vehicle as the most important business organisational form to ensure its rapid economic development since its market reforms in 1978. Adolf Berle and Gardiner Means's observation made over eight decades ago that large public companies dominate the world remains true today, not only in the West but also in China. The regulation and governance of such companies will have a material impact on the further development of the Chinese economy, which could in turn directly affect the world economy. Company law and corporate governance therefore receive much attention and have become a vital issue in China. Although the current focus is primarily on corporate performance, the fundamental question at the heart of corporate governance, namely the corporate objective, is still unresolved.

Contrary to the widely held belief that the corporate objective should be maximising shareholder wealth, this book seeks to demonstrate that the shareholder wealth maximisation approach is both descriptively inaccurate and normatively unsuitable. As an antithesis to it, stakeholder theory generally develops to be a more suitable substitute. Justifications and responses to its main criticisms are offered from descriptive, normative and instrumental aspects, whilst new techniques of balancing competing interests and more workable guidance for directors' behaviour are brought forward as essential modifications. Along with the unique characteristics of socialist states, the stakeholder model is expected to find solid ground in China and guide the future development of corporate governance.

This book will be important and useful to researchers and students of corporate law, corporate governance, business and management studies.

Min Yan is a Lecturer in Business Law and the Director of the BSc Business with Law Programme at the School of Business and Management, Queen Mary University of London, UK. His research interests are generally in the fields of corporate law, corporate governance and comparative business law studies.

Routledge Research in Corporate Law

Beyond Shareholder Wealth Maximisation

Towards a More Suitable Corporate Objective for Chinese Companies

Min Yan

LONDON AND NEW YORK

First published 2018 by Routledge

2 Park Square, Milton Park, Abingdon, Oxfordshire OX14 4RN
52 Vanderbilt Avenue, New York, NY 10017

Routledge is an imprint of the Taylor & Francis Group, an informa business

First issued in paperback 2019

British Library Cataloguing in Publication Data
A catalogue record for this book is available from the British Library

Library of Congress Cataloging in Publication Data
Names: Yan, Min (writer on corporate law), author.
Title: Beyond shareholder wealth maximisation : towards a more suitable
    corporate objective for Chinese companies / Min Yan.
Description: Abingdon, Oxon [UK] ; New York : Routledge, 2017. |
    Series: Routledge research in corporate law | Includes bibliographical
    references and index.
Identifiers: LCCN 2017022756| ISBN 9781138288867 (hbk) | ISBN
    9781315267616 (ebk)
Subjects: LCSH: Stockholders—Legal status, laws, etc.—China. |
    Stockholder wealth—China. | Corporate governance—Law and
    legislation—China. | Corporation law—China.
Classification: LCC KNQ1077 .Y33 2017 | DDC 346.51/0666—dc23
LC record available at https://lccn.loc.gov/2017022756

ISBN: 978–1-138–28886–7 (hbk)
ISBN: 978–0-367–88583–0 (pbk)

Typeset in ITC Galliard Std
by Swales & Willis, Exeter, Devon, UK

Contents

For Becky and Allen

Table of cases

Table of statutes

UK statutes and regulations

US statues and regulations

Chinese statues and regulations

Abbreviations

BLE	Behavioural Law and Economics
BOD	Board of Directors
BOS	Board of Supervisors
CA	Companies Act
CLRSG	Company Law Review Steering Group
CPC	Communist Party of China
CSRC	China Securities Regulatory Commission
CUP	Cambridge University Press
DGCL	Delaware General Corporate Law
DTI	Department of Trade and Industries
ESV	Enlightened Shareholder Value
FRC	Financial Reporting Council
IPO	Initial Public Offering
JSLC	Joint Stock Limited Company
KMT	*Kuomingtang* (Nationalist Party of China)
LLC	Limited Liability Company
LTSD	Long-Term Sustainable Development
NRC	National Resource Commission
OECD	Organisation for Economic Co-operation and Development
OUP	Oxford University Press
PRC	People's Republic of China
R&D	Research & Development
SEC	Securities and Exchange Commission
SOE	State-Owned Enterprise
SWM	Shareholder Wealth Maximisation

Acknowledgements

Some of the material in this book draws on my previous articles. I am grateful to Kluwer Law International and Sweet & Maxwell for their kind permission to use materials reproduced in the book. The articles are:

'The Corporate Objective Revisited: Part I' (2017) 38 *Business Law Review* 14–20.

'The Corporate Objective Revisited: Part II' (2017) 38 *Business Law Review* 55–60.

'Agency Theory Re-examined: An Agency Relationship and Residual Claimant Perspective' (2015) 26 *International Company and Commercial Law Review* 139–144.

'Evolution of the Corporation and the Shareholders' Role in China' (2015) 26 *International Company and Commercial Law Review* 355–363.

'The Failure of the Entity Model' (2013) 34 *Company Lawyer* 272–280.

Foreword

The struggle to provide an acceptable corporate objective has challenged company law scholars and law makers for many years. Many of these debates can be traced back to earlier periods, such as the debate between Berle and Means in the 1930s. Dr Min Yan sees the debate over the corporate objective as being the most important theoretical and practical issue facing the corporation today. By asking in whose interests a company should be run, Yan seeks to re-examine the priority that is given to shareholder wealth maximisation and its tendency to foster short-termism and externalisation.

Yan is not alone in looking at the effects of shareholder wealth maximisation, as the debate over the short-termism in public companies has raged in recent times, especially since the recent global financial crisis. This problem was highlighted in the United Kingdom by the Kay Review in 2012, which noted that the survival of the modern public company is much less dependent than it once was on shareholder equity and physical capital. This has focused attention upon significant changes that have taken place in the role of modern shareholders in public companies. Many observers, such as Margaret Blair, have therefore called for a rethinking of corporate governance to ensure that it is fit for the twenty-first century and allow it to take into account the contributions to the corporation that are made by non-shareholders of the company.

Yan's powerful and impressive analysis focuses attention on the degree to which the rhetoric of the shareholder wealth maximisation model of the corporation has been challenged by changes in the nature of shareholder roles in "mature" widely held companies. At a time when shareholders in such companies hold their shares for increasingly short periods of time, accelerated by the effect of electronic technology, they have been more concerned with trading shares or the income streams that they derive from their shares than with efforts to affect the governance of the companies in which they invest. At the same time, shareholders have been prepared to play a passive role in companies, rather than being active participants in internal governance. This has been especially so with companies in Anglo-American markets. But, as Yan effectively demonstrates, the shareholder wealth maximisation model has also had a powerful influence on the model of corporate governance adopted for Chinese public companies. As we will see, he argues that it is time for this to be reassessed.

Yan argues that the dominant shareholder wealth maximisation model is heavily reliant upon agency theory, even though the foundations of this theory are legally questionable. The rhetoric of agency theory has empowered directors and needs to be seen in the context of fiduciary duties that provide the basis for directors to proclaim the centrality of serving shareholder value at the expense of other objectives. As Yan demonstrates, instead of a separation of ownership and control in widely held companies, there has been a progressive insulation of boards from effective shareholder intervention, leading to the emergence of a shareholder primacy model of corporate governance. The reliance upon agency theory has also fostered short-termism in companies and led to management efforts to manipulate share prices, despite the questionable nature of this enterprise, as critics such as Roger Martin pointed out in *Fixing the Game* in 2011.

Whilst shareholders in public companies are able to limit their risks by diversifying their shareholdings amongst a portfolio of companies; others who provide contributions to the corporation, such as employees and creditors, are not able to limit their risks to the same degree. As a result of shareholder diversification of their investment portfolios, they are susceptible to externalisation whereby they are prepared to take excessive risks as their liability will be limited in the event of an investment failure, in contrast to other stakeholders who may be much more vulnerable to corporate risk taking. The lop-sided focus upon shareholder interests in the shareholder wealth maximisation model is seen by Yan as all too readily leading to negative externalities, such as the transfer of company costs to stakeholders, whilst allowing shareholders to retain any received company benefits.

This provides room for arguments in favour of greater reliance upon stakeholder theory, as pioneered by R Edward Freeman in 1984. Yan notes that an instrumental stakeholder model allows stakeholder value to be used to improve corporate performance. This provides room for greater reliance upon trust and irrational altruism, as Lynn Stout has also demonstrated in her consideration of corporate purposes and the myth of shareholder wealth maximisation. Yan provides an illuminating discussion of the advantages of stakeholder theory.

In this book, Yan also provides a nuanced discussion of the evolution of China's company law and its seeming embrace of shareholder wealth maximisation ideas. As an autocratic state-centred legal system, China has fostered powerful state-owned enterprises in which the State is the dominant shareholder and stakeholder. The language of Article 1 of the PRC Company Law 2005 (as amended) speaks of protecting the interests of shareholders in the context of protecting a range of other stakeholders, such as the company and creditors, as well as the importance of "maintaining the socialist economic order". Shareholders are however given special importance through other provisions (such as Article 4) and the centrality of the shareholder meeting which is able to give directions regarding the management of the company. Regulators in China have also fostered the importance of shareholder interests.

However, given the difficulties that shareholders face in giving directions in regard to the management of the company, the board of directors is in a better position to make decisions on behalf of the company. Moreover, as Yan argues, in China shareholders are not in a strong legal position to make directors liable by bringing effective legal action against them through the courts. Not surprisingly, he argues that the dominance of the shareholder centred model in China is far from settled.

Given the importance of other interests, such as the imperative of preserving social stability and improving living standards in China, Yan argues that it is more likely the government will attach more weight to stakeholder factors, such as employment, than to the goal of increasing the profits of shareholders. The strong emphasis in Chinese Company Law (Article 5) upon fostering corporate social responsibility is likely to limit the extent to which companies will be allowed to maximise the interests of shareholders at the expense of other stakeholders and the community. There is much more useful discussion on this theme in this book.

This is a well-argued and important book that engages with major policy questions that currently confront company law reform internationally. The comparative insights presented by Yan in this book strengthen the analysis and enhance the basic theoretic arguments and critique that are its greatest strengths.

Roman Tomasic
Professor of Law, School of Law,
University of South Australia
Visiting Professor of Company Law,
Durham Law School, Durham University

1 Introduction

Today corporate governance has become the single most important issue on the business agenda with incalculable political and social consequences both domestically and globally.[1] What the corporate objective is, namely, in whose interests should a company be run, remains the fundamental question at the heart of corporate governance[2] and the most important issue in corporate governance study today.[3] Despite decades of debate, there is no consensus regarding what the corporate objective is or ought to be. However, clarity on this issue is necessary in order to explain and guide corporate behaviour, as different objectives could lead to different analyses and solutions to the same corporate governance problem. Contrary to the widely held belief that the corporate objective should be shareholder wealth maximisation, this book seeks to look beyond maximising shareholder wealth and demonstrate that it is both descriptively and normatively unsuitable. This book also intends to critically discuss the corporate objective for Chinese companies due to the importance of China's role in the global economic and political arena.[4] After revisiting shareholder wealth maximisation and stakeholder theory, the book advocates the stakeholder model as the basis for Chinese corporate law and corporate governance.

1.1 What is corporate objective and why should we study it?

A company, as any rational activity, requires an objective to justify its behaviour,[5] and its performance can only be measured and evaluated after establishing such

---

1 Stephen Bloomfield, *Theory and Practice of Corporate Governance: An Integrated Approach* (CUP, Cambridge 2013) 3.
2 It is argued that "at the heart of the current global corporate governance debate is a remarkable division of opinion about the fundamental purpose of the corporation". Michael Jensen, 'Value Maximisation, Stakeholder Theory, and the Corporate Objective Function' (2001) 7 *Journal of Applied Corporate Finance* 8, 8.
3 James Walsh, 'Introduction to the "Corporate Objective Revisited" Exchange' (2004) 15 *Organization Science* 349, 349.
4 The World Bank, 'China Overview' at www.worldbank.org/en/country/china/overview [accessed 1 March 2017]. However, as discussed below, the subject of corporate objective is not sufficiently studied or explored by Chinese domestic scholars.
5 It is worth noting that contractarians who believe the company is merely a form of legal fiction question the validity of corporate objective by denying that it possesses an independent legal personality

a criterion. If no goals or expectations exist, it would be impossible to judge the performance of a company and to evaluate how well the directors of the board have performed. Moreover, the key to how obligations/responsibilities should be allocated to achieve the best corporate governance[6] largely depends on such an objective. If, for example, the ultimate corporate objective is the welfare of all stakeholder groups, then a good corporate governance structure should underlie their interests,[7] and board directors should run the company for all stakeholders. Accordingly corporate performance should no longer be solely determined by the share price and the like. In contrast, if shareholder wealth maximisation is the corporate objective, i.e. shareholder interests are the primary concern of the company, then the focal point would turn to understanding shareholders' roles and interests.[8] In this context, directors should run the company to maximise shareholder wealth, and the basic issue in terms of corporate governance therefore becomes whether shareholder interests can be effectively protected and maximised. Consequently, it is of vital importance

with motivations and intentions. The behaviour of the company is paralleled with the behaviour of the market. For example, see Michael Jensen and William Meckling, 'Theory of the Firm: Managerial Behavior, Agency Costs and Ownership Structure' (1976) 3 *Journal of Financial Economics* 305, 311. This idea will be discussed shortly in this chapter as well as in the following chapter. Suffice it to say here that the company has a will to be recognised in law. A company can be held criminally liable where mens rea is required. For example, a company can be indicted for a conspiracy to defraud. See *R v. ICR Haulage Ltd* [1944] KB 551. Also see Sarah Worthington, *Sealy and Worthington's Text, Cases and Materials in Company Law* (11th edn OUP, Oxford 2016) 146–157.

6 Corporate governance is principally about how companies should be structured and directed, which is indeed a rather broad field. For example, issues regarding how companies should be structured include which body within the company should be entitled to make particular decisions, who is eligible to be elected to enjoy such power, how the rights and duties are allocated among various corporate constituents and so forth. Further, which rules, norms or best practices should guide the corporate decision-making, and how to monitor the performance of corporate constituents among others also belong to the realm of corporate governance.

Pursuant to the definition by the *OECD Principle of Corporate Governance 2004*, "[c]orporate governance is the system by which business corporations are directed and controlled. The corporate governance structure specifies the distribution of rights and responsibilities among different participants in the corporation, such as the board, managers, shareholders and other stakeholder, and spells out the rules and procedures for making decisions on corporate affairs. By doing this, it also provides the structure through which the company objectives are set, and the means of attaining those objectives and monitoring performance". This is in fact not materially different from the classic definition in the UK produced by the Cadbury Committee in 1992: "[c]orporate governance is the system by which companies are directed and controlled. Boards of directors are responsible for the governance of their companies. The shareholders' role in governance is to appoint the directors and the auditors and to satisfy themselves that an appropriate governance structure is in place. The responsibilities of the board include setting the company's strategic aims, providing the leadership to put them into effect, supervising the management of the business and reporting to shareholders on their stewardship. The board's actions are subject to laws, regulations and the shareholders in general meeting".

7 The issue of whether it is essential to grant them substantial right for remedies among others will be dealt with in detail in Chapter 5 below.

8 Again it may arguably include the issue of how to protect and improve their rights.

to clarify the ultimate objective of the company, especially the large public ones, in order to solve corporate governance improvement issues, determine the extent to which companies should be directed and managed, and provide guidance to directors.

The corporate objective is arguably one of "the most important theoretical and practical issues confronting us today" because we need it to explain and guide corporate behaviour.[9] In the words of Professor Henry Hu, "the core objectives animate or should animate every decision a corporation makes".[10] Different objectives can lead to different diagnoses and solutions to corporate governance problems.[11] It is also argued that "at the heart of the current global corporate governance debate is a remarkable division of opinion about the fundamental purpose of the corporation".[12] And the answer to this issue becomes increasingly important as the business influences both individuals and societies.[13] If directors take a company in the wrong direction as a result of the corporate objective being incorrect, then this might produce worse results. Put simply, a governance theory cannot begin without a purpose.[14]

Unfortunately, company law in most jurisdictions fails to set out a corporate objective.[15] Though in theory members of companies are able to determine the corporate purpose by including it in the company's constitution (e.g. articles of association), few demand mandatory shareholder primacy. The vast majority of companies' articles do not include a corporate objective.[16]

Moreover, today's large public companies can hardly be seen as entirely private concerns, further complicating the issue. Companies, especially large public ones, are no longer private organisations – they have the ability to exercise social decision-making power.[17] In Professor Parkinson's words, "companies

---

9 James Walsh, 'Introduction to the "Corporate Objective Revisited" Exchange' (2004) 15 *Organization Science* 349, 349.

10 Henry Hu, 'Buffet, Corporate Objectives and the Nature of Sheep' (1997) 19 *Cardozo Law Review* 379, 380.

11 Steve Letza, Xiuping Sun and James Kirkbride, 'Shareholding Versus Stakeholding: A Critical Review of Corporate Governance' (2001) 12 *Corporate Governance: An International Review* 242.

12 Jensen, 'Value Maximisation, Stakeholder Theory, and the Corporate Objective Function' (n 2) 8.

13 Ronald Colombo, 'Ownership, Limited: Reconciling Traditional and Progressive Corporate Law via an Aristotelian Understanding of Ownership' (2008) 34 *Journal of Corporation Law* 247, 248.

14 John Carver, 'A Case for Global Governance Theory: Practitioners Avoid It, Academics Narrow It; the World Needs It' (2012) 18 *Corporate Governance: An International Review* 149, 152.

15 Andrew Keay, *The Corporate Objective* (Edward Elgar, Cheltenham 2011) 9.

16 The distinction between corporate objective and object clauses should be highlighted here. Object clauses, for example as formerly required under English company law, are mainly to define the scope of business and restrict directors' authority. Directors' actions outside these objects are *ultra vires* the company and therefore void. Corporate objective is, however, about the more fundamental and metaphysical issue of corporate governance, namely in whose interests the company should be run.

17 John Parkinson, *Corporate Power and Responsibility: Issues in the Theory of Company Law* (OUP, Oxford 1993) 22.

are able to make choices which have important social consequences: they make private decisions which have public results".[18] More concretely, Mary Stokes points out that:

> The company has become an organization whose significance almost rivals that of the state. It is the primary institution for organizing and employing much of our capital and labour resources and the primary supplier of goods and services in our community.[19]

Thus, as corporate behaviour is limited by political, social and economic environments, the extent to which members can determine the purpose of their company is not unrestricted.

Admittedly, during the preliminary stage of a newly established company, it is usually those entrepreneurial shareholders who take the initiative to seek and recruit essential resources to run the start-up. Whilst other corporate participants also play an important role and contribute indispensable investment, shareholders are more likely to exert a leading role at this stage. Shareholders' contribution is crucial when a new company desperately needs initial monetary capital to purchase machines, raw materials and invest in business projects, which is often the case for a start-up. More importantly, it is not uncommon for a start-up company to have overlapping management and shareholder bodies. Although other corporate participants like employees and suppliers afford equally or more valuable support to the success of the company and thereby should not be subordinated, due to this overlap, shareholders who maintain control (or directly manage the company) normally have a larger role to play at this stage.[20]

However, alongside corporate growth, the contribution and role of shareholders gradually becomes less important, though it is difficult to mark exactly at which point. On the one hand, the company is no longer heavily dependent on equity capital to finance new business projects and corporate expansion. A mature company relies more on accumulated corporate profits after years of operation, and debt funds.[21] On the other, the classic separation of ownership from control

18 Ibid. 10 (footnote omitted).
19 Mary Stokes, 'Company Law and Company Theory' in Sally Wheeler (ed), *The Law of the Business Enterprise* (OUP, Oxford 1994) 107.
20 But this does not necessarily mean companies at this stage are more likely to focus on their self-interest maximisation at the expense of others. It is not uncommon to see many start-ups focus more on customer satisfaction and other stakeholders' interests instead of purely share values. Indeed, it is very difficult in practice for a start-up to succeed if it only looks to shareholder returns. However, it is also understandable that small closed companies may primarily serve the purposes of their members.
21 A start-up company without a track record and explicit profit scenario finds it very difficult and costly to raise debt capital. In contrast, for a mature company, it is much easier and less costly to do so. But also noteworthy is that more and more high-tech start-ups are financed by venture capital nowadays.

is almost inexorable as the company expands. Widely dispersed shareholders can become rationally apathetic. In particular, after adopting strategies of diversified and balanced portfolios, shareholders or institutional investors are less concerned about the success of any one particular company than with their overall portfolio. As will be discussed later, the interests of diversified shareholders can be different from those of the company. Furthermore, it is not impossible for a shareholder to wish for one of her investee companies to fail in order to obtain higher aggregated proceeds from the portfolio. For example, if a hedge fund were to sell short a particular company's shares, there are then ample grounds for it to wish the company to be poorly run or even fail. Due to the alienation of the interest in those shares as a result of having sold them short or some other modern financial arrangement, certain shareholders' personal interests, particularly certain types of funds, may run completely counter to the interests of a given company. Consequently, "the old language of property and ownership no longer serves us in the modern world because it no longer describes what a company really is".[22]

On the contrary, other corporate participants continue to provide indispensable resources and actively participate in corporate activities in pursuit of success. Unlike shareholders, who are able to mitigate risks through diversification, most other corporate participants cannot do so. Consequently, shareholders may not be particularly concerned about the success of a given company whilst the welfare of other corporate participants is still closely tied to the very company to which they have contributed and in which they have invested. As a result, for large public companies which are of course mature enough, there are few grounds for the shareholders to determine the corporate objective. Indeed, when a company transitions into a "mature" stage, it is questionable whether the original founder's objective, if any, remains unchanged.[23]

The corporate objective is not a new issue – the debate has been continuing for years. Berle and Dodd's debate in the 1930s about corporate purpose[24] continues today: is the sole aim of companies to create benefits for shareholders at

---

22 Professor Charles Handy explained: "[t]he old language suggests the wrong priorities, leads to inappropriate policies and screens out new possibilities. The idea of a corporation as the property of the current holders of shares is confusing because it does not make clear where power lies. As such, the notion is an affront to natural justice because it gives inadequate recognition, and who are, increasingly, its principal assets". Charles Handy, 'The Citizen Corporation' (1997) 75 *Harvard Business Review* 26, 26–27. Also, it would be too narrow to define the property only as financial assets, as human capitals and such like provided by stakeholders should also be counted.

23 It should be noted that this book focuses on the corporate objective of those large public companies which can be defined as mature. There is an interesting issue here: most large public companies have arisen from small closed companies. At some point, the corporate purpose may therefore have changed. However, when this occurred is difficult to explicitly quantify, and so the criterion of the mature company might be a direction for further study.

24 E Merrick Dodd, 'For Whom Are Corporate Managers Trustees?' (1932) 45 *Harvard Law Review* 1145–1163; Adolf Berle, 'For Whom Corporate Managers Are Trustees: A Note' (1932) 45 *Harvard Law Review* 1365–1372.

all times, or should broader concerns be taken into account? In the beginning, Berle asserted that all powers granted to corporation and management alike should always be exercised in the interests of the shareholders as sole beneficiaries. But not long afterwards, Dodd questioned Berle's doctrine of corporate power in trust, arguing that a company should perhaps consider the interests of people other than the owners, particularly in the public utility field.[25] Berle responded that if the company is not run solely in the shareholders' interests, then in practice managerial power could not be effectively controlled, or worse, the power of unchecked management might become absolute.[26] However, it is not difficult to see that in his seminal work *The Modern Corporation and Private Property*, co-authored with Gardiner Means, corporate power serves more than just the shareholders' interests; it might also be regarded as in trust for society as a whole to a certain extent, as the so-called "owners" have surrendered their control and responsibility over the corporation and corporate property. As a social institution, in the authors' view, large modern corporations should at least in theory consider other corporate participants' interests rather than solely the shareholders' interests.

The source of confusion here is that Berle's trust theory, which facilitates the development of fiduciary duties,[27] is one of the most powerful weapons for the shareholder primacy approach. But in concluding *The Modern Corporation and Private Property*, Berle opened the question by suggesting that the corporation might have a broader responsibility to the wider community. In fact, Berle does not totally disagree with Dodd's view. His main concern is that if managers are not solely accountable to stockholders, their discretionary power may become absolute in practice, because no alternative and reasonably enforceable mechanism exists for them to be accountable to multiple or other constituents (e.g. employees, creditors, suppliers, customers, local community or environment) as well.

Over time, two opposing academic schools have emerged: one is the shareholder wealth maximisation approach (i.e. the shareholder model), which argues that the primary goal of commercial companies is to maximise shareholder wealth; and the other is the stakeholder theory (i.e. the stakeholder model), which argues that the interests of non-shareholding stakeholder groups should not be subordinated to those of shareholders, otherwise society as a whole would suffer.

---

25 Dodd (n 24) 1160.
26 Indeed, Berle makes the point clearer in a slightly later paper where he argues that until an alternative, reasonably enforceable scheme of responsibilities is introduced, the purpose of the company to maximise profits for shareholders remains unchanged, even though shareholders have already surrendered the control and exert a less significant role. Berle, 'For Whom Corporate Managers Are Trustees: A Note' (n 24) 1367.
27 Fiduciary duties generally refer to actions taken in good faith and in the best interests of the beneficiaries. For example, the court held in *Re Smith and Fawcett Ltd* [1942] Ch 304 that directors must act in a bona fide manner in what they consider . . . is in the interests of the company.

1.2 Shareholder wealth maximisation as corporate objective

Shareholder wealth maximisation (hereafter, SWM), or shareholder primacy,[28] is generally viewed by most people in the Anglo-American legal sphere as the primary, if not the only, corporate objective, especially under the prevalent thought that "an organization should have a single valued objective".[29] According to neoclassical economics, shareholders are regarded as residual claimants for the income stream after all fixed claims are met; as a consequence, it is argued that their interests can be aligned with the interests of the company, and therefore maximising their interests would be equal to maximising corporate interests as a whole. Aggregate social welfare is also deemed to be increased when shareholders' interest is enhanced. The board of directors and their delegates of daily management, executive officers, are as a result expected to serve shareholder value. Providing better employee welfare, improving customer services, and contributing more to communities among other things, are not considered proper for managers to pursue unless these activities can serve as a means to maximise shareholder value in due course. By the same token, when conflicts arise between shareholders and non-shareholders, directors and corporate officers are only required to address the interests of the former and to take actions to produce the highest possible returns for them, even at the expense of non-shareholder groups' interests.

Companies are thought of as economic entities which should "strive to maximise value for shareholders", and profit maximisation thereby becomes the baseline goal for directors and executives.[30] When asked, "who owns the large public companies", most senior managers of companies in the US answer: it is the shareholders.[31] Similarly, according to a survey of course syllabuses of US law schools, many faculties to this day still believe the focus on shareholder financial returns is *settled law*.[32] When those law or business students grow up

---

28 According to Professor Bainbridge, shareholder primacy is not exactly the same as SWM. In his mind, SWM just means the corporate objective, whilst shareholder primacy also requires the ultimate control of the company resting in the hands of the shareholders in addition to shareholder wealth maximization; Stephen Bainbridge, *The New Corporate Governance in Theory and Practice* (OUP, New York 2008) 110. However, as shareholder primacy will inevitably cause shareholder wealth maximisation, this book is not going to distinguish these two terms unless the context explicitly indicates.

29 Jensen, 'Value Maximisation, Stakeholder Theory, and the Corporate Objective Function' (n 2) 10.
    Although the impact of German law on China, for instance its dual board structure, should not be ignored, China's corporate governance structures in general emulate the stylised Anglo-American model. For example, see On Kit Tam, 'Ethical Issues in the Evolution of Corporate Governance in China' (2002) 37 *Journal of Business Ethics* 303, 303. Therefore, this book will primarily focus on the Anglo-American jurisdictions.

30 Jonathan Macey, *Corporate Governance: Promises Kept, Promises Broken* (Princeton University Press, Princeton 2008) 2.

31 Ibid. 4.

32 Darrell West, 'The Purpose of the Corporation in Business and Law School Curricula' (July 19, 2011) Governance Studies at Brookings 18 at www.brookings.edu/~/media/research/files/papers/2011/7/19%20corporation%20west/0719_corporation_west.pdf [accessed 30 October 2015].

and become corporate executives, they will undoubtedly view the corporate objective – namely, their main responsibility – as serving shareholder interests in all circumstances. Managing companies for purposes other than SWM is as a result seen at best as unethical and at worst as illegitimate. It is not surprising then when Professors Hansmann and Kraakman claim "there is no longer any serious competitor to the view that corporate law should principally strive to increase long-term shareholder value",[33] or when Milton Friedman asserts:

> In a free enterprise, private-property system, a corporate executive is an employee of the owners of the business. He has a direct responsibility to his employers. That responsibility is to conduct the business in accordance with their desires, which generally will be to make as much money as possible while conforming to the basic rules of society.[34]

In *Dodge v. Ford Motor Co*, often cited by shareholder primacists as the classic case for supporting shareholders' preeminent position, the Michigan Supreme Court asserted the superior position of shareholders by stating: "the ultimate objective of companies as currently enshrined in law – i.e. to generate maximum value for shareholders – is in principle the best means also of securing overall prosperity and welfare".[35] More recently, Chancellor Leo Strine of the Delaware Chancery Court also wrote: "the corporate law requires directors, as a matter of their duty of loyalty, to pursue a good faith strategy to maximize profits for the stockholders".[36]

Although pivotal contributions from various corporate stakeholders such as employees, suppliers and communities should not be ignored as regards the survival and prosperity of a company, taking their interests into account is a means of facilitating the end of maximising shareholder wealth in the eyes of most people, including the general public, business professionals, corporate lawyers and even policy makers. This point is well exemplified by the so-called "enlightened shareholder value" (hereafter, ESV) approach in section 172(1) of the UK's *Companies Act 2006*. As Professor Paul Davies argues, non-shareholder interests would not be taken into consideration unless "it is desirable to do so in order to promote the success of the company for the benefit of its members as a whole".[37] Logically, it might not be unacceptable under certain circumstances to sacrifice non-shareholders' interests for the sake of shareholder primacy.

---

33 Henry Hansmann and Reinier Kraakman, 'The End of History for Corporate Law' (2001) 89 *Georgetown Law Journal* 439.
34 Milton Friedman, 'The Social Responsibility of Business Is to Increase Its Profits' *New York Times* magazine (13 September 1970) 32, 33.
35 (1919) 170 NW 684 (US). An in-depth review of this case will be provided in Chapter 2.
36 Leo Strine, 'Our Continuing Struggle with the Idea that For-Profit Corporations Seek Profit' (2012) 47 *Wake Forest Law Review* 135,155.
37 Paul Davies and Sarah Worthington, *Principles of Modern Company Law* (10th edn Sweet & Maxwell, London 2016) 503. Some more detail discussion on the ESV is provided in Chapter 2, section 2.5.1 and Chapter 6, section 6.4.

SWM as a corporate objective and norm of corporate governance is regarded as the fundamental view of modern corporate law scholarship.[38] Even opponents of this approach concede its prevalence and dominance.[39] The most direct impact of SWM is to require board directors and corporate officers to strive for the highest possible shareholder profits; any behaviour that is inconsistent with SWM is subsequently considered as *corporate deviance*.[40] Basically, such an objective and governance norm determine that company law and good corporate governance practice should endeavour to design a system which on the one hand centres on shareholders' interests, and on the other incentivises those who run the company to make as much profit as possible by aligning the interests of directors and managers with the interests of shareholders.

A straightforward way to ensure the central position of shareholders within the company is to empower shareholders or disempower directors,[41] for example, by shifting the decision-making power from the board of directors to shareholders, increasing the involvement of shareholders and/or strengthening directors' responsibilities. Many people, including academics and policy makers, consider shareholder powerlessness to be a main reason for the 2008 global financial crisis, since managerial power had not been effectively checked.[42] This also explains why after recent financial crises, Western governments have responded by empowering shareholders. Increasing shareholder power by expanding their participatory rights encourages them to be more active and play a larger role.

1.2.1 What are the problems?

Although agency theory[43] has replaced traditional proprietorship theory[44] and has been generally regarded as the theoretical basis for SWM since the 1970s,

---

38 For example, see D Gordon Smith, 'The Shareholder Primacy Norm' (1997) 23 *Journal of Corporation Law* 277, 278. A norm (social norm) is, according to Professor Posner, "neither promulgated by an official source, such as a court or legal sanctions, yet is regularly complied with". Richard Posner, 'Social Norms and the Law: An Economic Approach' (1997) 87 *American Economic Review* 365, 365.

39 For example, see Kent Greenfield, 'Saving the World with Corporate Law' (2007) 57 *Emory Law Journal* 947, 948–949.

40 Macey, *Corporate Governance* (n 30) 2.

41 Namely, by giving them less power which is most obvious in some emerging countries like China.

42 Though there are oppositions to this view which will be discussed in Chapter 3, the viewpoint that directors and managers should be more closely monitored is shared by the vast majority. In short, neither the collapse of Enron nor the global crisis has changed the prevalence of SWM in principle.

43 The Chicago school of neoclassical economists has deeply influenced the ideology of SWM since the 1970s. In particular, Jensen and Meckling develop the agency theory based on Alchian and Demsetz's contractarianism which regarded the firm as a nexus of contracts. Directors and managers are elected and employed to run the company on behalf of and for the benefit of shareholders. Jensen and Meckling, 'Theory of the Firm' (n 5). Armen Alchian and Harold Demsetz, 'Production, Information Cost, and Economic Organization' (1972) 62 *American Economic Review* 777, 777–795.

44 I.e. the concept of ownership provides a doctrinal justification for the shareholder-centric model. The traditional logic is one of property rights, which is based on the theory that owners have the

the principal-agent model is indeed problematic. There are no explicit or implicit contracts between directors and shareholders, and the former are employed by the company instead of by the latter – owing fiduciary duties to the company is the general principle.[45] Issues such as separate legal personality and extensive board autonomy cannot be explained by agency theory – this is fully explored in Chapter 2. Suffice it to say here, the economic terms 'principal' and 'agent' do not bear the exact same meaning as their juridical counterparts; moreover agency theory fails to provide a rationale for *sui generis* power or board autonomy.[46]

Since the separation of control from ownership in modern companies, shareholders no longer operate the business in person or take direct control of the company.[47] In this context, is it meaningful to contend the agent nature of directors where shareholders as "principals" have little right to order or instruct their agents? Along with the changing nature of ownership, relinquishing control rights by shareholders is seen as achieving optimum efficiency by authorising directors to manage companies for a good return on their investment. From this perspective, it is necessary to grant directors independent positions and unrestrained power to make corporate decisions, whilst only being subject to the most fundamental principles, such as fiduciary duties. If shareholders are allowed or able to constantly interfere with management, along with the risk that majority shareholders may procure disproportionate profits at the expense of minority ones, efficiency would be substantially compromised. The "empowerment of centralized management" is one vital element to ensure the effectiveness of widely held public companies in terms of the significance of "business decisions with . . . speed and efficiency".[48] Even in the most traditional principal-agent model, directors as agents equally need decision-making powers to run the company; they must retain at least some discretion. As Professor Bebchuk opines, in

right to force the company to be run in their interests. As will be fully discussed in the next chapter, it is now well established in modern company law that the company cannot be owned and what shareholders have are only shares in the company.

45 Per Dillon LJ in *Multinational Gas & Petrochemical Co Ltd v. Multinational Gas & Petrochemical Services Ltd* [1983] Ch 258, 288: "the directors indeed stand in a fiduciary relationship to the company . . . and they owe fiduciary duties to the company though not to creditors, present or future, or to individual shareholders". Also section 170 of the *Companies Act 2006* explicitly provides that directors' general duties are owed to the company.

46 Though there appears to be a trend for shareholder empowerment, as will be discussed in Chapter 2 most corporate decisions remain in the hands of the board of directors.

47 It should be noted that in some closed private companies, shareholders will usually also be the directors/managers, or a comparatively high concentration of ownership structure exists. Under these circumstances the agency cost is comparatively lower and easier to control since the divergence is smaller and there is more incentive for shareholders to monitor. However, since most literature on corporate governance including corporate objectives either explicitly or implicitly assumes that only publicly traded companies are subject to analysis, this book will mainly focus on those public companies where shares are dispersed and shareholders are separated from management in general.

48 Leo Strine, 'Toward a True Corporate Republic: A Traditionalist Response to Bebchuck's Solution for Improving Corporate America' (2006) 119 *Harvard Law Review* 1759, 1762–1764.

the US, the power of the board comes not as a result of separating ownership and control; but rather, is partly as a result of legal rules that insulate boards from shareholder intervention.[49] Otherwise, it would be pointless to elect directors to run companies in the event that every decision had to be made by, or negotiated with, shareholders who are the so-called "principals".

Besides, SWM means, as the term itself suggests, generating the highest possible returns for shareholders, which mainly encompasses maximising the value of shares of the company and the dividends to shareholders. In practice, these are frequently simplified into one assignment for the directors – to maximise the share price for shareholders in order to secure their highest possible utility from the investment. The emphasis on SWM gives rise to the almost unavoidable inclination towards short-termism, as discussed in Chapter 2, which means directors and their delegated managers are explicitly or implicitly forced to adopt short-term strategies in order to boost the immediate share price to satisfy shareholders. Short-termism is difficult to resist if management's personal wealth is closely tied to corporate performance measured by share price. Management may subsequently have a strong inducement to manipulate the share price to acquire larger bonuses and the like, which are principally based on those share prices. High trading frequency is a typical example of the lopsided focus on immediate profit from the fluctuations in the stock markets. Empirical studies clearly show that the average holding period of shares has significantly decreased in recent decades.[50] It is not infrequent for certain institutional investors[51] to use a price index or computer software to complete a stock transaction without getting any details of the investee companies. Directors would therefore be under pressure to adopt corresponding strategies to satisfy shareholders' appetites.

The fact that companies are not able to succeed or achieve business goals in the absence of various non-shareholding stakeholders' contributions cannot be ignored either. Apart from equity capital provided by shareholders, other stakeholders' investments such as the credit provided by creditors, the labour and know-how provided by employees, the services and products provided by suppliers, and the infrastructure provided by the government are indispensable. More importantly, these stakeholders become increasingly more critical to the survival and prosperity of modern companies, whilst the importance of shareholders is

---

49 Lucian Bebchuk, 'Letting Shareholders Set the Rules' (2006) 119 *Harvard Law Review* 1784, 1784 and 1804.

50 Paul Farrow, 'How Long Does the Average Share Holding Last? Just 22 Seconds' *The Telegraph* (London 18 January 2012) www.telegraph.co.uk/finance/personalfinance/investing/9021946/How-long-does-the-average-share-holding-last-Just-22-seconds.html [accessed 1 March 2017].

51 Institutional investors are regarded as "professional investors which invest on behalf of or for the benefit of beneficiaries". Normally, they have a larger role to play in corporate governance due to their comparatively concentrated shareholdings. Although it is thought institutional shareholders are beneficial to improve the level of corporate governance, Professor Blair insightfully argues, they have a limited role to play and may even exacerbate the so-called agency problem due to the added intermediation. Margaret Blair, *Ownership and Control: Rethinking Corporate Governance for the Twenty-First Century* (The Brookings Institution, Washington 1995) 145–201.

constantly decreasing.[52] The role of equity issues and physical capital in investment "is much less important than it was" in modern public companies at present.[53] An individual shareholder is less concerned about the success of any one particular company than in the success of her overall portfolio, especially after establishing a diversified and balanced portfolio, and it is not impossible from time to time for a shareholder to wish that one of her investee companies would fail in order to obtain higher aggregated proceeds from the portfolio.[54]

Meanwhile, the welfare of non-shareholding stakeholders cannot be unaffected by corporate performance.[55] For example, when a company is badly run or becomes insolvent, creditors may not get back any interest or the principal loaned, and employees may be made redundant. They have an interest in the company but cannot obtain enough protection from the contracts between themselves and the company. These contracts are inevitably incomplete by virtue of the unbalanced bargaining power, informational asymmetry and bounded rationality. On the grounds that the liability of shareholders would not exceed their initial investment, if the company is approaching bankruptcy, shareholders may take excessive risks. Given that they have no material interests (namely, they get few chances to be paid), shareholders could possibly choose to gamble on risky investment projects. There is a severe potential for externalisation as shareholders are able to "reap all of the benefits of risky activity but do not bear all of the cost".[56] Worse still, in the event that shareholders have little chance of recovering anything, they will have a much stronger preference for high-risk activities, especially if their so-called residual claim has gone under water in this setting.[57] Moreover, the empty voting facilitated by modern financial and hedging techniques may further exacerbate the negative externalisation.

Many problems occur when SWM is given as the corporate objective. This is especially prominent after the corporate scandals and financial crisis of the 2000s. At best, it may not lead to the best corporate governance practice, and at worst it may provide the wrong emphasis on company law.[58] Both the theoretical foundation and the rationale can be questioned. The problems in the context of SWM, *inter alia* short-termism and externalisation, also drive a serious reconsideration

---

52 In particular, for knowledge-based or high-technology companies, human capital plays a much more important role than financial capital.

53 John Kay, 'The Kay Review of UK Equity Markets and Long-term Decision Making' (2012) 25.

54 Such as by selling short an investee company's shares.

55 For example, see Margaret Blair and Lynn Stout, 'Specific Investment and Corporate Law' (2006) 7 *European Business Organization Law Review* 473, 480. Their investment is also at risk, albeit with arguably different levels compared with shareholders'.

56 Frank Easterbrook and Daniel Fischel, *The Economic Structure of Corporate Law* (Harvard University Press, Cambridge 1991) 49–50.

57 Ibid. 69.

58 The corporate objective exerts a significant role in corporate governance. As mentioned earlier, it would be impossible to judge corporate performance or directors' performance if no goals or expectations existed. Accordingly, such an ultimate objective is instrumental in deciding how to allocate obligations or responsibilities in order to achieve the best corporate governance.

of the current shareholder-centred model. The argument that relying on external law to protect stakeholders and control negative externalities is flawed. The recent Volkswagen emission scandal is a good example. The German car giant[59] has admitted cheating emissions tests in the US by using devices in diesel-powered cars that could detect when they were being tested and change the performance accordingly to improve results.[60]

Regulatory slack and gaps, among other weaknesses in external regulation, have been well exposed by the Volkswagen scandal. First, Volkswagen admitted it started to install the cheating devices as early as 2008, but were only caught by the US Environmental Protection Agency eight years later. The ineffective or even impotent function of external regulations was thus revealed. Second, due to different legislative levels and techniques, the same cheating device causing the same pollution may not be regulated in some jurisdictions even after the scandal's exposure in Western countries.[61] Third, Volkswagen lobbied hard for governments to "promote the adoption of diesel engines as a way to reduce carbon emissions", which led to diesel cars constituting more than 50 per cent of the European car market.[62] Although this is an extreme case where Volkswagen misled regulators and policymakers to make suboptimal or even incorrect regulations or policies, it is not difficult to see the potential for companies to lobby regulators rather than change their own behaviour as a cost-saving measure.

The play in this case is between profits and the environment. When in 2008 Volkswagen found that a new diesel engine developed at great expense would not meet environmental standards in the US and other countries, the company

59 Volkswagen, the German car manufacturer, is now the second-largest auto maker in the world. Andrea Murphy, '2015 Global 2000: The World's Biggest Auto Companies' *Forbes* (New Jersey 6 May 2015) www.forbes.com/sites/andreamurphy/2015/05/06/2015-global-2000-the-worlds-biggest-auto-companies/ [accessed 1 March 2017].

60 In other words, using software to manipulate results in order to pass the environment test. Russell Hotten, 'Volkswagen: The Scandal Explained' *BBC Business* (London 25 September 2015) www.bbc.co.uk/news/business-34324772 [accessed 1 March 2017]; Tom Morgan and Melanie Hall, 'Volkswagen Crisis: Car Giant Warned against Emissions Rigging Eight Years Ago' *The Telegraph* (London 27 September 2015) www.telegraph.co.uk/motoring/car-manufacturers/volkswagen/11894672/Volkswagen-crisis-Car-giant-warned-against-emissions-rigging-eight-years-ago.html [accessed 1 March 2017].

Of course, it could be argued that Germany has a two-tier board structure with strong employee representation and that therefore they are less shareholder-oriented. This is generally true. But the Volkswagen case along with the Ford Pinto case in the US, which is explored in Chapter 5, is mainly to demonstrate that when a company adopts a corporate objective, its corporate decision-making would be subsequently shaped by that.

61 For example, so far in China, except for a small amount of media coverage there has been no formal investigation or intention to open an official probe into this case. This may be largely due to the law for environmental protection still lagging behind. And, bear in mind, Volkswagen vehicles are sold in 153 countries, which means this problem is staggering. Many countries are not able to effectively tackle Volkswagen's cheating behaviour due to a regulatory gap.

62 David Bach, 'Seven Reasons Volkswagen Is Worse than Enron' *Financial Times* (London 27 September 2015) www.ft.com/cms/s/0/cf9f73e8–62d6–11e5–9846-de406ccb37f2.html#axzz3n1SYu0Ea [accessed 1 March 2017].

was confronted with a difficult choice.[63] To adopt this new engine and pollute the environment or throw it out and redevelop? The company chose to use the cheating device to shirk their environmental responsibilities and maximise immediate profits. This is not surprising if profit is the most important focus and only external law is relied on to control negative externalities. If a broader objective had been adopted and the environment had a higher priority, Volkswagen may have avoided this scandal. Apart from the benefits to the environment and human health, even in terms of financial performance, the overall costs of throwing it out and redeveloping a new engine would be much cheaper than the loss Volkswagen has suffered so far. Less than ten days after the scandal went public, Volkswagen's shares lost 40 per cent of their value, and the company's reputation has been tarnished.[64] Moreover, in the US, which represents 5 per cent of Volkswagen's total sales, it will face a fine up to US$18 billion, plus numerous customers' lawsuits for compensation.[65]

The rationale claimed by shareholder primacists can be challenged and therefore may not be as valid as expected. On the other hand, the pressure to pursue immediate profits or externalise costs may be released if SWM were to be replaced by a broader objective. Meanwhile, other important values including fairness and justice can also be better preserved in the context of a broader corporate objective. Following on from this, the book endeavours to answer the fundamental question of corporate governance, i.e. for whose interests should the company be run, by re-examining the current shareholder model first. This book contributes to the recurring theme of corporate objectives by reconsidering and reassessing SWM and seeking an alternative model for the corporate objective when the former is no longer working properly. The outcome could become a starting point for future corporate governance discussion; in particular, it could address the regulatory gap and functional limitation of external measures regarding the control of short-termism and externalisation.

63 Jack Ewing, 'Volkswagen Engine-Rigging Scheme Said to Have Begun in 2008' *New York Times* (New York 4 October 2015) www.nytimes.com/2015/10/05/business/engine-shortfall-pushed-volkswagen-to-evade-emissions-testing.html [accessed 30 October 2015].
64 Tom Morgan, 'Volkswagen Crisis: Car Giant Removes 4,000 New Diesel Cars from Showrooms in Britain' *The Telegraph* (London 1 October 2015) www.telegraph.co.uk/motoring/11905543/Volkswagen-crisis-Car-giant-removes-4000-new-diesel-cars-from-showrooms-in-Britain.html; Julia Bradshaw, 'VW Scandal: 2.1 Million Audi Cars Worldwide Fitted with Volkswagen Emissions Cheat Device' *The Telegraph* (London 28 September 2015) www.telegraph.co.uk/finance/newsbysector/industry/11895848/BREAKING-2.1-million-Audi-cars-fitted-with-VW-emissions-cheat-devices.html [accessed 1 March 2017].
65 It is estimated that the cost will be at least several hundred billion dollars. For example, see Wolfgang Münchau, 'Volkswagen's Threat to the German Model' *Financial Times* (London 4 October 2015) www.ft.com/cms/s/0/82315c6a-68fe-11e5-a57f-21b88f7d973f.html#axzz3ng8bH4Az [accessed 1 March 2017]; Elizabeth Anderson, 'Volkswagen Crisis: How Many Investigations Is the Carmaker Facing?' *The Telegraph* (London, 29 September 2015) www.telegraph.co.uk/finance/newsbysector/industry/11884872/Volkswagen-crisis-how-many-investigations-is-the-carmaker-facing.html [accessed 1 March 2017].

1.3 The rise of stakeholder theory

Modern companies are very different from the primitive factory model "when the typical corporation owned and operated a canal, a railroad, or a big manufacturing plant".[66] A company consists of not only equity capital, but also other financial and non-financial resources, and its wealth-generating capacity increasingly depends on various different types of resources contributed by various stakeholders.[67] This means the company needs the support of all its diverse stakeholders in order to sustain and prosper. As Freeman's seminal book *Strategic Management* demonstrated, ignoring stakeholders could give rise to disastrous consequences.[68] It is fair and essential to take the interests of stakeholders into account in order to obtain their support. The only viable way to preserve competitive advantage and profitability is to encourage every corporate stakeholder to make a wholehearted effort, especially given today's competitive economic environment.

Human capital or intangible investment by stakeholders is of increasing importance, whereas the significance of the shareholder's role is decreasing.[69] There is also a simultaneous trend that shareholders are more willing to be *passive and functionless investors* rather than *active participants*, concerned only with receiving "a return on their capital accruing with the mere passage of time",[70] which indicates that they would come to be more opportunistic and apathetic. As Professor Ireland aptly notes, "the great majority of share dealings involve not issues raising capital for new investment but the buying and selling of titles to revenue issued long ago".[71] Most shareholders, including institutional investors, only put an insignificant amount of their money into any individual company in terms of a diversified portfolio strategy, and they do not commit to a company in

---

66 In these traditional form of companies, that the initial investors (shareholders) were the only parties whose significant assets including "some inventories and receivables, the entrepreneurial know-how of the owner-manager, and, most important, the canal, the roadbed and railcars, or the factory" were tied up and at risk. Margaret Blair, *Ownership and Control: Rethinking Corporate Governance for the Twenty-First Century* (The Brookings Institution, Washington 1995) 232–233.

67 For example, see the team production analysis. Margaret Blair and Lynn Stout, 'Specific Investment and Corporate Law' (2006) 7 *European Business Organization Law Review* 473, 491. Notwithstanding the full contribution by stakeholders would not ensure the survival or success of a company, deficiencies in their contribution would definitely lead to inferior corporate performance or even failure.

68 R Edward Freeman, *Strategic Management: A Stakeholder Approach* (Pitman Publishing, Boston 1984) 204. This has also been acknowledged in the *Hampel Report.* Committee on Corporate Governance, *Final Report* (1998) para 1.18.

69 Even for manufacturing companies which were heavily dependent on physical plant and equipment invested by shareholders, the intangibles contributed by stakeholders such as intellectual property rights, brand reputation, service capabilities and the like make up a rapidly increasing share of the assets. Blair, *Ownership and Control* (n 66) 234. Furthermore, it is not infrequent to hear top management say "our wealth is our people". Ibid. (footnote omitted). Also see the discussion in footnotes 52–54 and accompanying text above.

70 Paddy Ireland, 'Company Law and the Myth of Shareholder Ownership' (1999) 62 *Modern Law Review* 32, 42.

71 Ibid. 54.

either a moral or practical sense.[72] The role of equity issues and physical capital in investment "is much less important than it was" in modern public companies at present.[73] Based on Berle's observation in the preface to the revised edition in 1968 that shareholder investment by way of purchasing stock does not contribute savings to a company or undertake the residual risk of a new/increased economic operation,[74] Professor O'Sullivan further points out:

> Shareholders in these economies generally invest their money in the securities issued by successful enterprises on the basis of investments in productive assets that have already been made. In other words, public shareholders do not "wait" until the developmental investments that these companies make bear fruit but buy shares in these companies after they have paid off.[75]

Meanwhile, Professor Deakin illustrates, "most trades of shares in listed companies consist of movements from one shareholder to another with no new capital being supplied to the company".[76] Net contribution of new equity to the corporate sector has become negative.[77] By contrast, stakeholders' firm-specific investment might be, on the one hand, much greater[78] and on the other, more valuable[79] than the financial investment.

As a result, for large public companies, which are of course "mature" enough,[80] the contribution made by stakeholders and the role performed by them is obviously no less important to corporate success. Shareholders are not materially different from any other stakeholder group from a resource provider perspective. They are not the only group which bears risks, since stakeholders suffer as well when the company runs badly.[81] In fact, shareholders can take advantage of diversification to reduce and dilute idiosyncratic risks (i.e. non-systematic risks),

---

72 Ronald Green, 'Shareholders as Stakeholders: Changing Metaphors of Corporate Governance' (1993) 50 *Washington and Lee Law Review* 1409, 1414.

73 John Kay, 'The Kay Review of UK Equity Markets and Long-term Decision Making' (2012) 25.

74 Adolf Berle and Gardiner Means, *The Modern Corporation and Private Property* (Transaction Publishers, New Brunswick 1991, originally published 1932) xxii–xxiii.

75 Mary O'Sullivan, *Contests for Corporate Control: Corporate Governance and Economic Performance in the United States and Germany* (OUP, Oxford 2001) 49.

76 Simon Deakin, 'The Coming Transformation of Shareholder Value' (2005) 13 *Corporate Governance: An International Review* 11, 15.

77 Ibid.

78 For example, Professor Williamson concludes that employees work longer and make much more investment. Oliver Williamson, 'Corporate Governance' (1984) 93 *Yale Law Journal* 1197, 1200 (footnote omitted).

79 For example, Professor Zingales argues that the human capital investment in today's company is more important than any of the others. Luigi Zingales, 'In Search of New Foundations' (2000) 55 *Journal of Finance* 1623, 1643.

80 For the discussion of different stages of corporate development and the corresponding role of shareholders during these stages, see *supra* footnotes 19–23 and accompanying text.

81 *Infra* Chapter 2, section 2.3.2.

whilst other stakeholders cannot. As explained above, shareholders are not the only residual claimants either. Any increased earnings, namely, the residue may go to the creditors when the company cannot afford all of its debt. Even in a well-run company, the residue can go to employees as bonuses or go to customers in the form of improved service, instead of directly going to shareholders as dividends.[82] It is therefore inappropriate to overstate the role and importance of shareholders, especially in a large public company.[83] Moreover, it is necessary to look beyond maximising shareholder wealth, and the argument that stakeholders have a right to be treated as an end rather than a means is worth serious consideration. By virtue of stakeholders' important roles and intrinsic value, their interests should not only be an instrument serving as a means for shareholder interests.

Stakeholder theory is antithetical to the shareholder model and requires directors of the company to be *accountable* to more than just the shareholders; directors should take all stakeholder interests into account and not sacrifice them simply for the interests of shareholders. Whilst the origin of "stakeholder" is difficult to trace, it is generally agreed that the term did not formally appear until 1963.[84] Stakeholders first meant "those groups without whose support the organization would cease to exist" such as shareholders, employees, customers, suppliers and so forth.[85] With continuous evolution, Professor Freeman's classic definition is "any group or individual who can affect or is affected by the achievement of the organization's objective".[86] Stakeholder theory as a theory of the firm is intended to "explain and guide the structure and operation of the established corporation".[87] Generally speaking, a company is viewed as an entity through which various participants accomplish multiple purposes, thereby ensuring the interests of those with a stake in the company are taken into account and not automatically subordinated to any other group's interests; accordingly, the company should create value for all stakeholders rather than solely for the shareholders.

Unfortunately, as aptly noted by some stakeholder theorists, there is a multitude of different stakeholder models, since they are explained or used by different

---

82 Because shareholders in general have no right to claim the dividends and directors have the right to decide how to allocate the increased earnings. Ibid.
83 The examples made by Professor Blair also clearly show that only in the simplest and most primitive factory model might maximising shareholder wealth be equivalent to maximising total social wealth. As soon as specialised human capital and other intangible inputs are added in, the conclusion would change significantly. Blair, *Ownership and Control* (n 66) 245–259.
84 Freeman, *Strategic Management* (n 68) 31.
85 Ibid. 31–32.
86 Ibid. 46. However, it should be noticed there are various different definitions of stakeholder. A more critical and detail discussion of the concept of the stakeholder will be offered in Chapter 5.
87 Thomas Donaldson and Lee Preston, 'The Stakeholder Theory of the Corporation: Concepts, Evidence and Implication' (1995) 20 *Academy of Management Review* 65, 70.

proponents in different ways.[88] In order to avoid confusion, this book mainly adopts Professors Donaldson and Preston's categorisation of descriptive, normative and instrumental aspects of the theory,[89] as developed from Professors Mitchell, Agle and Wood's identification of power, legitimacy and urgency as characteristic of stakeholders.[90]

The descriptive aspect explains what the company is and how it operates in order to predict future corporate behaviour. As summarised, stakeholder theory has been used to describe the following: "(a) the nature of the firm, (b) the way managers think about managing, (c) how board members think about the interests of corporate constituencies, and (d) how some corporations are actually managed".[91] As John Kaler argues, being descriptive explains the reality of business; it is "about making a factual claim about a theory".[92] The descriptive stakeholder theory is based on its descriptive accuracy.

The normative stakeholder theory emphasises the intrinsic value of stakeholders and acknowledges that the shareholder's role is not materially different from that of other stakeholders – they are simply one group of resource investors/providers.[93] Each stakeholder agrees to put their valuable resources, labour or both together with that of others to pursue the success of the business and derive benefits from it.[94] The morals and values perceived as fundamental to running companies, including fairness, are emphasised.[95] Meanwhile, the welfare of all

---

88 For example, "the concepts stakeholder ... and stakeholder theory are explained and used by various authors in very different ways and supported (or critiqued) with diverse and often contradictory evidence and arguments". And it is sometimes also called the pluralist approach. See ibid. 66.

89 Ibid.

90 They propose that stakeholders can be identified pursuant to whether they possess any of the following characteristics: (1) the stakeholder's power to influence the firm, (2) the legitimacy of the stakeholder's relationship with the firm, and (3) the urgency of the stakeholder's claim on the firm. Ronald Mitchell, Bradley Agle and Donna Wood, 'Toward a Theory of Stakeholder Identification and Salience: Defining the Principle of Who and What Really Counts' (1997) 22 *Academy of Management Review* 853, 854.

91 Donaldson and Preston, 'The Stakeholder Theory of the Corporation' (n 87) 70 (footnote omitted). According to them, the stakeholder theory describes the company as "a constellation of cooperative and competitive interest possessing intrinsic value". Ibid. 66.

92 John Kaler, 'Differentiating Stakeholder Theories' (2003) 46 *Journal of Business Ethics* 71, 73.

93 For example, see Donaldson and Preston, 'The Stakeholder Theory of the Corporation' (n 87) 67. Some scholars go further and argue that shareholders, like punters at the races, just place their money on the financial runners without any interest in "stay[ing with] that horse through its career, or to give their advice to its trainer". They will choose another runner if they are not happy with the current one. For example, see Charles Handy, 'What Is a Company For?' (1991) 139 *RSA Journal* 231, 234.

94 According to Professor Freeman and his co-authors, "business is about putting together a deal so that suppliers, customers, employees, communities, managers, and shareholders all win continuously over time". R Edward Freeman, Andrew Wicks and Bidhan Parmar, 'Stakeholder Theory and "The Corporate Objective Revisited"' (2004) 15 *Organization Science* 364, 365.

95 For example, see Robert Phillips, 'Stakeholder Theory and a Principle of Fairness' (1997) 7 *Business Ethics Quarterly* 51–56. Robert Phillips, R Edward Freeman and Andrew Wicks, 'What Stakeholder Theory Is Not' (2003) 13 *Business Ethics Quarterly* 479, 481.

stakeholders cannot be unaffected by the performance of the company. In the words of Janet Williamson:

> Employees are affected by the wide range of decisions that impact upon their employment with the company; customers are affected by decisions on the price, specifications and standards of products; suppliers are affected by purchasing decisions; creditors are affected by financial procedures; and the local community is affected by recruitment policy and environmental impact.[96]

Like shareholders, stakeholders' investment is also at risk. For example, when a company is badly run or becomes insolvent, creditors may not get back the capital as well as the interest, and employees may be made redundant. They have an interest in the company – in Freeman's terms, each stakeholder has a stake in the company.[97] And these stakeholder groups cannot obtain enough, if any, protection via the incomplete contract, as explained earlier.[98] Corporate decisions can lead to significant social consequences by affecting others and the economy at large.[99] Due to its involvement and influence in various aspect of social life,[100] a large public company is expected to be more aware of its social obligations, including fairness, justice and the like.[101]

It thus implies that directors' duties and accountability are not limited to ensuring returns to shareholders, but extend to those who are interested in, and affected by, the company and whose role is no less significant.[102] Furthermore, under certain situations, so the argument goes, directors are even required to possess "a willingness to exhaust the resources of the company" to satisfy stakeholders' interests.[103] The shareholder-centred model is criticised for "using the *prima facie* rights claims of one group – shareholders – to excuse violating the rights of others".[104] Opponents of the shareholder model contend this damages other stakeholders' interests, and argue that the shareholders as one group of various constituents of a company have no reason to override other groups' interests. In terms of the stakeholder model, every stakeholder has a right to be treated as an end and not simply a means or instrument to facilitate the benefits

---

96 Janet Williamson, 'The Road to Stakeholding' (1996) 67 *Political Quarterly* 209, 212. Also see *infra* Chapter 2, section 2.3.2.
97 Freeman, *Strategic Management* (n 68) 25.
98 In particular, during financial difficulties, directors would probably choose excessively risky programmes since shareholders have little to lose in this setting.
99 Parkinson (n 17) 16.
100 Letza, Sun and Kirkbride (n 11) 250.
101 Ibid. In addition, the normative stakeholder theory originated from the entity theory in contrast to the aggregate or fiction theory.
102 William Allen, 'Our Schizophrenic Conception of the Business Corporation' (1992) 14 *Cardozo Law Review* 261, 265.
103 Ronald Green, 'Shareholders as Stakeholders: Changing Metaphors of Corporate Governance' (1993) 50 *Washington and Lee Law Review* 1409, 1421.
104 Freeman, Wicks and Parmar (n 94) 365.

of the shareholder.[105] Reputation, positive relationships with customers and suppliers, and motivated employees are consequently not just for fostering business goals, as in the context of the shareholder model. All stakeholder interests should be considered by directors of the board, even if they go against shareholders' sectional interests. To treat stakeholders as an end implies they are no longer merely a means for maximising shareholder wealth; instead, stakeholders' welfare should be seen as an ultimate and intrinsic objective of the company.[106]

In contrast to normative stakeholder theory's emphasis on moral values and fundamental human rights, instrumental stakeholder theory focuses on how stakeholder value can be used as a means to improve corporate performance. It finds the stakeholder model more economically efficient than its rival approach. First, it recognises that companies are not able to succeed or achieve business goals in the absence of stakeholders' contributions, whether pecuniary or not. Apart from shareholders, other non-shareholding stakeholders' investments are equally indispensable. Second, as Professor Thomas Jones observes, there is a distinct competitive advantage:

> This instrumental theory of stakeholder management essentially turns the neoclassical theory of the firm upside down. It implies that behaviour that is trusting, trustworthy, and co-operative, not opportunistic, will give the firm a competitive advantage. In the process, it may help explain why certain "irrational" or altruistic behaviours turn out to be productive and why firms that engage in these behaviours survive and often thrive.[107]

In other words, the stakeholder model is beneficial to fostering both existing and future contributors' potential, which subsequently helps advance aggregate wealth.[108] The shareholder model would, however, damage other stakeholders' incentive by virtue of their inferior position vis-à-vis shareholders. They might worry about being subordinated by shareholders' interests. This may also explain the claims that the stakeholder model is – in contrast to the argument from a traditional, purely ethical perspective – the key to allowing businesses to make more profits.[109] When stakeholders know their interests will be fully considered during the corporate decision-making process, they will be more likely to invest in that company and "go the extra mile". Specifically, creditors might charge a lower interest rate or lend more when they are confident that it would be safe

---

105 Donaldson and Preston, 'The Stakeholder Theory of the Corporation' (n 87) 67; Freeman, *Strategic Management* (n 68) 97.

106 R Edward Freeman and Robert Phillips, 'Stakeholder Theory: A Libertarian Defense' (2002) 12 *Business Ethics Quarterly* 331, 333.

107 Thomas Jones, 'Instrumental Stakeholder Theory: A Synthesis of Ethics and Economics' (1995) 20 *Academy of Management Review* 404, 432.

108 Andrew Keay, 'Stakeholder Theory in Corporate Law: Has it Got What It Takes?' (2010) 9 *Richmond Journal of Global Law and Business* 249, 256.

109 Andrew Campbell, 'Stakeholders: the Case in Favour' (1997) 30 *Long Range Plan* 446, 446.

to put money into the company; employees may be more loyal to the company and work more passionately; suppliers may also be more willing to make firm-specific investments and so forth. Whilst shareholder model advocates insist that stakeholders would be better off under SWM,[110] opponents doubt its validity and believe that such an approach may not necessarily benefit other stakeholders or society as a whole.[111] The lopsided focus on shareholder interests could be easily conducive to negative externalities, such as transferring the costs of the company to the stakeholders and retaining the benefits for the shareholders.[112]

Public companies, unlike closed ones, are of broad public concern,[113] so only serving the interests of one group in the company would be too narrow to be justified. Rather, the company should be run for the interest of all stakeholders rather than solely for shareholders. Max Clarkson sums this up well: "the economic and social purpose of the corporation is to create and distribute wealth and value to all its primary stakeholder groups without favouring one group at the expense of others".[114] Following on from this, the book critically analyses the stakeholder model in order to see whether it could be a more suitable corporate objective than SWM.

1.4 The corporate objective in China

China has become the second largest economy in the world and is exerting an increasingly significant role in global affairs.[115] Though a socialist state, since the market reforms of 1978 China also relies heavily on the corporate vehicle as the most important business organisation to ensure its rapid economic development. Adolf Berle and Gardiner Means' observation in the 1930s[116] that large public companies dominate the world remains true today, not only in the West[117] but

---

110 One of the strongest arguments for supporting SWM is that to generate maximum value for shareholders is "in principle the best means also of securing overall prosperity and welfare". CLRSG, *Modern Company Law for a Competitive Economy: The Strategic Framework* (DTI, London 1999) 37.
111 Dodd (n 24) 1152.
112 Ian Lee, 'Efficiency and Ethics in the Debate about Shareholder Primacy' (2006) 31 *Delaware Journal of Corporate Law* 533, 539. *Infra* Chapter 2, section 2.4.
113 Roberta Karmel, 'Implications of the Stakeholder Model' (1992) 61 *George Washington Law Review* 1156, 1171.
   But it is worth noting that Professor Phillips, Freeman and Wicks hold a view that the stakeholder model should be applied not only to the large public companies, but to all other organizational forms including small closed companies, family owned firms, partnerships and so forth. Phillips, Freeman and Wicks, 'What Stakeholder Theory Is Not' (n 95) 481. Also see footnote 47 above.
114 Max Clarkson, 'A Stakeholder Framework for Analyzing and Evaluating Corporate Social Performance' (1995) 20 *Academy of Management Review* 92, 112.
115 The World Bank (n 4). In addition, US President Trump's trade protectionism may make the role of China in the world economy even more prominent.
116 Adolf Berle and Gardiner Means, *The Modern Corporation and Private Property* (Transaction Publishers, New Brunswick 1991, originally published in 1932).
117 For example, see Keay, *The Corporate Objective* (n 15) vi.

also in China. The regulation and governance of such companies will have a significant impact on the further development of the Chinese economy, which could in turn directly affect the world economy. Company law and corporate governance are therefore vital issues in China. Although the current focus is primarily on corporate performance, the fundamental question at the heart of corporate governance, namely for whose interests these large public companies should be run, remains unresolved.

China was historically renowned for disregarding private property. The government had long played a very significant role in corporate management. Nonetheless, lack of private property and overemphasis on state control over a prolonged period may have to some degree intensified the desire and yearning for shareholder primacy. As soon as private-sector investors were allowed to engage in corporate activities during the reform period of the Late Qing Dynasty (1861–1894), a game has endlessly played out between the state/government on one side and private shareholders including merchants, individual investors and alike, on the other. Most of the time the state has dominated, even after the establishment of the People's Republic of China in 1949, where collectivism prevailed over individualism. Nevertheless, the importance and benefits of non-government shareholders are becoming conspicuous. Subsequent to several enormous reforms in recent decades, it is interesting to see that shareholder rights are receiving increasingly more attention and concern. SWM is also increasingly accepted as the orthodox objective of Corporate China and the norm of corporate governance, not only by the general public but also by academics and practitioners.[118] Both company laws and corporate governance codes, among others, adopt the shareholder-oriented approach, which is discussed in Chapter 4. Such predisposition is to a great extent influenced by the Western mainstream idea that shareholder primacy is the best corporate governance practice and of benefit to overall economic efficiency, as most neoclassical economists and contractarians would argue.

However, there is little critical discussion in China about ultimate corporate objectives and SWM.[119] Even within the limited articles that do, most take the

---

118 For example, see Roman Tomasic and Neil Andrews, 'Minority Shareholder Protection in China's Top 100 Listed Companies' (2007) 9 *Australian Journal of Asian Law* 88, 96–97; Ping Wang, Guanggui Li and Fangliang Gong, 'Study on Cost of Capital, Shareholder Wealth Maximization and Its Realization – Based on the Empirical Analyses of Chinese Listed Companies' [2008] 4 *China Industry Economy* 110, 117; Qiao Liu, 'Corporate Governance in China: Current Practices, Economic Effects and Institutional Determinants' (2006) 52 *CESifo Economic Studies* 415, 449; On Kit Tam, 'Ethical Issues in the Evolution of Corporate Governance in China' (2002) 37 *Journal of Business Ethics* 303, 311; Shuangge Wen, *Shareholder Primacy and Corporate Governance: Legal Aspects, Practices, and Future Directions* (Routledge, Oxford 2013).
119 When the terms "corporate objective", "shareholder primacy", "shareholder wealth maximisation", "stakeholder", "stakeholder theory", "corporate governance" and "directors' duty", both in Chinese and in English, were searched in the CNKI China Academic Journals Database, which is allegedly the largest full-text Chinese journal database in the world, few articles seriously dealt with the question of in whose interests should the company be run in China. Available at http://eng.oversea.cnki.net/kns55/ [searched on June 1, 2016].

shareholder model for granted or fail to analyse stakeholder theory thoroughly.[120] But the importance of ultimate corporate objectives warrants a similar study in the Chinese context. The timing is apt: Chinese corporate governance currently faces many problems,[121] and proposals including ownership reform, board reform and market reform have been raised or are being adopted. Nonetheless, these efforts could be misguided. There is always the risk that China's corporate governance reforms may be based on ill-considered corporate objectives with potentially damaging consequences. Measures to reinforce shareholder primacy, including shareholder empowerment and stock options, may exacerbate corporate governance levels if the company should not run solely for the interests of shareholders.

Thus, apart from reconsidering SWM as a corporate objective in a general way, the book also discusses SWM in China to see whether it is any different from the Anglo-American version. In addition to problems in SWM such as short-termism and negative externalisation, the largely imperfect market system and socialist nature would add extra weight to the argument that a stakeholder model should be more suitable than SWM as a corporate objective for Chinese large public companies.

From an economic perspective, in a perfect market where the competition is fierce and the information is available cost-effectively, a company has no choice but to follow the market.[122] In such a market, owing to a sufficiently large pool of companies, it is assumed that none of them can charge more for its goods than the current market price; instead, a company can only passively accept the prevailing market price if it does not want to lose its business to competitors. According to the classical and neoclassical economic theory, price is determined by the laws of supply and demand. State interference is therefore unwelcome, since the market is deemed to be the price-setter. By the same token, companies are also forced to follow the quality and the like demanded by the market. If a company's production costs exceed the average market cost, i.e. its production costs are higher than most of its rivals, it will not survive. In short, such a market is

---

120 It should be noted that some Chinese scholars have started to study stakeholder theory as a management discipline, but they are still mainly in the introductory stage of this theory. For example, see Longjie Zhou, 'Modern Revision of the End of Corporation' (2005) 112 *Contemporary Law Review* 30–36; Hongtao Shen and Yifeng Shen, 'Modernization of Corporate Governance Theory – From Shareholder Maximisation to the Stakeholder Theory' [2008] 6 *Economic Survey* 108–111; Haiping Jin, 'Subversion of the Tradition of Shareholder Primacy – Comment on Foreign Corporate Stakeholder Theory' [2007] 3 *Social Sciences in Nanjing* 25–30; Shenyu Wang, 'From Stakeholder Influence, Stakeholder Participation to Stakeholder Co-governance – A Review and Revelation to Stakeholder Theory Development' [2008] 11 *Journal of Xiangtan University* (Philosophy and Social Sciences) 28–35; Yongjun Xiao and Biqing Li, 'The Applied Research Review on Stakeholder Theory' [2008] 7 *Commercial Research* 36–39; Liming Liu and Songmei Zhang, 'On Stakeholder Thinking of the Corporate Governance' (2005) 7 *Journal of Southwest University of Political Science and Law* 96–104.
121 Min Yan, 'Obstacles to China's Corporate Governance' (2011) 32 *Company Lawyer* 311, 319–320.
122 Parkinson (n 17) 22.

the perfect discipline for the control of companies.[123] However, the real market is not perfect.[124] The competition is not unlimited. It is not uncommon for a small number of large companies to dominate the market, and barriers to entry in certain industries are not yet completely removed. Therefore even if one company is not operating efficiently, potential rivals may find it difficult to enter the market to challenge it. Second, information is asymmetric and most of the time is not available cost-effectively to all economic actors. It becomes more difficult to shift to alternative producers and resource suppliers who may be cheaper in price or better in quality. Third, products and services increasingly focus on individuality, making substitution less practical. In other words, less homogeneous products mean companies have less competitive pressure, and thereby may raise prices without leading to customers shifting to their rivals. This is even more pronounced in China, where market mechanisms have only recently been established.[125]

Meanwhile, requiring directors to take all stakeholders' interests into account is thought by some to be a form of communism or thinly veiled socialism.[126] Such a standpoint may be a misinterpretation of the stakeholder theory,[127] but viewing it as a socialist theory does not affect socialist countries', such as China's, decision to adopt it. Whilst more justification may be needed to tame the harsher aspects of capitalism in the West,[128] focusing more on the lives of ordinary people and other non-economic-related issues is less difficult for China. Prioritising social goals such as full employment, improvement of infrastructure and environmental protection above pure economic efficiency can be more easily justified.

Thus shareholder supremacy and economic efficiency, central tenets of classic capitalism, are worth more careful reconsideration in China. The political and social pursuits of the state, which is normally the majority shareholder in the largest public companies,[129] do not differ substantially from the legitimate interests of employees, the local community, the environment and so on. In addition to maintaining the ruling position, the key political interest of the

---

123 Corporate governance at its broadest concerns the question of who should own and control the company. Alan Dignam and John Lowry, *Company Law* (9th edn OUP, Oxford 2016) 379.
124 For example, see Brian Cheffins, *Company Law: Theory, Structure and Operation* (OUP, Oxford 1997) 8.
125 *Infra* Chapter 4.
126 Stakeholder theory is usually attacked as socialism by Anglo-American scholars. For example, see Phillips, Freeman and Wicks, 'What Stakeholder Theory Is Not' (n 95) 491–492.
127 Ibid. Anthony Barnett argues: "stakeholding is not a socialist argument. It is a capitalist argument that observes a chronic inadequacy and danger in leaving all wealth creation to the hidden hand of the free market". Anthony Barnett, 'Towards a Stakeholder Democracy' in Gavin Kelly, Dominic Kelly and Andrew Gamble (eds), *Stakeholder Capitalism* (Macmillan Press, Basingstoke 1997) 83.
128 Janice Dean, *Directing Public Companies: Company Law and the Stakeholder Society* (Cavendish, London 2001) 117.
129 *Infra* Chapter 4. As a consequence, state controlled companies are expected to undertake social and even political responsibilities. For example, see Baocai Yu, 'What are the Responsibilities of State-Owned Enterprises' *Xinhua* (Beijing 16 November 2006) at http://news.xinhuanet.com/fortune/2006–11/16/content_5338255.htm [accessed 1 March 2017].

Chinese government is to preserve the social stability and continuously improve living standards. As a result, the state or government pursues the welfare of the general populace. This potentially embraces interests of creditors, employees, the local community and other stakeholders. Take cutting jobs, for example: it is definitely not beneficial to employees and local communities, though shareholders may profit from it. Leaving aside the corporate objective, when comparing these competing interests, it is more likely for the Chinese government to see stakeholding factors, such as employment, as more important than increasing shareholder profits. After all, the principle of law and public policy should be inclined to protect comparatively vulnerable groups, especially in socialist China. As recent history shows, rich people are getting richer whilst most poor are getting poorer.[130] Most commentators overemphasise the significance of shareholders' economic interests whilst ignoring other stakeholders' interests pursued by countries like China.

From the perspective of the development of corporate governance, the improving status of shareholders since the 1990s could be seen as progress from the previous bureaucratic control and state intervention. However, the shareholder-centred model is by no means the final destination; further development is still essential, especially considering the problems in the SWM and the unique Chinese characteristics. Therefore, after examining SWM and the stakeholder model, this book endeavours to look beyond SWM and suggest the stakeholder model is more suitable for Chinese companies.

1.5 Structure of the book

This book is divided into six chapters. Following Chapter 1, the introduction, Chapter 2 re-examines SWM as a corporate objective. In order to obtain a clearer understanding of SWM in the West, it first explores its current theoretical foundation. SWM is justified by theories ranging from the traditional corporate aggregate theory and proprietorship theory to the current contractarian theory and agency theory – all of these will be critically examined. Those taken for granted, for example the belief that the company should be run solely for shareholders' interests because shareholders own the company, could be defective. Current theoretical bases such as agency theory, efficiency argument and the like are mainly economic in nature: this is not surprising since companies are important economic actors, and changes in the global economy have significantly affected corporate governance structures. Chapter 2 therefore incorporates

---

130 The issue of increasing income inequality and low wages has been discussed by Professor Greenfield, see Kent Greenfield, 'Using Behavioral Economics to Show the Power and Efficiency of Corporate Law as Regulatory Tool' (2002) 35 *University of California Davis Law Review* 581, 601–604. It has been identified that other industrialised countries, except the US and UK where shareholder interests are prioritised, have lower poverty rates, and people in those countries find it easier to move into the middle class out of poverty. Ibid. 604.

an economic analysis of law to examine SWM as the corporate objective.[131] Following a thorough discussion, it is found that agency theory – including the principal-agent relationship, the so-called residual claimant argument and efficiency argument – clash repeatedly with some long-established corporate governance mechanisms. The merits claimed by shareholder primacists, such as economic efficiency or social wealth maximisation, may be merely illusory.

Furthermore, Chapter 2 discusses externalisation and short-termism as unavoidable defects in the shareholder model, implying that relying on external rules is not enough to control these problems. They are detrimental not only to other corporate stakeholders but also to the interests of the company and society as a whole. The regulatory gap and the inability of external rules to control externalisation propel us to consider using the internal corporate governance system as an alternative to deal with the problem. A full reconsideration of SWM is provided at the end of this chapter. No laws require directors to only serve shareholder interests. The heterogeneous expectations of different types of shareholder groups could further impair the so-called merit of single-minded measurability of the shareholder model. It is then natural to consider that the corporate objective may not be maximising shareholder wealth at all.

Whilst short-termism and negative externalisation can be seen to reflect SWM at the micro level, shareholder empowerment reflects SWM at the policy level. Empowering shareholders and enabling them to be the locus of corporate governance is not only stressed in China but is also seen by most professionals, academics and policy makers in the UK and US alike as good practice and the best solution for overcoming the kind of corporate failures exemplified by recent global financial crises.[132] In fact, China's emphasis on shareholder power is in large measure affected by Western practice.[133]

From the opposite perspective, increasing shareholder power implies diminishing directors' discretion. Indeed, shareholder power and director power are

---

131 Indeed, an economic analysis of corporate governance and company law has been easily accepted and has dominated the study of many law areas including company law. Stephen Bottomley, 'From Contractualism to Constitutionalism: A Framework for Corporate Governance' (1997) 19 *Sydney Law Review* 277, 278.

132 It should be noted that even before the financial crisis, there was also a trend for increasing shareholder powers and restraining directors' authority. For example, in 2006, the Committee on Capital Markets Regulation recommended increasing shareholder rights for the purpose of enhancing managerial accountability in their *Interim Report of the Committee on Capital Markets Regulation* (2006). In academia, a high-profile debate on increasing shareholder rights can also be found in a 2006 special edition of *Harvard Law Review*. For example, see Lucian Bebchuk, 'The Case for Increasing Shareholder Power' (2005) 118 *Harvard Law Review* 833, 833; Bebchuk, 'Letting Shareholders Set the Rules' (n 49) 1784. The growth in institutional shareholders and the emergence of non-dispersed institutional shareholders also advance the issue of shareholder empowerment.

133 In particular the US and UK as it is argued China's corporate governance structures emulate the stylised Anglo-American model. For example, see Tam (n 29) 303. Though it does not necessarily mean shareholders in Western countries have extensive power, the mere focus on shareholder value makes China put shareholders at the centre of the corporate governance structure.

at opposing ends of the spectrum; it is impossible to have more of one without having less of the other. By emphasising shareholder empowerment, authority is reallocated from directors to shareholders; some limitations on shareholder participation are also removed. Granting shareholders adequate power to interfere in board decision-making, i.e. making boards of directors and their delegates more dependent on shareholders, cannot ensure an enhanced decision-making process. Even assuming SWM is the only proper and legitimate corporate objective, it remains questionable whether shareholder empowerment is *the* way to achieve it.[134] Shareholder empowerment ignores the value of centralised authority in large companies with hundreds or thousands of dispersed shareholders as well as the potential cost of shareholders' opportunistic or short-term behaviour. Further, apathetic, uninformed shareholders, without the necessary skills or time, may not necessarily lead to better corporate governance practice. Negative effects, such as the added pressure for directors to pursue short-term profits at the expense of corporate interests, long-term development and other stakeholders' interests, cannot be disregarded either. Worse yet, the interest of other stakeholders and shareholders as a whole may be subsequently impaired.

In response to the conventional stance of shareholder empowerment as a means to SWM,[135] Chapter 3 examines shareholder empowerment including its large-scale application as well as its negative effects. Conventional shareholder rights in Anglo-American jurisdictions and the rationale behind them are explored first, followed by an analysis of empowerment through the legal approach. A critical assessment of shareholder empowerment concludes the chapter by discussing the value of authority as well as the balance between authority and accountability. Chapter 3 argues that shareholder empowerment is by no means the best approach to increase shareholder value, even if SWM were the appropriate corporate objective. The chapter's conclusion is also expected to enlighten the question of how to balance the power between stakeholders and directors under the stakeholder model.

After a re-examination of SWM and shareholder empowerment in the West, Chapter 4 focuses on shareholder powers and SWM in the context of China. Shareholder powers can be classified into two main categories: control of the decision-making process, including director election, and ex post remedies. The first

---

134 For example, see John Armour and Jeffrey Gordon, 'Systematic Harms and Shareholder Value' (2014) 6 *Journal of Legal Analysis* 35, 60–61; Stephen Bainbridge, 'Director Primacy and Shareholder Disempowerment' (2006) 119 *Harvard Law Review* 1735, 1735.

135 There are *prima facie* two main approaches to maximising shareholder wealth in terms of the internal governance structure. Apart from shareholder empowerment, the other way is through designing performance-based compensation to incentivise directors and executive officers to maximise shareholder profits. Such a method is principally implanted by tying executives' pay to corporate performance measured by the share price. However, scholars such as Professors Lynn Stout, John Armour and Jeffrey Gordon have already correctly pointed out that share options and the like might lead corporate managers to seek only short-term profits at the expense of the long-term interests of shareholders as a whole as well as the general public. More discussion can be found in the following chapters.

category is clear: shareholder powers can be established by the fact that significant transactions, constitutional change and other fundamental corporate decisions are premised on shareholders' approval. In addition to these ex ante sanction requirements, shareholders can initiate their own proposals. Moreover, shareholders in general meetings have the right to elect and remove directors and determine their remuneration, which could definitely be seen as having a material influence on the degree of directors' obedience. The second category is also straightforward. At first, directors' duties are essentially another way to express shareholder rights. Given that directors of boards are required to be accountable to shareholders under China's law,[136] any deviating behaviour by directors can be seen as a breach of duty and detrimental to shareholders. Shareholders can therefore enforce rights against directors and seek remedies to protect themselves. The ease of seeking such a remedy – including how soon an interim shareholders' meeting can be called, the threshold for filing a lawsuit, the expenditure of suing liable directors or whether they can be reimbursed and so forth – determines the effectiveness of shareholder remedy, which in turn affects shareholder powers in practice. Besides, the deterrents to directors, i.e. the potential liability for directors, can also deter them from serving their own interests and encourage more obedient behaviour.

In order to accurately construct a picture of China, Chapter 4 first charts the evolution of China's companies and private property rights, exploring the historical development of corporate forms and shareholder rights in the *Late Qing Dynasty* (1861–1911), *Republican Period* (1912–1948) and the *People's Republic of China* (1949 onwards). It is hoped this history could help us better understand the current situation. Although nowadays shareholder protection in China is comparatively undesirable, shareholders have the right to decide on a company's operational policy and investment plans, mergers, corporate bonds and many other issues, implying that they are indeed quite powerful. For further clarity, a comparison of shareholder powers between China and the UK/US is undertaken with reference to the control of the decision-making process and ex post remedies. Shareholder empowerment in the Anglo-American sphere, especially after the financial crisis, and entrusting extensive executive power to shareholders in China since the revised *Company Law* in 2005, are both meant to improve shareholders' position and their influence over corporate governance. The specific reasons behind each are not identical, but they share a desire to enhance shareholder value and are fundamentally based on conventional shareholder-centric thinking.[137]

---

136 It should be noted that in Anglo-American jurisdictions, directors owe fiduciary duties only to the company. For example, see *Multinational Gas & Petrochemical Co Ltd v. Multinational Gas & Petrochemical Services Ltd* [1983] Ch 258.

137 In other words, it is thought that shareholder interests should be served primarily and all the internal governance systems should emphasise maximising shareholder wealth. However, even such shareholder primacy can be justified as a legitimate and proper corporate objective, but as discussed in Chapter 3, shareholder empowerment may not serve that end.

Chapter 4 then examines the corporate objective in China to see whether any disparity exists compared with the mainstream viewpoint in the West.[138] In addition to the fact that the supremacy of shareholders could reflect the inclination towards SWM, company law statutes, corporate governance codes and other related regulations as well as the general opinion of corporate participants are discussed in order to more clearly identify the corporate objectives in China. This having been ascertained, Chapter 4 continues to analyse why China pursues a shareholder-oriented approach. The tradition of ignoring shareholder rights, along with the influence of shareholder primacy in the UK and US, precipitates the increasingly urgent demand for a shareholder-centred corporate law and governance structure. Apart from the extensive and far-reaching historical reasons, political, legal, economic and other factors are also considered in this chapter to explain why SWM became the corporate objective in China.

The stakeholder model is antithetical to the shareholder model and requires directors to be accountable to more than just shareholders. Generally speaking, the stakeholder model requests directors to consider the interests of those who hold a stake in the company and run the company for all stakeholders rather than solely for shareholders. None of stakeholder groups is born to be subordinated to shareholders. Thus Chapter 5 examines whether the stakeholder model is a more suitable corporate objective. Following a brief introduction, the chapter endeavours to first clarify the concept of stakeholders and then justify the stakeholder model from its descriptive, instrumental and normative aspects. The important role of the stakeholder, the issue of long-termism, firm-specific investment and the internalisation of negative externalities are analysed in turn. Following this, the main problems of stakeholder theory are discussed. In particular, the balance of different stakeholders' interests, the accountability of management and enforcement of this model are explored in detail. Although these problems cannot be ignored, they can be mitigated. And, if the criteria of urgency and long-term sustainable development are adopted, many defects claimed by shareholder primacists could be alleviated or even overcome, even under the current legal framework.

Apart from problems inherent in SWM and benefits in the stakeholder model, China as a socialist country has added reason to look beyond maximising shareholders' interests. Chapter 6 considers the important role of employees and labour unions in Chinese companies, the mandatory rule for supervisory boards to have employee representatives, the requirement for directors to balance economic returns and social returns, and the political responsibility to support the government in achieving its political objectives, which potentially include

---

138 It should be noted that Continental countries in Europe such as Germany may have divergent views on corporate objectives though some scholars argue that there appears to be a convergence of the Anglo-American and Continental systems. This book mainly deals with corporate objectives and SWM in Anglo-American countries, namely the UK and US. As a result, the West or Western countries referred to in this book imply the UK and US unless explicitly specified in other ways.

providing employment opportunities, supporting the public good, protecting the environment and the like. All of these may indicate that the stakeholder model as corporate objective is more suitable than SWM in China. This chapter also finds that there is no explicit expression of SWM at the statutory level, which implies that replacing the current shareholder-centred inclination does not need a sea change of existing laws and regulations. Last but not least, some preliminary suggestions on the enforcement of the stakeholder model are offered and the lessons from shareholder empowerment are revisited for the better development of corporate governance in the Chinese context.

The final conclusion suggests that SWM should not be the corporate objective – especially in China – though private property needs to be better protected. On the other hand, there remains optimism that the stakeholder model has more valid grounds in China for the benefit of all stakeholders and long-term corporate value.

2 Shareholder wealth maximisation revisited

2.1 An overview

Shareholder wealth maximisation (SWM) is generally regarded as the primary, if not *the* only, corporate purpose. The board of directors and its delegates of daily management, executive officers, are therefore expected to maximise shareholder values. Such an objective and governance norm determine company law, and good corporate governance practice should endeavour to design a system with shareholders' interests at the centre. Providing better employee welfare, improving customer services, contributing more to communities and the like are not seen as proper ends for managers to pursue unless these activities can serve as a means to maximise shareholder value in due course. When conflicts arise between shareholders and non-shareholders, directors are only required to address the interests of shareholders and take actions to produce the highest possible returns for them, even at the expense of non-shareholder groups. Any behaviour that is inconsistent with SWM is subsequently considered *corporate deviance*.

However, many problems occur when SWM is the objective of the company; these became especially prominent after the recent financial crises. At best, it may not lead to the best corporate governance practice, and at worst it may provide the wrong emphasis on company law. Both the theoretical foundation and the rationale can be questioned. The principal-agent model is indeed problematic and the argument of residual claimants is untenable. In fact, there are increasingly more occasions where shareholder interests are in conflict with, or completely opposed to, corporate interests; the development of modern financial derivatives and the alienation of interest from shares is a good example. Along with externalisation, SWM is neither equivalent to maximising social welfare nor the best way to achieve it. It is therefore the main purpose of this chapter to re-examine and reassess SWM in detail.

Before entering into the formal discussion of SWM, the rest of this section explores some key corporate theories.[1]

---

1 Due to the fact that it is impossible to detail all of the theories of the company, the following paragraphs only focus on the main corporate theories and those directly related to corporate objective or SWM.

(1) *Concession theory.* In the very beginning, incorporation was regarded as a concession granted by the state. For instance, companies in the UK were initially formed by charters or grants from either Crown or Parliament.[2] The company therefore owed its existence to the state; such a privilege could only be legitimised on the basis that the company would serve the public good during its business.[3] In the context of concession theory, the state has a dominant role in the creation of the company, which justifies state intervention and regulation of corporate activities. The state could thus define the corporate objective to include other corporate stakeholders' interests and require the company to promote public interests in addition to shareholders' private interests.[4]

(2) *Aggregate theory.* However, with the arrival of general incorporation in the mid-nineteenth century, incorporation only required registration instead of a charter or grant, and the role of the state in corporate creation became irrelevant. Incorporation was no longer a privilege and became available to all. As Professor William Bratton argues, "the source of all firms' economic energy" is located in "individuals".[5] Incorporation was thought to stem from the right to own property and write contracts.[6] The public interest was thus no longer of concern and a company could be formed to only pursue private interests. In other words, the state lost the legitimacy to interfere with the corporate objective.

In contrast to concession theory, which fails to address the real people behind the corporation, aggregate theory admits the company is a voluntary association created by an aggregate of contracting individuals.[7] The company was considered a private arrangement by members, which is also why this theory can be seen as the ancestor of modern contract theory.[8] Accordingly, it is not surprising for the company to only serve shareholders' interests.

Aggregate theory, however, fails to explain the independent legal personality of the company. The company can make contracts, own property in its

---

2 For example, see Alan Dignam and John Lowry, *Company Law* (9th edn OUP, Oxford 2016) 144–145. It is pointed out that such charters or grants were awarded specifically to organizations with public-related works like Churches or local authorities. Ibid.

3 This is also why companies at that time were viewed as "a socially useful instrument for the state to carry out its public policy goals". For example, see Anant Sundaram and Andrew Inkpen, 'The Corporate Objective Revisited' (2004) 15 *Organization Science* 350, 351.

4 It was the same in the US, when a company could only be incorporated through state legislative action, the purposes were limited to "to promote a public interest or purpose". For example, see Lynda Oswald, 'Shareholders v. Stakeholders: Evaluating Corporate Constituency Statues under the Takings Clause' (1998) 23 *Journal of Corporation Law* 1, 11.

5 William Bratton, 'The New Economic Theory of the Firm: Critical Perspective from History' (1989) 41 *Stanford Law Review* 1471, 1475.

6 William Allen, 'Our Schizophrenic Conception of the Business Corporation' (1992) 14 *Cardozo Law Review* 261, 266–267.

7 David Millon, 'Theories of the Corporation' (1990) 39 *Duke Law Journal* 201, 213.

8 More discussion will be provided in the next section.

own capacity, sue or be sued, and directors' fiduciary duties are owed to the company rather than to shareholders (namely, only the company is eligible to be regarded as a victim in derivative actions). The weakness of the aggregate theory became more apparent with the advent of the separation between ownership and control. As observed by Berle and Means in the 1930s in *The Modern Corporation and Private Property*, the dispersed shareholders in large modern companies are both unable and uninterested in exercising control.[9] In contrast, the board of directors and its delegated managers had emerged into an important force in the corporate governance system and became protected from shareholders' interference in making most decisions.[10]

(3) *Corporate realism theory.* The company at this time was no longer thought of as a legal fiction created by the state in the context of concession theory, or dependent on members of the company in the context of aggregate theory; rather, it was argued to be a real entity after incorporation in accordance with corporate realism theory. According to the nineteenth-century German theorists, the company was regarded as a real person with a separate existence from shareholders. Due to such independence, the sum of private contracting individuals was not equivalent to the interests of the company.[11] Rather, the company had its own interests and shareholders had no superior position.

This solved the difficulty of explaining the independent corporate personality confronted by aggregate theory. But the core question is: what are the interests of this real person if they cannot be equated with the shareholders? The assumption is that the unaccountable directors will serve their own interests at the expense of others. Unaccountable discretionary managerial power, especially during financial crises, significantly challenges this theory.

(4) *Economic theories.* Economic theories primarily focus on the issue of efficiency, including the allocative and productive aspects. Since Professor Coase raised the question of corporate nature from the perspective of transaction costs,[12] economic theories have largely influenced corporate governance and corporate law scholarship. Maximisation of utility becomes the criterion. SWM is also justified mainly from an economic perspective. For example, the main economic justification for SWM is that, as acknowledged by the Company Law Review Steering Group (CLRSG), shareholders have greatest exposure to residual risk as a consequence of mismanagement.[13] As discussed later, contractarian theory, agency theory, economic efficiency

---

9 Adolf Berle and Gardiner Means, *The Modern Corporation and Private Property* (Transaction Publishers, New Brunswick 1991, originally published 1932).

10 *Infra* Chapter 3.

11 See Dignam and Lowry (n 2) 384.

12 Ronald Coase, 'The Nature of the Firm' (1937) 4 *Economica* 386.

13 CLRSG, *Modern Company Law for a Competitive Economy: The Strategic Framework* (DTI, London 1999) 34.

argument and the like are all used to support the superior position of the shareholder in the corporate governance system. This is not surprising, since companies are important economic actors, so an economic analysis of corporate governance and company law has been easily accepted.[14] In fact, the scholarship of law and economics, which significantly embraces economic theories of the company, largely dominates the academic study of corporate law – this is arguably a very important reason for the rise of SWM.[15] Thus, this chapter also incorporates an economic analysis of law to re-examine SWM as a corporate objective.

2.2 Logic of shareholder wealth maximisation

2.2.1 Proprietary justification

According to aggregate theory, whereby a company's independent existence is denied and everything is explained by reference to its members, the company is just an extension of the shareholders' hand. In other words, companies are seen as the private property of their shareholders or something transferred from shareholders collectively. In contrast to the later development of proprietary justification which is more likely to focus on the "entitlement to exercise *residual rights of control*",[16] the traditional proprietary justification of the nineteenth and early twentieth centuries tended to ignore the independent legal personality of the company. Historically, the concept of proprietorship, in other words the traditional logic of property, was the strongest justification for SWM. Since companies were viewed as the property of shareholders, directors and corporate executives should accordingly run companies exclusively in shareholders' interests. Put simply, the belief in proprietorship entitles shareholders to the right to control (though it may still need directors/executives to manage) and use the company to enhance their own benefits.[17] Such shareholder ownership remains the central doctrinal explanation of shareholder primacy, even after the recognition of the company as a separate legal entity.[18] The persisting notion, as Professor Sappideen points out, is that the company could be owned, and owned

---

14 Stephen Bottomley, 'From Contractualism to Constitutionalism: A Framework for Corporate Governance' (1997) 19 *Sydney Law Review* 277, 278.

15 It is argued that the law simply reflects the economic system with which it is suited.

16 John Armour and Michael Whincoup, 'The Proprietary Foundations of Corporate Law' (2007) 27 *Oxford Journal of Legal Studies* 429, 437. It will be discussed in some detail later in this section.

17 It should be noted that "the right of ownership is not an unrestricted right", namely the harmful use of property rights is restricted. Svetozar Pejovich, *The Economics of Property Rights: Towards a Theory of Comparative Systems* (Kluwer Academic Publishers, Dordrecht 1990) 27–28. But enhancing shareholder value at the expense of employees, creditors and other stakeholders is normally not restricted both in law and in practice. This point will be further developed in the section regarding externalisation below.

18 Ross Grantham, 'The Doctrinal Basis of the Rights of Company Shareholders' (1998) 57 *Cambridge Law Journal* 554, 555.

by the shareholders.[19] Indeed, the status of shareholder ownership seems to be the central and orthodox assumption of company law scholarship.[20]

Prior to the rise of large modern public companies in the late nineteenth century, entrepreneurs normally not only set up the business but also managed it by themselves for their own interests. Furthermore, before separate corporate personality had been established[21] and shareholders were unable to fully enjoy the protection of limited liability: if a company was badly run, shareholders risked losing everything, which could be far beyond the share capital they had initially invested. As a result of this, shareholders were keen on managing their companies. More interestingly, at that time, directors were usually requested to be shareholders of the company[22] in the traditional single-unit firms before the arrival of multi-unit ones. In Alfred Chandler's words, "owners managed and managers owned".[23] It is therefore not surprising that directors who were elected by shareholders would be required to operate the company in the interests of the shareholder as "owner".

Even after separate legal entity status was granted to incorporated companies in the UK in 1844, shareholders were still viewed as not substantially different from the company. According to section 3 of the *Joint Stock Companies Act 1856*, "seven or more persons . . . may . . . form themselves into an incorporated company"; in other words, the company at that time was seen as being made up of people rather than by people.[24] In the words of John William Smith, a company after incorporating comprised "several individuals, united in such a manner that they and their successors constitute but one person in law, a person distinct from that of any of the members, though *made up of them all*".[25] Put simply, *the shareholders were the company*.[26] Company law was deemed to be "a mere statutory development" of partnership law, and incorporation simply added several legal privileges.[27] Similarly, during roughly

19 Razeen Sappiedeen, 'Ownership of the Large Corporation: Why Clothe the Emperor' (1996) 7 *King's College Law Journal* 27, 27.
20 For example, see David Millon, 'New Directions in Corporate Law: Communitarians, Contractarians and the Crisis in Corporate Law' (1993) 50 *Washington and Lee Law Review* 1373, 1374.
21 Paddy Ireland, 'Capitalism without the Capitalist: The Joint Stock Company Share and the Emergence of the Modern Doctrine of Separate Corporate Personality' (1996) 17 *Journal of Legal History* 41, 45, referred to John Smith, *A Compendium of Mercantile Law* (3rd edn Saunders and Benning, London 1843) 81.
22 D Gordon Smith, 'The Shareholder Primacy Norm' (1997) 23 *Journal of Corporation Law* 277, 300. Similarly, there was also a share qualification to become a director in the UK at that time.
23 Alfred Chandler, *The Visible Hand: The Managerial Revolution in American Business* (Harvard University Press, Harvard 1977) 9.
24 Ireland, 'Capitalism without the Capitalist' (n 21) 47.
25 Benedict Sheehy, 'Shareholders, Unicorns and Stilts: An Analysis of Shareholder Property Rights' (2006) 6 *Journal of Corporate Law Studies* 165, 189 referred to John Smith, *A Compendium of Mercantile Law* (3rd edn Saunders and Benning, London 1843) 47 (emphasis in original).
26 Paddy Ireland, 'Company Law and the Myth of Shareholder Ownership' (1999) 62 *Modern Law Review* 32, 39.
27 Ibid. 39–40, referred to Nathaniel Lindley, *A Treatise on the Law of Partnership, including its Application on Joint Stock Companies* (4th edn Maxwell, London 1878) 22–23.

the same period in the US, companies were also regarded as "little more than limited partnerships, every member exercising through his vote an immediate control over the interests of the body".[28] The then chancellor of Delaware Court of Chancery William Allen also pointed out that companies at that time were like a limited partnership: "its property is equitably the property of the shareholders".[29] Naturally, a corollary is that shareholders comprise the ownership of the corporate property, and, as a result, the directors were elected by shareholders and bound to act on their behalf.[30]

However, in section 6 of the *Companies Act 1862*, the words "themselves into" were deleted. Consequently, just as a chair or table is made by, not of, a craftsman, a company is seen to be made *by* people.[31] Incorporation, then, in the late nineteenth century could be explained by creating an independent legal entity separate from shareholders.[32] Interestingly, the depersonalisation from the subtle linguistic changes also reveals the separate legal personality, as aptly noted by Professor Ireland and other scholars: in earlier periods when companies were deemed to be aggregations of people, a company was referred to as "them", in contrast to "it" used in modern company law exposition.[33]

Due to the later distinction between companies and shareholders, the role of shares became more important as the sole property left to shareholders. Correspondingly, at first, shares were viewed as "equitable interests in the property of the company", i.e. ownership of company assets.[34] A share of a company still indicated "a share of the totality of the company's assets".[35] Until then, shareholders continued to be regarded as the owners. The *Bligh* case, however, demonstrated that shareholders no longer have direct legal or equitable rights over company assets.[36] Or as the court in *Macaura v. Northern Assurance Co. Ltd* pointed

---

28 Professor Horwitz has further pointed out that: "as late as 1890, the leading decision of the United States Supreme Court did not see that the rights of the parties in regard to [the sale of] the assets of [a] corporation differ from those of a partnership on its dissolution". Morton Horwitz, 'Santa Clara Revisited: The Development of Corporate Theory' (1985) 88 *West Virginia Law Review* 173, 202.

29 Allen (n 6) 267.

30 Ibid. Also see Ireland, 'Company Law and the Myth of Shareholder Ownership' (n 26) 40.

31 Ireland, 'Capitalism without the Capitalist' (n 21) 47 (emphasis in original).

32 From the cases *Salomon v. A Salomon & Co Ltd* [1897] AC 22 (House of Lords) and *Gramophone and Typewriter Co Ltd v. Stanley* [1908] 2 KB 89 (Court of Appeal) to the more recent case *Prest v. Petrodel Resources Ltd and others* [2013] UKSC 34, there should be few doubts on this point.

33 Ireland, 'Capitalism without the Capitalist' (n 21) 46.

34 Paddy Ireland, Ian Grigg-Spall and Dave Kelly, 'The Conceptual Foundations of Modern Company Law' (1987) 14 *Journal of Law and Society* 149, 152.

35 Unlike "dividing capital into an indeterminate number of shares of fixed nominal capital" in modern companies, in early companies, the number of shares was fixed and "the sum called up on each of them varied". Therefore, in order to increase capital, the only way is to increase "the amount already called up on the fixed number" of those existing shares. Ireland, 'Capitalism without the Capitalist' (n 21) 48–49.

36 *Bligh v. Brent* (1837) 160 ER 397. Also see Ireland, 'Company Law and the Myth of Shareholder Ownership' (n 26) 41.

out: "the corporator even if he holds all the share[s] is not the corporation, and that neither he nor any creditor of the company has any property legal or equitable in the assets of the corporation".[37] The shares have been generally recast into the interests of company profits.[38] The assets are owned and only owned by the company; shareholders therefore have no right to them. Shareholders own shares in the company, which are an independent form of property, distinguished from company assets. The separate personality of the company implies a company is both the legal and the beneficial owner of its property. As summarised by Lord Evershed in *Short v. Treasury Commissioners*, "shareholders are not in the eyes of the law part owners of the undertaking. The undertaking is something different from the totality of its shareholdings".[39] Therefore, shareholders are only owners of shares and have no direct proprietary rights against corporate assets. It thus creates a significant legal space, i.e. companies own the assets and shareholders own the shares.[40]

Shares are property themselves, with their own value autonomous from companies' assets. They are, as Professor Ireland notes, "readily marketable commodities, liquid assets, titles to revenue easily converted by their holders into money".[41] Unlike partners, who have equitable ownership of partnership assets, shareholders only own shares – items of intangible property. Shares are legal property in their own right, which can be freely bought and sold. At present, it is rather explicit that shares are no longer an interest in the company's property. Ownership of the capital should not be confused with ownership of a company. Much as a BP or Apple shareholder is not allowed to visit a petrol station or Apple store to get free petrol or a free iPhone, shareholders cannot use or access corporate property simply because of the shares they own. Suffice it to say, shareholders do not own companies from any legal perspective and the property of companies cannot be owned by shareholders. The company is "no longer subject to the demands of private ownership".[42] Not least, the corporate separate legal personality, as illustrated in the *Salmon* case,[43] implies that the company as an

---

37 [1925] AC 619, 633.

38 Ireland, Grigg-Spall and Kelly, 'The Conceptual Foundations of Modern Company Law' (n 34) 152–153.

39 [1948] 1 KB 116, 122.

40 Ireland, 'Company Law and the Myth of Shareholder Ownership' (n 26) 41.

41 Paddy Ireland, 'Corporate Governance, Stakeholding, and the Company: Toward a Less Degenerate Capitalism' (1996) 23 *Journal of Law and Society* 287, 303. According to Professor Bainbridge, the ownership of shares represents "only a proportionate claim on the corporation's net assets in the event of liquidation, the right to a pro rata share of such dividends as may be declared by the board of directors from time to time, and limited electoral rights". Stephen Bainbridge, *Corporate Governance after the Financial Crisis* (OUP, Oxford 2012) 235.

42 Lorraine Talbot, *Critical Company Law* (Routledge, Oxford 2008) 113.

43 Per Lord Halsbury LC: "it seems to me impossible to dispute that once the company is legally incorporated it must be treated like any other independent person with its rights and liabilities appropriate to itself, and that the motives of those who took part in the promotion of the company are absolutely irrelevant in discussing what those rights and liabilities are". *Salomon v. A Salomon and Co Ltd* [1897] AC 22, 30–31.

independent entity cannot be owned. Meanwhile, from the economists' perspective, the concept of ownership is closely tied to "the possession of the residual rights of control" over the given assets.[44] Nevertheless, as soon as control became separated from ownership in the early twentieth century along with the independent legal personality, the so-called ownership right became incomplete.[45] Shareholders could no longer possess, use or control corporate property. Accordingly, if one could not unrestrictedly utilise the assets in the way one would like (unless subject to any previous agreement and regulatory rules), then no meaningful ownership right could exist either in law or in the economic domain.

Moreover, due to the limited liability rule, the liabilities of the company could not be attributed to its shareholders in full beyond a certain extent; therefore, in law, corporate property became separate from shareholders' property.[46] As a result, the traditional argument from the ownership perspective turned out to be less convincing than before.

Modern proprietary justification

Influenced by economic thought, modern proprietary justification identifies the company as a set of property rights which focus on the nonhuman assets that belong to it,[47] and "ownership" is defined by law and economics scholars as the right to exercise "residual rights of control".[48] The owner of the asset has residual rights of control over it and uses it in any way he or she wishes provided it is not inconsistent with prior contracts or laws. As Professor Hart observes, in a world full of transaction costs and where contrasts are inevitably incomplete, residual rights of control will influence both ex ante incentives to invest in a relationship and ex post bargaining power, as well as the division of ex post surplus in that relationship through their influence on asset usage.[49] Seeing the limitations of contractarian theory,[50] Professors Armour and Whincoup argue that proprietary rights could better protect their holders' rights, which could in turn

---

44 Oliver Hart, 'An Economist's Perspective on the Theory of the Firm' (1989) 89 *Columbia Law Review* 1757, 1765; Oliver Hart and John Moore, 'Property Rights and the Nature of the Firm' (1990) 98 *Journal of Political Economy* 1119, 1120.

45 Take one simple example, the owner of a stock is totally different from the owner of a horse, from levels of the control to the responsibility. As famously noted by Professors Adolf Berle and Gardiner Means, "If the horse lives, he [the owner] must feed it. If the horse dies, he must bury it. No such responsibility attaches to a share of stock". Berle and Means, *The Modern Corporation and Private Property* (n 9) 64.

46 For example, see *Macaura v. Northern Assurance Co. Ltd* (n 37). Also Patrick Fitzgerald, *Salmond on Jurisprudence* (12th edn Sweet and Maxwell, London 1996) 247.

47 Hart (n 44) 1765–1766; Hart and Moore (n 44) 1120.

48 Armour and Whincoup (n 16) 437.

49 Hart (n 44) 1766.

50 Namely a theory seeing a company as no more than contracts or a nexus of contracts, and which will be discussed soon in subsection 2.2.2 as it is another important justification for SWM.

facilitate more effective utilisation of corporate governance mechanisms.[51] They elaborate how property rights facilitate the sharing or petitioning of control of assets between various corporate participants.[52] In contrast to the aggregate theory and the traditional proprietary justification discussed earlier, both of which ignore corporate personality, the modern proprietary justification acknowledges the role of the independent legal personality of the company, though its role is considered limited.[53] But similar to the former justification, shareholders with residual rights of control could still order the directors to maximise their wealth, which is still thought to be legitimate.

Interestingly, one of the main attacks from Armour and Whincoup on contractarian theory is that savings offered by legal default rules only fit the smallest firms;[54] their own model suffers exactly the same problem, namely it only fits small partnership-like companies. Even the hypothetical example they provide is a single-member company.[55]

However, in the context of large public companies – the subject of this book – the situation will be significantly different. A typical diversified shareholder may not care about the company or its assets at all.[56] Take the UK, for example, it is practically impossible for shareholders in large public companies to direct directors. In addition, according to the latest *Share Register Survey Report*,[57] an estimated 54 per cent of the value of the UK stock market was held by investors outside the UK at the end of 2015. This follows a trend, up from 30.7 per cent in 1998 and 43.4 per cent in 2010.[58] It means a significantly large proportion of shareholders are not ready for a proper engagement in corporate governance, which is reflected in advocation in *Myners Review of Institutional Investment in the United Kingdom* (2001) as well as in the recent *UK Corporate Governance Code* and *UK Stewardship Code*.[59]

On the other hand, the critical and indispensable contributions made by non-shareholding stakeholders, such as human capital and intangible investment, are becoming more important to the success of a company, whilst the monetary capital

---

51 Armour and Whincoup (n 16) 431.

52 Also see Henry Hansmann and Reinier Kraakman, 'The Essential Role of Organizational Law' (2000) 100 *Yale Law Journal* 387, 407–408; Henry Hansmann, Reinier Kraakman and Richard Squire, 'Law and the Rise of the Firm' (2006) 119 *Harvard Law Review* 1333, 1337–1339.

53 Armour and Whincoup (n 16) 460–461.

54 Ibid. 435.

55 Ibid. 460.

56 They can diversify firm-specific risks by adopting diversified portfolio. See *infra* Chapter 2, section 2.5.2.

57 Office for National Statistics, Statistical bulletin: Ownership of UK Quoted Shares: 2014 (2 September 2015) at www.ons.gov.uk/economy/investmentspensionsandtrusts/bulletins/ownershipofukquotedshares/2015–09–02 [accessed 1 March 2017].

58 Ibid.

59 More details could be found in the FRC's website, at www.frc.org.uk/Our-Work/Codes-Standards/Corporate-governance.aspx [accessed 1 March 2017].

provided by shareholders is becoming comparatively less significant. Particularly in knowledge-based industries, employees who own the knowledge or specialised skills are the key "assets" of the company. The increasing importance of human capital cannot be ignored: "companies used to be physical assets, run by families and their helpers. Nowadays they are largely people, helped by physical assets".[60] It would be unfair to state that only shareholders are able to be the owners, not other stakeholders; they are all resource providers, and shareholders from this aspect are not fundamentally different from other stakeholders.

2.2.2 Contractarian theory and agency theory

With the development of law and economics disciplines, contractarian theory became the dominant theoretical understanding of corporate governance. In particular, Alchian and Demsetz's seminal paper *Production, Information Cost, and Economic Organization* and Jensen and Meckling's *Theory of the Firm: Managerial Behaviour, Agency Cost and Ownership Structure* in the 1970s introduced the contractual understanding of the company. In the eyes of Alchian and Demsetz, the company does not own any of its inputs; rather, it is the owner of various resources both tangibly and intangibly through "co-operative specialization" to increase productivity. As a result, the company is viewed as no different from "ordinary market contracting between any two people".[61] For example, a relationship between an employer and an employee within a company is deemed equivalent to the relationship between a customer and a grocer. A customer can fire their grocer by no longer buying from them, can assign the grocer the task of obtaining any item to sell at a mutually agreeable price and even punish the grocer by filing a lawsuit if defective goods are provided by the grocer – these are all matters an employer can do to their employee.[62] Alchian and Demsetz question the role of authority within the company raised by Professor Coase,[63] and parallel the role of authority with the role of consensual trade in the context of a free market. In other words, a company is deemed to be an artefact of continuously renegotiated contracts, or a "legal fiction which serve as a nexus for a set of contracting relationships among individuals".[64] The ownership of the company becomes irrelevant when seen from this contractarian perspective.

Shareholders are therefore regarded as the input owners of equity, similar to the input owners of labour, credit, raw materials and others. Input owners

---

60 Charles Handy, 'What Is a Company For?' (1991) 139 *RSA Journal* 231, 235.
61 Armen Alchian and Harold Demsetz, 'Production, Information Cost, and Economic Organization' (1972) 62 *American Economic Review* 777.
62 Ibid.
63 Coase (n 12) 404.
64 Michael Jensen and William Meckling, 'Theory of the Firm: Managerial Behavior, Agency Costs and Ownership Structure' (1976) 3 *Journal of Financial Economics* 305, 310. Similarly Professor Fama argues "the firm is just the set of contacts covering the way inputs are joined to create outputs and the way receipts from outputs are shared among inputs". Eugene Fama, 'Agency Problems and the Theory of the Firm' (1980) 88 *Journal of Political Economy* 288, 290.

co-operate within the company to strive for enhanced productivity with their respective comparative advantages, and thereby for higher rewards. However, there is a problem in ascertaining the rewards when all those input owners work as a team instead of working separately. The final output is usually not separable, which means each individual's contribution to the output is difficult to iden-tify. As Alchian and Demsetz point out, when the productivity and rewards are highly and accurately related, then the input productivity will be enhanced; oth-erwise input productivity will become smaller if there is only a loosely correlated relationship.[65] Put simply, given that one can shirk without being punished, the incentive to shirk will be great since only a small percentage of losses caused by the shirker will be borne by them and the rest would be shared by others. So it is of significance to reward each input owner as a team member correctly in order to incentivise higher productivity.

One option is to observe the behaviour of individual input owners to ascer-tain their contribution.[66] But monitoring is costly and cannot completely rely on the market owing to information asymmetry and any less incentive for new substitutes to shirk.[67] Alchian and Demsetz therefore suggest entitling the ulti-mate monitor the *net earnings of the team, net of payments of other inputs.*[68] That is, let the ultimate monitor be the residual claimant to earn "his residual through the reduction in shirking that he brings about, not only by the prices that he agrees to pay the owners of the inputs, but also by observing and directing the actions or uses of these inputs"; with this enhanced incentive, the monitor with residual claims would no longer shirk as before.[69] Shareholders are chosen to be such monitors, thereby entitling them to all the residual claims. Maximising shareholder returns is thereby equated with maximising overall team productivity, which is ultimately beneficial to society as a whole.

Based on Alchian and Demsetz's contractual theory, as well as the tricky problems of observing shirking and monitoring in team production, Jensen and Meckling developed the theory of agency costs in 1976. The agency problem emphasises the need for utility maximisation from the perspective of the holding agents who are accountable,[70] for the reason that the contracts between principals and agents are inevitably incomplete owing to transaction costs and, more impor-tantly, the uncertainty of future contingencies. The agency problem arises when

---

65 Alchian and Demsetz (n 61) 780.
66 For instance, "when lifting cargo (by more than one man) into the truck, how rapidly does a man move to the next piece to be loaded, how many cigarette breaks does he take, does the item being lifted tilt downward [on] his side?" Ibid. 780.
67 This is because the new substitute "still bears less than the entire reduction in team output for which he is responsible". Ibid. 781.
68 Ibid. 782.
69 The logic is "the lower is the cost of managing, the greater will be the comparative advantage of organizing resources within the firm". Ibid. 782–783.
70 This is also the fundamental reason why Professor Jensen claims no measurable objective would lead to directors' unaccountability. Michael Jensen, 'Value Maximisation, Stakeholder Theory, and the Corporate Objective Function' (2001) 14 *Journal of Applied Corporate Finance* 8, 8–9.

directors as the agent may possibly have a different agenda from the principal and maximise their own utility due to the conventional assumption of self-interested utility maximisation.[71] As Jensen and Meckling point out:

> One or more persons (the principal(s)) engage another person (the agent) to perform some service on their behalf which involves delegating some decision making authority to the agent. If both parties to the relationship are utility maximizers there is good reason to believe that the agent will not always act in the best interests of the principal.[72]

Correspondingly, the agency problem becomes an inevitable consequence after allowing directors and their delegated managers to run the company, especially in public companies with substantially dispersed shareholders and where professionals have almost unchallenged power. The costs incurred when the directors act in their own interests at the expense of the principals are referred to as agency costs, which include: (1) the monitoring expenditures by the principal; (2) the binding expenditures by the agent; and (3) the residual loss.[73] In other words, they are mainly "the costs resulting from agents misusing their position as well as the costs of monitoring and disciplining them to try to prevent abuse".[74] Trying to structure private contracts to control the behaviour of agents is extremely expensive and difficult by virtue of the changing future of the company[75] and the problem of the "free ride".[76] As others have argued, on the one hand, it is likely never to be optimal for agents to act in a way that is best for the principals' interests,[77] and on the other, agents are much better informed about both their own

---

71 However, there are increasing doubts against this conventional assumption. Just as Professor Lynn Stout argued, most people are not psychopaths, they are neither purely rational nor purely selfish. Indeed the "prosocial behaviour" is omnipresent: the vast majority of people are at least prosocial to a certain extent and would make modest personal sacrifices for their overall well-being. Lynn Stout, *The Shareholder Value Myth* (Berrett-Koehler Publishers, San Francisco 2012) 96–97. This point will be further explored later in this chapter.

72 Jensen and Meckling, 'Theory of the Firm' (n 64) 308.

73 Ibid.

74 Professor Mallin more generally describes the agency costs including the agent misusing its power for its own benefits; the agent not taking appropriate risks in pursuance of the principal's interests; the problem of information asymmetry. Christine Mallin, *Corporate Governance* (5th edn OUP, Oxford 2016) 17.

75 Put simply, even the most comprehensive contract today would not cover the new circumstances tomorrow, and wasting effort identifying or dealing with issues which might never happen is unavoidable if attempting to elaborate such contracts. Frank Easterbrook and Daniel Fischel, 'The Corporate Contract' (1989) 89 *Columbia Law Review* 1416, 1444–1445.

76 No one could seize all the benefits from working out all problems in advance, because other companies could simply copy these answers without paying the first solver, or say share part of the first solver's expenditure. Ibid. 1445–1446.

77 Andrew Tylecote and Francesca Visintin, *Corporate Governance, Finance and the Technological Advantage of Nations* (Routledge, New York 2008) 16.

actions as well as the outcomes. In addition, as Professor Bainbridge points out, "while the principal reaps part of the value of hard work by the agent, the agent receives all of the value of shirking".[78]

There may be opportunities for an agent to put their own interests first after calculating they would be better off doing so – unless the agent can reap the entire benefits of their efforts, which is of course impossible. By virtue of the difficulties in observability and information asymmetries, as identified by agency theory, conflicts between principals and agents as differing economic actors always exist.[79] Likewise, in the corporate context, problems arise when those who run the company are not "owners". Directors, including executives, are treated as agents of shareholders, managing companies for the latter. Shareholders are thought to have the best interests in monitoring. As the so-called residual owners, they have, as argued, higher impetus to assure the wealth maximisation of a company. Specifically, both the residual risk and the variability of the cash flow stream provide shareholders with enough incentive to monitor. Any other non-measurable objectives for directors are deemed to leave loopholes for managerial deviation. As a consequence, in the opinion of contractarians, shareholder interests should be the sole objective for management, in particular from the perspective of ensuring managerial accountability and lowering agency costs.

2.3 Problems in agency theory

However, such a principal-agent model is both descriptively and normatively problematic. First of all, there is indeed no legal agency relationship between shareholders and directors, and the *sui generis* position of directors cannot be justified either. Subsequently, the residual claimant argument and economic efficiency argument developed from agency theory are also flawed. This section discusses the main problems of agency theory in detail.

2.3.1 Agency relationship

The economic term "agency relationship" does not bear the exact same meaning as its juridical counterpart. The economic concept of "agency" is concerned with the costs that arise from delegation rather than with the precise nature of the juridical relationship to which delegation gives rise.[80] In law, agency is the fiduciary relationship that arises when one person (the principal) manifests assent to

78 Stephen Bainbridge, *The New Corporate Governance in Theory and Practice* (OUP, New York 2008) 74. For example, the shirker would receive all the benefits of leisure and other non-pecuniary income from his shirking but only bear a fraction of the loss from the reduced output.
79 Hart (n 44) 1758–1759.
80 Law Commission and Scottish Law Commission, 'Company Directors: Regulating Conflicts of Interest and Formulating a Statement of Duties' (Law Com No 261, 1999) para 3.11.

another person (the agent) that the agent shall act on the principal's behalf, and subject to the principal's control, and the agent manifests assent or otherwise consents to act.[81] There are two implications in the agency relationship: first, the agent should perform an act on behalf of the principal; second, and more importantly, the principal should have the authority to control their agent. In the corporate context, it is problematic to treat directors as agent of shareholders on the grounds that shareholders are no longer the owners of the company.[82] Furthermore, there is no direct or explicit contractual relationship between both parties, since it is the company rather than the shareholders that enters into the relationship with the directors. Directors therefore are not agents who follow the shareholders' direction.

Moreover, shareholders, the so-called principals, have little control over directors, the so-called agents. As discussed in Chapter 3, although not all countries accept that the powers of the directors are *original and undelegated*, it is widely agreed that directors' managerial prerogative as a general rule does not need the shareholders' assent. Directors are required to exercise their independent business judgement. In other words, so-called agency theory cannot explain the *sui generis* position of directors. An agent is the person who is employed to perform an act on behalf of the principal, so at least the principal should have the right to control the behaviour of their agent. However, shareholders cannot give directors of boards binding instructions in general. Shareholders as principals cannot even force directors as agents to pay them dividends. The *duty of obedience* as a rule of agency does not exist in the shareholder-director relationship.[83] While directors are seen as agents by contractarians, they do not strictly fit the definition of agents from the law of agency.

Though it could be argued that directors are generally more specialised than shareholders, and that consequently "ceding authority to the board" is "in shareholders' interest and is part of a public company's optimal structure";[84] for the sake of economic efficiency, the authority and power of the board are only subject to the law and the company's constitution instead of to the shareholders, who are regarded as principals. As long as the directors of public companies are not pursuing personal interests, it is then very hard for the court to blame the directors for not maximising shareholder wealth. Both the business judgement

81 The American Law Institute, Restatement (Third) of Agency section 1.01.
82 In law, it has already become clear directors should no longer be regarded as mere agents of shareholders. For example, see *Automatic Self-Cleansing Filter Syndicate Co. Ltd v. Cuninghame* [1906] 2 Ch 34; *Gramophone and Typewriter Co Ltd v. Stanley* [1908] 2 KB 89. Moreover, directors' duties are in principle owed to the company instead of the shareholders.
83 Margaret Blair and Lynn Stout, 'Specific Investment: Explaining Anomalies in Corporate Law' (2006) 31 *Journal of Corporation Law* 719, 726.
84 Lucian Bebchuk, 'Letting Shareholders Set the Rules' (2006) 119 *Harvard Law Review* 1784, 1792; also see Bainbridge, *The New Corporate Governance in Theory and Practice* (n 78) 7–8.

rule in the US[85] and case law in the UK[86] tell us that whenever self-serving is not involved and a reasonable effort has been made, courts in both countries will not second-guess the business judgement of directors. That is to say, under such a situation, the court shows a great deference to the board's decision and a noticeable reluctance to overturn them, even if the decisions are not the best ones or harm shareholders' economic interests.[87] The *sui generis* position of the board of directors, namely directors' autonomous managerial power and discretion, is therefore inconsistent with authentic agency theory.

From a normative perspective, the so-called rational actor assumption, which is seen as the basis of contractarianism, is challenged by behavioural law and economics (BLE). Human beings make decisions for many different reasons, which are not necessarily economic-based. If one makes decisions on non-economic values or beliefs, then the efficiency-focused justification of shareholder primacists becomes less convincing.[88] BLE experiments, including ultimatum games and public good games, show that economically rational strategy is not always favoured; instead, reciprocal altruism, fairness and cooperation are frequently reflected.[89] At the very least, such a perspective adds significant insights to challenge the conventional standpoint of rational economic actors.

In fact, besides the problems discussed above, the contractarian theory itself suffers increasingly more criticism for its deregulatory claims as well as for its failure to explain corporate separate legal personality. It is noteworthy that contractarians argue that limited liability is a default rule provided by company law, which could be created by private arrangements to the same effect without the law.[90] However, the company's ability to own property in its own name as a legal consequence of the independent legal personality of the company cannot be explained by the so-called *nexus of contract* theory. The so-called entity shielding, or say affirmative asset partitioning, which protects corporate property

85 That is "directors of a corporation . . . are clothed with [the] presumption, which the law accords to them, of being [motivated] in their conduct by a bona fide regard for the interests of the corporation whose affairs the stockholders have committed to their charge". *Gimbel v. Signal Companies, Inc.* (1974) 316 A 2d 599, 608 (Delaware).

86 For example, see *Re Smith and Fawcett Ltd* [1942] Ch 304; *Howard Smith Ltd v. Ampol Petroleum Ltd* [1974] AC 821. Moreover, section 172(1) of the *Companies Act 2006* explicitly specifies that a director of a company must act in the way *he considers*, not what a court may consider, for the best interests of the company.

87 Of course, if an action caused substantial damage to the company, it may be under more careful and cautious scrutiny by the courts. However, the burden of proof is still on the person who wants to challenge the directors' good faith in making decisions. For example, see *Charles Forte Investments v. Amanda* [1964] Ch 240.

88 Kent Greenfield, 'Using Behavioral Economics to Show the Power and Efficiency of Corporate Law as Regulatory Tool' (2002) 35 *University of California Davis Law Review* 581, 586.

89 Ibid. 628–633.

90 For example, Professors Hansmann, Kraakman and Squire argue that the institution of limited liability for shareholders could possibly be realised merely through private contracts. Hansmann, Kraakman and Squire, 'Law and the Rise of the Firm' (n 52) 1337, 1339.

from its shareholders' personal creditors, must recourse to the fiat and decree of regulatory law due to the prohibitively high transaction costs and moral hazards.[91] In other words, although shielding shareholders' personal assets from the company's creditors might possibly be realised through private contracts, shielding the company's assets from the owners' personal creditors cannot be achieved merely through private contracts.[92] Moreover, regarding tort liability, it is ironic to argue that tort victims would consent to waive or limit their right to go after the personal assets of shareholders.[93] Last but not least, the increasing mandatory rules and regulations following the financial crisis in 2007/8 largely refute contractarian deregulatory claims.

Although an agency perspective could help to understand modern companies in many aspects, it is wrong and perilous to simply equate the relationships within the company to an agency relationship.[94] Directors are much more than agents. Insulating boards from shareholders' continuous intervention by giving boards of directors the *sui generis* position and extensive power could be seen as an important means to preserve the benefits of centralised management.[95] Thus, this principal-agent relationship fails to accurately describe the relationship between shareholders and directors, let alone other relationships between other participants within the corporate governance system.

2.3.2 Residual claim

In the context of agency theory, namely the contractarian framework, relationships between various stakeholders and the company are seen as contractual. The company has no owner; shareholders are just one group of investors, not different in nature from other stakeholders such as creditors or employees. Shareholders contribute equity capital in exchange for the right to profits. Equally, employees contribute labour and skills in exchange for their salary and creditors contribute credit in exchange for interest. By the same token, consumers, suppliers and even local communities and the like can all be regarded as making a certain investment in order to obtain a corresponding consideration, which could vary from products and services to payment and tax revenues. Further justification for granting shareholders a superior status is required.

Nonetheless, it is argued that the position of shareholders remains in contrast to other corporate stakeholders because they are residual claimants to the income generated by the company, which provides them with a different incentive compared to that of other stakeholders. Shareholders as residual claimants can then

---

91 Ibid. 1340 (footnote omitted).

92 Ibid. 1340–1343.

93 As admitted even by Professors Hansmann, Kraakman and Squire, limited liability to involuntary creditors cannot be achieved by contract alone, though they dismiss it by arguing it is "relatively unimportant". Ibid. 1341.

94 Or to put too much of a lopsided emphasis on the financial structure.

95 See *infra* Chapter 3, section 3.3.1 for the benefits of centralised management.

"reap the marginal dollar" of the corporate profits and "suffer the marginal dollar" of any corporate losses as well,[96] which means they are only entitled to what is left from the income stream after all fixed claims are met.

Assuming such a residual nature argument is valid, as the recipients of the residual cash flow and income stream in a healthy and solvent company, shareholders would have the greatest impetus to maximise the wealth of the company since they could receive the entire surplus (or at least most of it) after the fixed claims of other stakeholders have been satisfied.[97] Such a gain allocation rule allows shareholders to receive whatever is left from the income stream and thereby tightly ties their benefits to the performance of the company. Wealth of residual claimants would be maximised in the event that company wealth is maximised by virtue of that residual nature. As residual owners, shareholders would receive higher dividends and share value when the company is run well, and less or even losing all their investment if the company is run badly. In particular, the position in the allocation sequence of corporate profits underlines the shareholders' eagerness to pursue the success of the company. Contrary to the so-called definable and compulsory returns, such a residual risk-bearing nature could stimulate those residual claimants into choosing, and wholeheartedly supporting, the best investment projects for the development of the company. It follows that maximising the wealth of shareholders could be equated with maximisation of company wealth owing to this residual nature, which in turn would foster economic efficiency and benefit society as a whole. In short, this assumption suggests that corporate interests are best served when shareholders' interests are maximised.[98] As some scholars have commented, the aggregation of all shareholder interests in a company is equivalent to the company's interests.[99]

Unfortunately, there are several problems with this argument. To begin with, shareholders are normally not entitled to claim dividends or any profits in a solvent company. It is in fact the board of directors which has the sole control of its disposition and decides where the residue should go. Directors in most jurisdictions have the right to decide not to pay shareholders dividends, and instead deliver the benefits to non-shareholding stakeholders by retaining the profits for future business, increasing employee benefits, improving customer

---

96 Lynn LoPucki, 'The Myth of the Residual Owner: An Empirical Study' (2004) 82 *Washington University Law Quarterly* 1341, 1343–1344.

97 For example, see Jonathan Macey, 'Fiduciary Duties as Residual Claims: Obligations to Nonshareholder Constituencies from a Theory of the Firm Perspective' (1999) 84 *Cornell Law Review* 1266, 1267. In the meanwhile, as Professor Stephen Bainbridge argued, if directors just "siphon some portion of the corporation's free cash flow into their own pockets", the stakeholders' interests may not readily be harmed, but the shareholders as residual claimants would apparently be damaged. Bainbridge, *The New Corporate Governance in Theory and Practice* (n 78) 68–69.

98 It is because if the interests of other stakeholders were to be fixed by their contracts, maximising the shareholders' residual claim means maximising the total social value of the firm. Lynn Stout, 'Why We Should Stop Teaching *Dodge v. Ford*' (2008) 3 *Virginia Law Business Review* 163, 173.

99 For example, see JiLian Yap, 'Considering the Enlightened Shareholder Value Principle' (2010) 31 *Company Lawyer* 35, 35.

service and expanding Research and Development (R&D), among other things. Shareholders cannot receive anything, at least directly, unless the board decides to distribute dividends. The increasing share price can be seen as an indirect benefit, since shareholders can sell the shares to realise the added value. But this is still subject to the board's decision – it can change the earnings into expenses by increasing employee benefits, improving customer service, and expanding R&D, thereby making the share price decline.[100] In other words, due to the corporate independent personality, shareholders cannot enjoy corporate profits directly in most jurisdictions unless directors so decide; moreover, they are denied the ability to direct companies, including forcing the board to declare dividends. Rules empowering the directors with the right to determine how to utilise and allocate assets in all major jurisdictions fatally destroy the argument that shareholders are the residual claimants who are entitled to "every penny of profit left over after the firm's contractual obligations to creditors, suppliers, and employees have been met".[101]

Only in insolvency law will shareholders receive the residue after the claims of employees, creditors and other stakeholders have been fully satisfied. Nevertheless, even under such circumstances, shareholders are by no means the only, or most appropriate, residual owners. Just like the simple and straightforward example illustrated by Professor LoPucki, in a company which is on the brink of insolvency, if the unsecured debts owed by the company are much more than its assets, it will be the unsecured creditors who own the residue, namely the remaining assets after the outstanding taxes, employees or secured creditors are fully paid off.[102] All of the gains and losses from action taken during the reorganisation, for example, would therefore fall to the unsecured creditors instead of the shareholders in these circumstances. For instance, if an insolvent company with £1,000,000 in assets owes £2,000,000 to unsecured creditors, it is in fact those unsecured creditors who have the right to any residue. In addition, stakeholders such as employees who have made a firm-specific investment[103] could also be seen as the residual claimants, because under such a situation they would also lose out. According to LoPucki's empirical study, the identity of the residual owner is difficult to ascertain, and indeed, multiple residual owners exist with differing priority levels.[104]

Another important justification for the proponents of the residual claimant argument is the issue of incentive. As shown above, shareholders are argued to have the greatest incentive to maximise company wealth and monitor directors' accountability owing to the so-called residual characteristic. On the other

---

100 For more discussion, see Stout, *The Shareholder Value Myth* (n 71) 41.
101 Blair and Stout, 'Specific Investment: Explaining Anomalies in Corporate Law' (n 83) 728 referred to Robert Clark, *Corporate Law* (Little, Brown 1986) 594–602.
102 LoPucki (n 96) 1342.
103 More detailed discussion on firm-specific investment is on offer in Chapter 5, section 5.3.3.
104 LoPucki (n 96) 1352. The scope of the identity is further complicated by the corporate group. Ibid. 1354–1355.

hand, non-shareholding stakeholders, as argued,[105] have no incentives to advance corporate success. Their interests are regarded as barely, if at all, aligned with corporate performance. The main basis for this incentive argument is that since stakeholders have fixed claims, such as monthly salaries among other fixed pay-outs, creating any marginal profits cannot make any difference to fixed claimants. As a result, they have little impetus to maximise company value. It is argued that stakeholders as fixed claimants "do no better whether the firm performs *spectacu-larly well* or *just well*".[106]

However, apart from the problems with the residual claimant argument, stake-holders can be at least partly better off when the company runs *spectacularly well* than *just well*: they can receive benefits over and above their fixed claim. Take government for example: if a company is run well, it can definitely collect more tax revenues. This means that the local administration will endeavour to improve infrastructure and provide more convenient facilities, etc. to encourage the com-pany to stay in its area and help corporate growth, allowing them to receive more in addition to the so-called fixed claims. Similarly, employees may also have the right incentive to help the company perform better, as it is not uncommon for employees in a well-performing company to receive generous bonuses on top of wages, and the better run the company, the bigger the bonuses employees can obtain. Creditors and suppliers will also gain more security for their contribu-tion when companies are run well. Thus, stakeholders are in effect able to obtain a fraction of the extra benefits, namely the residue, apart from the fixed rights to a particular flow of income stream. Such an incentive can be made explicit in advance, for instance in the design of performance-related bonuses. In other words, stakeholders' claims are not entirely fixed.[107] They also have a material incentive to compel directors to run companies better.

It should be equally clear that shareholders are not the only group that under-takes residual risks, although it is often asserted by financial economists "as if it were a self-evident fact".[108] A creditor will lose their interest as well as their principal when a company fails. A supplier will lose out in view of the fact that its specialised production line and machinery might be useless if the company is run badly or fails.[109] Similarly, an employee who wishes to join a certain company may invest a large amount of time, energy and money in developing special-ised and unique skills required by the company. Such an employee's fate would

---

105 Sundaram and Inkpen, 'The Corporate Objective Revisited' (n 3) 354.

106 Ibid. (emphasis in original).

107 Take employees for example: although their wages are normally fixed claims, other rewards such as the bonuses mentioned before and certain retirement benefits are definitely not fixed. For example, see Jingchen Zhao, 'The Curious Case of Shareholder Primacy Norm: Calling for A More Realistic Theory' (2012) 15 *International Trade and Business Law Review* 1, 18.

108 For example, see Mary O'Sullivan, *Contests for Corporate Control: Corporate Governance and Economic Performance in the United States and Germany* (OUP, Oxford 2001) 50.

109 The supplier may provide highly specialised products and services to a given company which may be devaluated or completely worthless to other companies.

then be closely linked with the company on the grounds that their specialized, firm-specific skill may be less useful or even useless to other companies. Stakeholders therefore assume risks as well.

Moreover, the limited liability of shareholders means part of the residual risk has already been shifted to other stakeholders, such as creditors. On the grounds that the liability of shareholders would not exceed the initial investment, around some critical point, such as in the vicinity of corporate bankruptcy, shareholders may take excessive risks. Under these circumstances, shareholders have no material interests – namely, they have few chances to be paid, and as economic actors they have no reason to resist very risky investing projects. There is then a serious potential of externalisation because shareholders are able to "reap all of the benefits of risky activity but do not bear all of the cost".[110] Even worse, in the event that shareholders have possibly no chance of receiving anything, they would have a more vociferous preference for high-risk activities, especially when these shareholders lose the incentive to increase any margin, since in this situation their residual claim has gone under water.[111] As Professor Crespi points out, there is a problem in the case of impending insolvency of incentives for inefficient investment.[112] Of course, even in an ordinary situation, such a phenomenon of disproportionate gain by externalising costs remains.[113]

As a result, the point at which shareholders have the most to lose or gain is not always accurate. In particular, when considering that shareholders nowadays usually diversify their investment and thereby the risk by adopting a diversified portfolio strategy, their interests are not always identical to the company's best interests, as previously discussed.[114] The incentive argument for shareholders is not invulnerable. The preferred risk strategy for shareholders when they are able to diversify unsystematic risks or when, close to bankruptcy, there is little hope of being paid might be correspondingly different from the interests of the company and other stakeholders.[115] We can see that unsecured creditors own the residue

110 Frank Easterbrook and Daniel Fischel, *The Economic Structure of Corporate Law* (Harvard University Press, Cambridge 1991) 49–50.
111 Ibid. 69.
112 Gregory Crespi, 'Maximizing the Wealth of Fictional Shareholders: Which Function Should Directors Embrace?' (2007) 32 *Journal of Corporation Law* 381, 392.
113 On the one hand, their losses would never exceed what they had already paid; and on the other, the costs are borne partly by creditors among other stakeholders. For example, see Frank Easterbrook and Daniel Fischel, 'Limited Liability and the Corporation' (1985) 52 *University of Chicago Law Review* 89, 104. An in-depth discussion of externalisation is provided in the next section.
114 John Armour and Jeffrey Gordon, 'Systematic Harms and Shareholder Value' (2014) 6 *Journal of Legal Analysis* 35, 36.
115 It is argued that mechanisms outside the company law regime could be adopted to restrain such tendency. For instance, directors could be held personally liable for causing creditors increasing losses by virtue of their negligence or fraud under such circumstances. Directors are required to take reasonable care to protect the interests of the creditor when the company is nearly insolvent. Furthermore, the rule of wrongful trading in the *Insolvency Act* could be regarded as another effective deterrent against directors who dare to take excessive risks which may enlarge creditors' losses. However, the workability of these mechanisms is doubtful in practice. See *infra* Chapter 2, section 2.4.1.

of what secured creditors have left, whilst shareholders could still be called the ultimate residual claimants by definition. In other words, shareholders are always deemed to be the last persons who have a claim on whatever is left after all other claims – secured and unsecured – have been met, even if they have little or no chance of receiving anything and cash flow has little possibility of moving to them. Under such circumstances, however, being a residual claimant does not provide any meaningful incentive. Thanks to the limited liability rule, in such a situation shareholders have much to gain and little to lose from taking excessive risks;[116] the conventional incentive argument becomes invalid and the residual claimant theory therefore can no longer support the shareholder-centred model.

In particular, with the development of financial derivatives, shareholders are not necessarily affected by a company's decision under certain conditions. Indeed, they can be indifferent to corporate performance and alienate their personal interests from their shares. Take hedge funds for example, shareholders may not care about the decline in share prices as it is possible for them to profit from poor performance – when they sell the shares short, a decline in the share price rather than an increase is desired.[117]

Last but not least, another argument in support of shareholders' superior position is that shareholders who provide capital do not demand immediate compensation, if other stakeholders can provide their contribution without requiring immediate compensation and agree to accept the compensation adjusted by corporate performance or "in the form of a share of whatever value is realized".[118] This seems to provide some justification for granting shareholders special status. On closer inspection, however, many stakeholders such as creditors also have to wait a long period until they can be paid off. It is not uncommon either for a supplier to have to wait some time to be paid after providing materials or services. Even for employees who usually rely on monthly salaries, there is still a significant annual bonus to award well-performing employees. This means that although employees, owing to their vulnerable position, have to claim a fraction of their compensation in a comparatively short period,[119] they still need to wait, normally a year, for another part of the payment in the form of annual bonuses. Moreover, the monetary capital contributed by shareholders is worth exactly the amount they invest, it would be meaningless to compensate shareholders immediately after they provide money. In fact, shareholders receive shares as soon as they provide capital. Shares are themselves valuable assets and they can be sold at any

---

116 Shareholders at that time would have almost nothing to lose. If the high-risk ventures succeed, they will gain substantial benefits; if they fail, the interests of the company and other stakeholders will be further damaged.

117 For example, activist hedge fund manager Carl Icahn only cares about his own wealth, not the interests of the company or other shareholders. Stout, *The Shareholder Value Myth* (n 71) 93.

118 For example, see Louis Putterman, 'Ownership and the Nature of the Firm' (1993) 17 *Journal of Comparative Economics* 243, 246.

119 This is mainly for supporting employees and their families' living in the contemporary society. It would be difficult to imagine a worker and their family having to wait a year or even longer for the income.

time, even immediately after being acquired. Therefore, this so-called distinction between shareholders and other stakeholders cannot be a reason to justify shareholders' preferential position or residual status.

A more accurate description as a result is that stakeholders other than shareholders can equally enjoy a fraction of the surplus and become residual owners, and shareholders are not the only risk bearers, owing to their limited liability and diversification, among other things. Also, excessive risk-taking by shareholders along with the alienation of share interests could harm the best interests of the company and society. Hence, apart from the problematic agency relationship, we can see that the argument of residual claimants is untenable as well.

2.3.3 Efficiency argument

Economic theories primarily focus on the issue of efficiency, and their rationales are to a great extent based on the justification of efficiency. More economic efficiency by way of effectively allocating financial resources is hoped to create more social wealth and benefit the economy as a whole. Not surprisingly, the efficiency argument is also utilised by advocates as a justification for SWM. Specifically, it is argued that efficiency will decrease if the goal is not straightforward or definite.[120] Given that directors fall into a position accountable to divergent interests of different corporate stakeholders, efficiency and effectiveness will inevitably reduce. Even worse, directors might always have an excuse for their self-serving behaviour under such circumstances, which implies a rise in the costs of directors' opportunism. As famously argued by Professors Easterbrook and Fischel, directors would be free and answerable to no one if they were required to take all stakeholders' interests into account.[121] It is thought that directors would pursue their own interests, and they would become blameless because they could always use an excuse to advance certain stakeholder interests which closely match their own. Apart from a less efficient decision-making process, the final decision may not be optimal to a large extent according to the economic efficiency argument. The worry is that if there are two or more 'masters', directors can play them off against each other. A clear directive is needed; as the argument goes, one cannot serve two masters at the same time. It is also believed that monitoring would be easier if there were only a single objective. When directors are required to run a company in all stakeholders' interests by balancing different or even countervailing interests, the difficulty of monitoring increases substantially, implying that more costs would be incurred.

This argument is, however, untenable. Such an argument is based on the premise that shareholder interests are homogenous. But different shareholders may have

---

120 Furthermore, it is believed that if the stakeholder model is applied, it would be impossible for the market or future investors to judge the performance of a given company since some costs could be seen as being justified to meet certain stakeholders' interests.

121 Easterbrook and Fischel, *The Economic Structure of Corporate Law* (n 110) 38.

different pursuits from different risk preferences to different expected returns. Directors will also confront difficulties in making decisions on the grounds of such divergence. Shareholder interests are more than economic profits; for example, some shareholders may be more concerned about environmental issues or community welfare in addition to a fair return. If directors cannot balance various different stakeholders' interests or efficiently work with a singular objective under the stakeholder theory, the same doubt could be raised here: how can directors do their job when different shareholder interests exist? To take one step back, even though the ultimate goal of shareholders could be roughly categorised into making economic interests in general, they could possibly have substantially dissimilar time frames and risk preferences in accordance with their degree of diversification, among other things. Different classes of shareholders have different specific requirements, and simple wealth maximisation cannot cover all situations. Unless further proof can be provided, Easterbrook and Fischel's statement that the preferences of diverse shareholders remain similar is not persuasive.[122] Shareholders do have divergent criteria when assessing corporate performance from time to time.[123] Indeed, requiring companies to focus on SWM is not necessarily consistent with all shareholders' welfare. A diversified shareholder's interest is not identical to the well-being of the company or the interests of undiversified shareholders.[124] Private equity and hedge funds may even have completely different interests from other shareholders as a result of certain financial arrangements.[125]

Even assuming that focus on a single objective is the only positive way to be efficient, this paradigm claims to be able to avoid the potential risk of being distracted by various stakeholder interests;[126] increased economic efficiency is by no means the same as enhanced higher corporate or social welfare. The advantage brought by increased efficiency can be diminished by the negative externalities and unchecked social costs caused by the process of pursuing SWM. This so-called efficiency is defined from the perspective of shareholder value, since benefits to stakeholders other than shareholders are usually deemed to be costs.

Moreover, shareholders are not the only group that provides firm-specific investment; the explicit contracts made in advance between other stakeholders

---

122 Easterbrook and Fischel, *The Economic Structure of Corporate Law* (n 110) 70. Similarly, Professor Reinier Kraakman and his co-authors have commented that those investors of pecuniary capital have, or at least are able to be induced to have, relatively homogeneous interests. Reinier Kraakman *et al.*, *The Anatomy of Corporate Law: A Comparative and Functional Approach* (3rd edn OUP, Oxford 2017) 13. Interestingly, in the previous edition, the authors use the phrase '*highly* homogenous interests'. See Reinier Kraakman *et al.*, *The Anatomy of Corporate Law: A Comparative and Functional Approach* (2nd edn OUP, Oxford 2009) 15.

123 For more discussion, see *infra* Chapter 2, section 2.5.2.

124 Henry Hu, 'Risk, Time, and Fiduciary Principles in Corporate Investment' (1990) 38 *University of California at Los Angeles Law Review* 277, 299.

125 Stout, *The Shareholder Value Myth* (n 71) 92–93.

126 Like the similar argument: "a venture is worth more if managers are tasked with a clear mission, such as the maximisation of the stock price than with a more amorphous mission involving the balancing of competing interests". Ian Lee, 'Efficiency and Ethics in the Debate about Shareholder Primacy' (2006) 31 *Delaware Journal of Corporate Law* 533, 537.

as one party and the company as the other would deter the incentive of other stakeholders from making those essential specific investments. Any ex ante sharing rules can inevitably lead to shirking since each party has an impulse to free ride on others' effort.[127] A fixed share will be distributed to the party regardless of how hard or how well they work. Even the ultimate output will be shrunk when any party/team member shirks; the shirker would only undertake a small portion of the diminished surplus whilst enjoying the entire benefits of shirking. On the other hand, any ex post sharing arrangement could give rise to another more serious problem – rent-seeking, which is that money and time among other resources may be wasted when various parties compete for a bigger slice of those already fixed surpluses.[128] Both situations would erode the aggregate wealth, either by sub-optimum efforts beforehand or wasting part of it afterwards. In order to achieve efficiency and utilise all corporate stakeholders' potential, it is only viable to confer the right of allocation and balance to directors and to allow them to have a broader and fairer concern. Finally, as Professor Mitchell aptly observes, "a single-minded focus on efficiency . . . sacrifices the human values of those who play a part in its functioning".[129] Values other than simply efficiency should be considered.[130]

Social wealth maximisation?

Similar to the efficiency argument, it is further argued that granting shareholder primacy is in society's interests. For example, Professor Deakin observes:

> Agency theory tells us that company law grants shareholders the right to call managers to account not because of an a priori ownership claim, but essentially because it is in society's interests.[131]

Nevertheless, the apparently powerful argument of maximising shareholder wealth through maximising company wealth fails to be valid due to one important

127 Margaret Blair and Lynn Stout, 'A Team Production Theory of Corporate Law' (1999) 85 *Virginia Law Review* 247, 249.
128 Ibid.
129 Lawrence Mitchell, 'Groundwork of the Metaphysics of Corporate Law' (1993) 50 *Washington and Lee Law Review* 1477, 1479. He continues to argue that: "the efficiency model does this by legally combining the actions of corporate actors within confining, distinctly nonhuman roles. It is this denial of humanity, which ultimately denies reality, that is at the heart of the current debate over stakeholder status". However, as already known, corporate behaviour can profoundly affect the lives of others.
130 Suffice it to say, efficiency is just one type of values, and it is best seen as a means rather than an end. The role of other values such as fairness and justice should not be ignored. Hence, even if the economic efficiency could be increased under the SWM model, it remains doubtful whether or not we should adopt it. This will be discussed further in Chapter 5.
131 Simon Deakin, 'The Coming Transformation of Shareholder Value' (2005) 13 *Corporate Governance: An International Review* 11, 13. Also see Stuart Cooper, *Corporate Social Performance: A Stakeholder Approach* (Ashgate, Surrey 2004) 13.

link that does not work as expected. With the collapse of the residual claimant argument, the causal relationship or association between generating maximum value for shareholders and increasing overall welfare no longer exists. By the same token, the argument that monitoring directors is in the best interests of shareholders in order to lower agency costs and maximise company wealth, is also flawed, since shareholders are not the only residual owners. The aforementioned argument of residual nature exhibits shareholder interests that are not always aligned with corporate interests in general. Maximising company wealth does not necessarily increase shareholder value. Neither can SWM lead to enhancing the best interests of the company.[132]

Companies can indisputably provide value not only to shareholders but also to other stakeholders. Interest to creditors, salaries to employees, goods and services to customers, tax revenues to governments, stability to communities and so forth are all values provided by the company. Consequently, "firm value will, by its nature, exceed shareholder value", but as Professor Fisch's argument goes, most or all of the value provided to non-shareholding stakeholders is explicitly excluded from shareholder-oriented concepts of the company value.[133]

Society as a whole includes various corporate stakeholders, and its welfare also includes values beyond economic profit to shareholders. The implication of enlarging social wealth could be reinterpreted – in the corporate context – as the aggregate wealth of all stakeholders, including shareholders.[134]

On the one hand, as the essence of SWM is to prioritise shareholder interests under all circumstances – even at the expense of other stakeholders' interests – it is obviously not beneficial to stakeholder interests. On the other, owing to the fact that shareholders are not the exclusive residual owners and sometimes have substantially different interests from those of the company, it is no longer convincing to argue that aggregate wealth, which includes both shareholders and other stakeholders, can be maximised by virtue of maximising shareholder wealth. It is clear that proponents of SWM would not use Pareto efficiency,[135] which emphasises that it is more efficient if an allocation makes at least one person better off

---

132 In other words, it is possible for SWM to increase shareholder value at the expense of the company and other stakeholders. The gain in wealth to shareholders may be outweighed by the costs incurred by them.

133 Jill Fisch, 'Measuring Efficiency in Corporate Law: The Role of Shareholder Primacy' (2006) 31 *Journal of Corporation Law* 637, 644.

134 This inference also aligns with the viewpoint that companies should be structured and operated for the interests of society, and indeed such a broad objective of advancing overall social welfare attracts few critics; even the most aggressive shareholder model advocates concede it. For example, see Reinier Kraakman *et al.*, *The Anatomy of Corporate Law: A Comparative and Functional Approach* (3rd edn OUP, Oxford 2017) 22–23; Henry Hansmann and Reinier Kraakman, 'The End of History for Corporate Law' (2001) 89 *Georgetown Law Journal* 439, 441.

135 Nicholas Barr, *The Economics of the Welfare State* (3rd edn Stanford University Press, Stanford 1998) 70–85. Also see Drew Fudenberg and Jean Tirole, 'Nash Equilibrium: Multiple Nash Equilibria, Focal Points and Pareto Optimality' in Drew Fudenberg and Jean Tirole, *Game Theory* (MIT Press, Cambridge 1991) 18–23. In the context of Pareto efficiency or Pareto optimality, it would be impossible for one to be better off without worsening others.

without making any other person worse off, to justify overall welfare enhancement. Instead, shareholder primacists would employ Kaldor-Hicks efficiency,[136] which is more 'lenient' for externalisation and puts forward that it is more efficient if the gain from those who are made better off could outweigh the loss suffered by those who are made worse off. In a corporate context, if the gains accruing to shareholders outweigh any losses stakeholders suffer, the outcome could be defined as efficient. Even if some stakeholders' interests were to be sacrificed at the expense of SWM, it could be argued that the overall welfare in society could still be increased in such a situation.

However, apart from distributive injustice and the difficulty in wealth redistribution,[137] the fact that shareholders may also externalise loss and excessive risks to other stakeholders, could in turn cause high transaction costs and low incentives for other stakeholders.[138] For example, shareholders only suffer a fraction of the costs caused by risky programmes owing to their limited liability, but they can obtain higher returns if the gamble succeeds. To achieve shareholder value enhancement, directors of the board could be forced to siphon value from one or several stakeholder groups.[139] Saving the situation of making the pie bigger for example, another potential tactic to obtain more benefits is to steal or extract other stakeholders' portions. Indeed, there are many alternative ways to achieve the goal of increasing dividends and capital appreciation other than through enhanced corporate earnings – for instance, lowering production costs or increasing added value, as discussed in detail in the next section. Directors can focus solely on share prices instead of on the welfare of the whole company. Despite these methods of maximising shareholders' benefits might not necessarily be what the shareholder model implies (in the minds of most advocates of the shareholder model, SWM should be achieved by increasing company value in the first place rather than redistributing interests from stakeholders to shareholders[140]), such a

---

136 Nicholas Kaldor, 'Welfare Propositions of Economics and Interpersonal Comparisons of Utility' (1939) 49 *Economical Journal* 549–552; John Hicks 'The Foundation of Welfare Economics' (1939) 49 *Economical Journal* 696–712; John Hicks, 'The Valuation of the Social Income' (1940) 7 *Economica* 105–124. Also see Brian Cheffins, *Company Law: Theory, Structure and Operation* (OUP, Oxford 1997) 14–16.

137 Social psychologists have found that people are not only concerned about the fairness of the final outcome but also care about the fairness of the distribution process itself. Research shows people are more accepting of a poorer outcome as long as the procedure for distribution could be perceived as fair. E Allan Lind and Tom Tyler, *The Social Psychology of Procedural Justice* (Plenum Press, New York 1988) referred to by Robert Phillips, R Edward Freeman and Andrew Wicks, 'What Stakeholder Theory Is Not' (2003) 13 *Business Ethics Quarterly* 479, 487.

138 If negative externalisation is to environment or such like, the weighting between benefits accruing to shareholders and the loss suffered by the public become nearly impossible.

139 Andrew Keay, 'Ascertaining the Corporate Objective: An Entity Maximisation and Sustainability Model' (2008) 71 *Modern Law Review* 663, 671. Also see the example of Wal-Mart's low employee wages, which can be regarded as transferring benefit from employees to shareholders. Kent Greenfield, 'New Principles for Corporate Law' (2005) 1 *Hastings Business Law Journal* 87, 101.

140 Therefore, social wealth may be increased through enhanced long-term and sustainable shareholder interests.

possibility could never be ignored or denied as it could happen in certain cases, especially when SWM is interpreted in the practical guidance for directors.[141]

In fact, it is in practice very difficult to include a long-term view in SWM, as short-termism has an advantage when competing with long-termism, as discussed later. Without explicit and practical guidelines, it is not surprising to see manipulation in the real business world. For this reason Professor Dodd argues that a company run for the interests of shareholders does not create wealth automatically for other stakeholder groups or society.[142] In other words, shareholders' wealth can be maximised by extracting wealth from other stakeholders without increasing corporate wealth.[143] Meanwhile, the emphasis on shareholders' superior position could impair other stakeholders' willingness and incentive to contribute firm-specific investment.[144] This will ultimately lead to higher negotiation costs and lower productivity. Therefore, both the company and society's benefits cannot be enhanced.

The conventional corporate accounting practice at present may further contribute to the misunderstanding.[145] Only the value provided to shareholders accounts for corporate value, whilst value to other stakeholders is regarded as expenditure or a cost to the company. This may easily mislead people into categorising shareholder interests as the only positive value for the company. But the true value of business includes not only profits to shareholders.[146] Also, shareholders are under no obligation to share their profits with other stakeholders; however, these stakeholders along with society have to bear the costs made by SWM, such as the transferring of wealth and other negative externalities.

In short, SWM is by no means the best approach for social wealth maximisation, and granting special treatment cannot ensure the enhancement of social welfare. Just as a company is able to create wealth for more than shareholders, it can also incur costs to more than shareholders. These costs to employees, customers, communities and other stakeholders must not be ignored, but count in the calculus.

---

141 For example, see Joseph Heath, 'Business Ethics without Stakeholders' (2006) 16 *Business Ethics Quarterly* 533, 542.

142 E Merrick Dodd, 'For Whom are Corporate Managers Trustees' (1931) 45 *Harvard Law Review* 1145, 1152.

143 Worse, as discussed earlier, shareholder value is possibly the opposite of corporate value as a result of the alienation of interests from the shares which arises from the development of modern financial derivatives.

144 It is also argued by some scholars that extracting other stakeholders' portions is not peculiar to the shareholder model. No matter the ultimate beneficiary, it would still occur. For example, see Sundaram and Inkpen, 'The Corporate Objective Revisited' (n 3) 356. Managing companies for the interests of any other stakeholder group may cause a potentially similar outcome. Although further discussion is required, the argument of other stakeholders as the ultimate beneficiaries causing a similar extraction or externalisation fails to make the case that shareholders could be the ultimate beneficiaries or that shareholders as the ultimate beneficiaries would maximise social wealth.

145 Such as earnings per share, return on capital employed, economic value added and similar.

146 In this regard, it can be argued that the current financial reporting system is incomplete.

2.4 Problems of externalisation and short-termism

Apart from the problematical bases of SWM, there are two severe problems surrounding the shareholder model, namely externalisation and short-termism. The current shareholder model and its rationale encourages both externalisation and short-termism. The pressure on directors and their delegated managers to pursue maximum profits will force them to focus only on the day-to-day share price at the expense of long-term value. A lopsided focus on share price will in turn distract management from true value creation. This section first explores the potential of externalising loss and excessive risks in order to transfer value to shareholders in the context of SWM, and then follows with a discussion about short-termism.

2.4.1 Externalisation

Externalities are usually referred to as "costs (or benefits) imposed by the physical effects of one person's action on others for which the actor does not bear the costs (or benefits)".[147] In addition to making the pie bigger, the possibility always exists for shareholders to siphon benefits from other stakeholders or, more frequently, pass on costs to a third party in order to increase their own revenue by lowering costs.[148] For instance, increasing share prices by introducing redundancies or reducing wages in fact transfers value from employees to shareholders. It is also possible for a company to let the negative impact of its operations on the natural environment go unchecked as long as the reduction in operation costs outweighs any potential fines (or a company may stop adopting any further steps to reduce pollution as soon as it meets the minimum legal requirements). Similarly, taking excessive risks which could be deemed to be costs to other stakeholders also belongs to negative externalities. As previously discussed, shareholders can obtain substantial benefits from high-risk projects whilst their risks are limited to a certain level due to the rule of limited liability.[149] Shareholders then transfer the costs of high-risk activity to stakeholders, such as creditors, by externalising such risks. The spectre of insolvency becomes a problem, owing to inefficient investment incentives. In short, externalisation can be seen as a process of decreasing corporate costs by passing on these costs to a third party, and social costs would concomitantly increase as a result.

Shareholder primacists argue that externalising costs is a universal method and not unique to shareholders.[150] Generally speaking, favouring one group may sometimes unavoidably decrease another group's interest no matter which group is favoured. Whoever becomes the beneficiary, they may have an incentive to

---

147 Michael Jensen, 'Non-rational Behavior, Value Conflicts, Stakeholder Theory, and Firm Behavior' in Bradley Agle *et al.* 'Dialogue: Toward Superior Stakeholder Theory' (2008) 18 *Business Ethics Quarterly* 167, 167.

148 Before discussing externalisation in detail, it should be borne in mind that profits could be enhanced by 1) increasing revenue and/or 2) decreasing costs.

149 They may also do so by increasing leverage ratios.

150 Sundaram and Inkpen, 'The Corporate Objective Revisited' (n 3) 357.

externalise.[151] Further, Professor Jensen argues that companies as such are not able to resolve externality issues voluntarily, since they would probably lose competitive advantage compared with those rivals who do not choose to do so.[152] Accordingly, companies are reluctant to rectify such behaviour even after recognising the *sin* of externalisation, which implies that relying on adjustment by voluntary agreement between parties is unworkable.

Function of external laws and regulations

In terms of the counter measures against externalisation, regulations and laws other than company laws are believed by shareholder primacists to be *the* viable solution. In other words, external rules are deemed to be a more appropriate battleground for controlling externalisation. It is often argued that company law is private law and should mainly concern shareholders and their interests; therefore protection of the interests of third parties, including stakeholders, from externalisation should be best achieved by measures outside company law.[153] Following on from this argument, dealing with externalisation to the environment should be left to environmental law, and externalisation to employees should be left to employment law.[154] It is argued that *external* laws or regulations are better placed to internalise externalities, and there is no necessity to rely on company laws to provide extra protection.[155] Put simply, shareholder primacists tend to think that stakeholder protection should be provided in other areas of law rather than in company law, and SWM is not considered a source of this problem in the realm of company law and corporate governance. As Professor Elhauge argues:

> It leaves corporate law scholars free to ignore issues about any effects the corporation may have on the external world as topics best addressed by other legal fields, and to focus on more tractable models about which corporate rules would maximize shareholder value.[156]

---

151 This is also why Chapter 5 is going to argue that the company should not be run for any particular group's interest.
152 Michael Jensen, 'Value Maximisation, Stakeholder Theory, and the Corporate Objective Function' (2001) 7 *Journal of Applied Corporate Finance* 8, 16.
153 For example, see Hansmann and Kraakman, 'The End of History for Corporate Law' (n 134) 441.
154 In other words, employees could be protected by minimum wage laws and employment law; the environment could be protected by environment law; and customers could be protected by consumer law.
155 For example, according to *The White Paper on Modernising Company Law*, "[t]he specific duties of care required of companies to their employees and society at large will normally best be set out in other legislation, covering areas such as health and safety, environmental and employment law". House of Commons Trade and Industry Committee, Sixth Report of Session 2002–03, *The White Paper on Modernising Company Law*, HC 439, para 22. Taking the protection of employees, for example, the *Health & Safety at Work Act 1974, Employment Relations Act 2004* as well as the *Employment Act 2008* are thought to play an adequate role in protecting employees' interests.
156 Einer Elhauge, 'Sacrificing Corporate Profits in the Public Interest' (2005) 80 *New York University Law Review* 733, 737.

However, company law should also consider other corporate stakeholders, since they are all indispensable to both a company's survival and success.[157] It would not be sufficient if company law or corporate governance only focused on the relationship between shareholders and companies. After all, shareholders can also obtain protection from contract law via the company's constitution and tort law among others. If one could argue such protection is not complete due to high transaction costs or bounded rationality, then it may also be reasonable to argue that stakeholders cannot effectively get full protection either. The so-called complete contract covering all contingencies is not cost-effective and indeed almost impossible.[158] Even in a free market, the unforeseen contingencies, cost of writing and enforcing contracts, among others, deter the formation of the so-called complete contract.[159] Incomplete contracts with missing provisions are the norm. This also applies to external laws and regulations.

Regulatory gaps are unavoidable. Although in theory external regulations may play a role in controlling externalisation by imposing negative externalities upon the company, its effectiveness in the real world is largely questionable. First of all, the hysteresis nature of the laws and legislative process is self-evident. It takes time for legislators or policy-makers to identify new problems, and even then, more time is needed to tackle them. Second, according to Professors Armour and Gordon, the "regulatory slack", such as under-specification of regulatory terms and under-enforcement of regulations, would be exploited by the company in order to lower costs.[160] Indeed, it may be more reasonable from an economic point of view to exploit the slack or even seek to lobby the regulator than to amend the original behaviour for reducing regulatory costs. The concern is that SWM will tend systematically to undermine the regulatory effort, as the easiest way to achieve SWM is to "exercise political influence to achieve a lower rate of regulatory tax" rather than seeking "innovation that reduces the social costs of one's activities in accordance with regulatory strictures".[161] Though the enforcement of internal structures may also be subject to a similar manipulation, if the current incentive mechanism could be modified, directors' personal interests would be better aligned with the long-term growth and success of a company than with the short-term rise in the share price.[162]

---

157 *Supra* Chapter 1 footnotes 67–69 and accompanying text.
158 As observed, the transactions costs in the real world are pervasive and large which leads to the result that "a consequence of the presence of such costs is that the parties to a relationship will not write a contract that anticipates all the events that may occur and the various actions that are appropriate in these events". Oliver Hart, 'Incomplete Contracts and the Theory of the Firm' (1988) 4 *Journal of Law, Economics, and Organization* 119, 123.
159 Jean Tirole, 'Incomplete Contracts: Where Do We Stand?' (1999) 67 *Econometrica* 741, 743–744.
160 Such regulatory slack has been exemplified by the recent financial crisis. Armour and Gordon (n 114) 48.
161 Armour and Gordon (n 114) 38. It is argued that inflecting "the production and enforcement of regulation" is much easier and more certain to price while the innovation in new processes may be exposed to the risk of renegotiation by the regulator afterwards. Ibid. 49.
162 *Infra* Chapter 5, section 5.3.3. In the meanwhile, the directors would still be subject to fiduciary duties among other restraints.

As exhibited by the Volkswagen scandal discussed in Chapter 1, external regulation and monitoring are not effective. Emission standards are legal requirements for governing air pollutants released from vehicles into the atmosphere; in fact there has been a set of laws to test, monitor and discipline vehicle emissions since the end of the twentieth century.[163] However, it took more than eight years for the US authority to discover this irregularity. And it is not an overstatement to say most other countries would have remained ignorant about such externalisation if the US Environmental Protection Agency had not identified it. Even after becoming the headline of mainstream media outlets, only a few countries have undertaken or intend to undertake formal investigations.[164] To some extent, this reflects the regulatory gap and ineffectiveness of legislative process, as many countries have not realised the harm of such externalisation. Therefore, it is not convincing to rely on external laws to regulate negative externalities.

By contrast, internal corporate governance has comparative advantages in addressing externalities over external regulations. First, directors have more information and expertise regarding the projects they are undertaking than legislators and policy-makers. It is obviously harder for outsiders to design regulations to discipline directors' behaviour. Meanwhile, external regulations are much more expensive than internal changes for reaching the same end. This is partly because external regulations require more ongoing enforcement costs compared to adopting internal governance changes to the same ends.[165] Furthermore, external regulations are mostly reactive in nature. Including the goal in the company's own objectives is more efficient than this reactive approach, since directors of the board would become more proactive in addressing problems like externalisation.[166]

Last but not least, internal corporate governance changes against externalisation may build more trust among various stakeholders who are vulnerable to the externalisation, which will in turn encourage reciprocal actions.[167] And external rules can never touch upon such "soft issues". For instance, if directors

---

163 For example, see Council Directive 91/441/EEC of 26 June 1991 amending Directive 70/220/ EEC on the approximation of the laws of the Member States relating to measures to be taken against air pollution by emissions from motor vehicles. Available at http://eur-lex.europa.eu/ legal-content/EN/ALL/?uri=CELEX:31991L0441 [accessed 1 March 2017].

164 For example, see Elizabeth Anderson, 'Volkswagen Crisis: How Many Investigations Is the Carmaker Facing?' *The Telegraph* (London, 29 September 2015) at www.telegraph.co.uk/finance/ newsbysector/industry/11884872/Volkswagen-crisis-how-many-investigations-is-the-carmaker-facing.html [accessed 1 March 2017]. Also see Chapter 1 footnote 61 and accompanying text.

165 Greenfield, 'Using Behavioral Economics to Show the Power and Efficiency of Corporate Law as Regulatory Tool' (n 88) 601.

166 In addition, the regulatory restraints have jurisdiction limitations since companies could choose to incorporate in other jurisdictions without such regulations, while internal governance changes do not have such limitations. Ibid.

167 It can be found in John Armour and Jeffrey Gordon's early version of 'Systemic Harms and Shareholder Value' *Columbia Law and Economics Working Paper No. 452* at http://papers.ssrn. com/sol3/papers.cfm?abstract_id=2307959 [accessed 1 March 2017] 19.

unilaterally end a long-term co-operative relationship with a supplier solely for shareholder interests, contract law and trade law could do little as no statutory remedies are available. For example, in *Baird Textile Holdings Ltd v. Marks & Spencer plc*, when Marks & Spencer (M&S) unilaterally terminated the long-term relationship with one of its major suppliers, Baird Textile Holdings, contract law could do nothing to protect the vulnerable stakeholders.[168] Nevertheless, most suppliers and other stakeholders would wish to maintain a long-term co-operative relationship with the company, especially after making a significant firm-specific investment. If directors are only required to maximise shareholder wealth, even at the expense of other stakeholders, the latter may be less willing to make contributions, which could in turn affect the success of the company. But such trust and reciprocal relationships cannot be entirely based on external laws. Only by including them in internal corporate governance systems would suppliers, for example, be more willing to make firm-specific investment, as they know companies would not externalise excessive risk to them simply to pursue SWM, and employees may become more loyal and productive by virtue of the fairer treatment.

Not only does internal corporate governance have these comparative advantages in controlling externalities – sometimes it may be the only viable way. Externalisation can be divided into direct and indirect forms. Direct externalisation includes current and imminent externalities caused by externalising costs or risks to third parties. Increasing shareholder interests by cutting employee welfare, for example, belongs to this category, as the externalities can be ascertained immediately. However, indirect externalisation may be more difficult to determine as long as the real costs are not raised. One typical example is incumbent shareholders influencing a company (at least indirectly) to inflate the current share price by short-term strategies such as accounting adjustments, stock buybacks, cutting R&D expenditure and increasing the leverage ratio,[169] which may not incur costs immediately.[170] This category of future externalities can be classified as indirect externalisation. Externalities are not readily generated until the future, which means no concrete victims occur until negative costs are crystallised or actually transferred onto them. Therefore, it is almost impossible for external

168 [2001] EWCA CIV 274. It is worth noting that in this case there was no contract formed between the two parties since M&S had deliberately abstained from concluding such a contract though they had 10-year on-going relationship. The question was whether there was an express or implied contract between them. Nothing could prevent M&S from terminating their co-operation to gain shareholder wealth maximisation. However, if a broad corporate objective had been adopted, the motion to sacrifice stakeholder interests simply for profit maximisation would be less likely to occur in the boardroom.
169 Namely, the proportion between debt and equity.
170 Short-termism can generally be seen, as current shareholders externalise costs or risks to future shareholders. More precisely, stakeholders other than future shareholders may also be negatively affected by short-termism either immediately or in the future.

laws and regulations to address externalisation in the context of such indirect externalisation.[171]

In short, the hysteresis nature, regulatory gap and slack, and the comparative ineffectiveness of external laws imply that it may be time to rethink the traditional logic and consider relying on internal corporate governance to control externalisation. More specifically, a broader corporate objective may be better positioned to internalise both direct and indirect externalisation.

Externalisation in the context of SWM

Professors Sundaram and Inkpen claim that externalisation in the type of value transference from one group to another is unavoidable, no matter whose interests predominate.[172] If a company is required to be run for employees' interests, they argue, value transference from other stakeholders to employees cannot be precluded. However, if the corporate interests can be distinguished from the interests of the shareholders, then no group is doomed to be subordinated in advance,[173] which in turn could effectively relieve the risk of such value transference.

In the context of SWM, not surprisingly, directors and their delegated managers have great incentive to externalise costs to those stakeholders whose interests are not counted. As Armour and Gordon point out, SWM will only push directors harder to undermine regulation.[174] Although increasingly more shareholder primacists claim that SWM should include long-term and sustainable shareholder value, until long-termism can be fully recognised not only theoretically but also pragmatically,[175] share prices and dividends as the only reportable metrics will remain the focus of directors.

It is very difficult to effectively solve externalisation by relying on external laws if SWM is the guiding principle.[176] Since the foregoing discussions show internal corporate governance is better suited for addressing externalisation, SWM as a corporate objective must be re-evaluated. If shareholder wealth is no longer *the* criterion, directors may be released from the pressure of solely focusing on shareholder value – or share price, to be more accurate. Assuming a broader goal could be adopted, then externalising costs or risks to stakeholders or society would

---

171 The internal governance systems may be the only available alternative to effectively tackle this kind of externalisation. *Infra* Chapter 5, section 5.3.3.

172 Sundaram and Inkpen, 'The Corporate Objective Revisited' (n 3) 356.

173 Although this does not mean all stakeholder groups should be treated equivalently, a balance is required case by case according to certain criteria, which are introduced in Chapter 5.

174 Armour and Gordon (n 114) 38–39.

175 The next subsection explains short-termism in detail and its attractiveness compared with long-termism in practice.

176 For example, the sought-after alignment of directors' interests with short-term shareholder interests could amplify risk-taking.

then become senseless. For example, if all stakeholders' interests matter, directors would definitely not maximise one group's interests at the expense of others', because under the new criterion, the costs of externality to stakeholders would be deducted from the aggregate profits.

If a company creates more social harm than good, as Professor Greenfield argues, no society would grant it formation or allow it to continue.[177] Even though shareholders can be made better off in the context of SWM, a company can still not be regarded as good or beneficial to society if it creates more costs to third parties. Severe problems exist. Not least is the distribution problem, as shareholders are under no obligation to share their profits even though they may have been obtained at the expense of other parties. Suffice it to say, in order to effectively tackle the issue, it is very important to have a broader and more balanced objective than a narrowly focused objective.

2.4.2 Short-termism

The other significant problem of SWM is its lopsided focus on short-term value. There exist two kinds of value in the company: the long-term fundamental value of the stock (i.e. real corporate value), and the market price of the stock. If the market is sufficiently effective and efficient, then the market price should be the same as the real value of the company. However, the recent financial crisis again demonstrated that the market price cannot reflect the real value. Overemphasising market price will unintentionally force management to increase the speculative component of the stock price at the expense of long-term fundamental value.[178] As Professors Scheinkman and Xiong point out, "the ownership of a share stock provides an opportunity (option) to profit from other investors' overvaluation".[179] Concurrently, given that future investors are able to optimistically overestimate the value of the company, current shareholders have an incentive to "cater to such potential sentiment even at the expense of firm long-term fundamental value".[180]

Short-termism in the corporate context can be generally defined as "foregoing economically worthwhile investments with long-term benefits in order to increase reported earnings for the current period".[181] It simply concerns the reported growth for the current period at the expense of worthwhile investment,

---

177 Greenfield, 'New Principles for Corporate Law' (n 139) 89–90. Professor Greenfield continues to argue that "a company cannot be considered a success if the total social value it creates is less than the social costs it throws off". Ibid. 90.

178 In other words, directors may manage the speculative factors which are unrelated to fundamental value in order to increase the immediate profits.

179 Jose Scheinkman and Wei Xiong, 'Overconfidence and Speculative Bubbles' (2003) 111 *Journal of Political Economy* 1183, 1184.

180 Patrick Bolton, Jose Scheinkman and Wei Xiong, 'Executive Compensation and Short-Termist Behaviour in Speculative Markets' (2006) 73 *Review of Economic Studies* 577, 597.

181 John Grinyer, Alex Russell and David Collison, 'Evidence of Managerial Short-termism in the UK' (1998) 9 *British Journal of Management* 13, 15.

which would advance benefits in the long run.[182] Short-term value is very different from the long-term fundamental value of a given company as the efficient markets hypothesis does not include real stock markets. Expenses such as R&D can be cut or delayed in order to claim the immediate rising profits, to increase dividends or to buy back stocks. Also, revenues from future years can be moved to the current year by booking orders earlier and other accounting adjustments.[183] Furthermore, profitable divisions can be sold for cash and a company's leverage can be substantially enlarged to make the financial reports look better. So long as a company is a going concern, any short-term action would harm all late comers. Though it can be categorised into one type of externalisation, due to its significance, this subsection specifically discusses this problem in SWM and its devastating impact.

Most shareholders, who have no intention of actively participating in corporate affairs, may concentrate solely on short-term gains. Apart from individual shareholders' short-term views on investment, institutional shareholders such as mutual funds and hedge funds also focus on short-term success, namely the current market price of the share.[184] And companies with dispersed shareholders are more likely to prefer risky and shorter-term investment. Empirical studies indicate companies with substantial outside shareholder interests invest less in R&D and focus less on long-term strategy than companies directly controlled by shareholders,[185] as the following suggests:

> In many cases, shareholders deemed the expected profits from taking these risks worthwhile and so implicitly supported excessive risk taking, especially through high leverage. The reason is that shareholders would fully benefit from the upside of such a strategy, while they participate in losses only until the value of shareholder equity reaches zero, after which further losses would be borne by the creditors.[186]

Therefore, it is not impossible for shareholders to deem excessively risky projects or short-term returns worthwhile. Further, by virtue of the dispersed shareholdings,

---

182 Ibid. For instance, shareholders with a short-term view would prefer a large dividend pay-out instead of R&D investment which could generate profits in the future. And, theoretically, short-term profit maximisation itself indicates it would reach the highest and largest point within a certain time limit, but that after that period, the quantity would reduce.

183 For example, by announcing future price increases, or by giving special discounts this year, or guaranteeing to repurchase goods. Michael Jensen, 'Paying People to Lie: The Truth About the Budgeting Process' (2003) 9 *European Financial Management* 379, 387.

184 Iman Anabtawi, 'Some Skepticism About Increasing Shareholder Power' (2006) 53 *University of California Los Angeles Law Review* 561, 579–580. More discussion on institutional shareholders' myopic focus on short-term performance and its rationale will be provided in Chapter 3 footnotes 125–134 and accompanying text.

185 Tylecote and Visintin (n 77) 95–96.

186 European Commission, 'Green Paper: The EU Corporate Governance Framework' COM (2011) 164 final, 11.

shareholders are increasingly prevented from exerting influence. From an economic perspective, a more rational strategy for the majority is to simply focus on profits and exit when they find any problems in the company. Diversification of shareholdings also makes it economically unworthy to understand and thereby monitor all the investee companies.[187] The cost for institutional shareholders to actively engage in governance makes it a less optimal choice. The stock market price index is then frequently utilised as a criterion.

Financial economists assume that today's share price can fully reflect the market value of all future profits and growth that will accrue to the company. The capital market, along with the product and labour markets, are regarded as the most effective discipline mechanism. The threat of hostile takeover, *inter alia*, will force directors to maximise shareholder return. When a company underperforms, its share price will drop, and this will in turn make it vulnerable to a hostile takeover. If the share price is lower than it should be, the more vulnerable the company. That is also why in their view, the best measure to address corporate governance problems is to remove the restriction on the market, such as increasing shareholder rights – especially in takeover issues – and to avoid state interference.

However, the market is far from perfect and share prices are erratic.[188] First, it is not uncommon to see a small number of large companies dominate the market or set up barriers to entry, so competition is limited. This implies rivals may be hard to challenge even if a given company does not run efficiently. Second, due to the asymmetry of information and transaction costs, it is not always easy to shift to alternative producers and resource suppliers who may be cheaper in price or better in quality. Further, the focus on individuality nowadays makes substitution even more difficult. Increasingly fewer products and services are homogeneous, which may lead companies to suffer little competitive pressure as well. Finally, new categories of shareholders have appeared due to the development of financial markets, and these shareholders are of little interest to long-termism.[189]

Corporate liquidity, which is preferred by most investors, is also largely contributed to by short-term investors.[190] This further presses short-term demands

---

187 Moreover, according to the prudent person rule, pension and insurance companies are required to diversify the assets in order to diversify the risks and avoid excessive reliance on any particular investee companies. For more discussion, see Jonathan Mukwiri and Mathias Siems, 'The Financial Crisis: A Reason to Improve Shareholder Protection in the EU' (2014) 41 *Journal of Law and Society* 51, 63–64.

188 Just as Professor Blair observed: "a joke common among economists is that the stock market has correctly predicted ten of the last five recessions. The point is that stock prices sometimes rise or fall quite markedly without a significant change in underlying fundamental factors". Margaret Blair, *Ownership and Control: Rethinking Corporate Governance for the Twenty-First Century* (The Brookings Institution, Washington 1995) 128.

189 European Commission, 'Green Paper: Corporate Governance in Financial Institutions and Remuneration Policies' COM (2010) 284 final, 8.

190 It is thought liquidity could give investors more options. On the other side, if shareholders can exit freely, they will also lose the incentive to make a long-term commitment which may require extra time and effort among others.

on the board of directors.[191] The much-needed liquidity causes high frequency trading, and this makes understanding all individual companies in the portfolio impractical. Most investors can only choose to follow the market. The subsequent pressure from the reporting of quarterly earnings can be exemplified by the statement as below:

> The two key earning benchmarks are quarterly earnings for the same quarter last year and the analyst consensus estimate for the current quarter ... Failure to meet earnings targets is seen as a sign of managerial weakness and, if repeated, can lead to a career-threatening dismissal.[192]

On the other hand, directors may fear that a long-term strategy will not immediately satisfy those investors who focus on share prices by comparing them with competing companies.[193] When facing a hostile takeover bid, short-term profit, in particular immediate cash flow, is appealing to the incumbent directors.[194] The threat of losing jobs due to such a hostile takeover and the competitive labour market for management also encourage directors to ensure a high share price, even if it may be unsustainable. Naturally, by virtue of the fact that the long-term strategy may make the share price increase less quickly than the short-term strategy, short-term profits would be preferable to innovation and long-term development.[195] In other words, directors are not necessarily short-sighted; they may just follow the signals of a short-sighted financial market.[196]

Performance-based remuneration also contributes to risk-taking and short-termism since directors could be rewarded with excessive remuneration when the share price increases. Directors, as the argument goes, have little incentive to make long-term strategic plans since share prices and dividends under such a strategy are not likely to rapidly and markedly increase by contrast with short-term plans, and all the benefits generated by long-term planning might be attributed to their successors.[197] As discussed in the next chapter, the average tenure of directors is shortened substantially; though this makes it less costly to remove a director, the problem is that they may have already left the company when it starts to reap the benefits from a long-term strategy. Instead, their successors would benefit from such long-termism, and therefore they may be less willing to adopt a long-term development strategy. The current executive compensation package in the form

---

191 Mukwiri and Siems (n 187) 60–61.

192 Alfred Rappaport, 'The Economics of Short-term Performance Obsession' (2005) 61 *Financial Analysis Journal* 65, 69.

193 This makes companies with long-termism "ripe" for hostile takeovers, which may encourage directors to adopt a short-term strategy. Kent Greenfield, 'The Puzzle of Short-termism' (2011) 46 *Wake Forest Law Review* 627, 636.

194 Simon Deakin and Giles Slinger, 'Hostile Takeovers, Corporate Law, and the Theory of the Firm' (1997) 24 *Journal of Law and Society* 124, 132.

195 For example, see Robert Sprague, 'Beyond Shareholder Value: Normative Standards for Sustainable Corporate Governance' (2010) 1 *William & Mary Business Law Review* 47, 80–82.

196 Blair, *Ownership and Control* (n 188) 126.

197 Franklin Allen and Douglas Gale, *Comparing Financial Systems* (MIT Press, Massachusetts 2001) 382.

of share options and the like could also be seen as an important inducement for directors and executives to maximise short-term earnings, since it is closely tied to share price. And indeed, the incentive structure is hard to design to prompt long-term interests as long as current accounting and reporting practices are not being materially transformed. Improper incentive mechanisms undoubtedly make the situation worse.

Unfortunately, focusing on quarterly or even monthly earnings is harmful for long-term development and success.[198] Not only may important R&D expenditures or loyal employees be cut as discussed above, but directors are likely to have greater impetus under such pressure to pursue reckless business strategies, especially in the context of diversified shareholdings. This kind of shareholder short-termism is criticised for leading "many companies to the brink of self-destruction".[199] Indeed, the US Congress opines that management's failure to regard "the long-term profitability of their institutions" and "the long-term health of their firms and their shareholders" are "the central causes of the financial and economic crises".[200]

For this reason it is often argued that directors are not forced to only pursue immediate profits for shareholders,[201] but in reality, shareholder value is frequently interpreted as their financial well-being, or, more accurately, the share price and dividends.

Simply stating that SWM should or could include a long-term view is not helpful, as it is very hard to implement in practice. And in the real business world, it is also very hard to distinguish what the inflated earnings are based on: a long-term or short-term strategy. As Professor Greenfield argues,

> Profits and earnings for a long-term-oriented company may be indistinguishable from profits and earnings for a short-term-oriented company. It is easy to show the numbers; it is rather difficult for most investors to determine the reason for such numbers.[202]

When a company adopts a long-term strategy, it may sacrifice immediate earnings, for example by increasing investment in customer service or R&D. This makes it

198 David Millon, 'Why is Corporate Management Obsessed with Quarterly Earnings and What Should be Done About it?' (2002) 70 *George Washington Law Review* 890, 902.

199 'Corporate Apocalypse', *Management Today* (1 January 2009) at www.managementtoday.co.uk/news/870435 [accessed 1 March 2017].

200 The Senate of the United States, 'Shareholder Bill of Rights Act (2009)' at www.govtrack.us/congress/bills/111/s1074 [accessed 1 March 2017].

201 This happens even under the Anglo-American system. For example, the Company Law Review Steering Group had claimed "we do not accept that there is anything in the present law of directors' duties which requires them to take an unduly narrow or short-term view of their functions". CLRSG (n 13) 40.

202 Greenfield, 'The Puzzle of Short-termism' (n 193) 635–636. As a result, "capital markets may not *punish* such short-term management if it is not clear that the inflated earnings are based on strategies that are costly in the long-term". Ibid.

difficult for most shareholders and investors to tell whether the low level or even decline of profits is due to a long-term strategy or merely due to bad management. By the same token, increased earnings may be based on good management and previous long-term investment, but it may also simply be due to short-term manipulation as explored earlier. The stock market is far from perfectly efficient at delivering the expected information; it is not easy for the market or most shareholders to distinguish the real reasons for a company's good or bad performance. A company may even camouflage a short-term strategy as a long-term one, which would make it more difficult for shareholders or the market to discover until the bubble is burst.[203] Consequently, until a short-term strategy becomes clear, maybe after a sufficient period of time, the market may not begin to respond to the factor of such short-termism by plummeting the share price. On the other hand, the long-term strategy may be not recognised by the market either. The sacrifice of immediate profits for the long-term development may easily be confused with, or thought of as, the result of incompetent management. And in practice it may be difficult to quantify the long-term benefits in a precise way whilst the short-term costs are much easier to measure. This could also lead to a long-term strategy being less attractive.

Even assuming it is possible for certain professional and sophisticated investors to figure out which is which after costly research, it will be more rational and profitable for them to buy shares of companies with short-term strategies for immediate earnings and sell them afterwards before their short-term strategies are understood by the market. They can also invest in companies with long-term strategies not at the beginning but when the timing is ripe.[204] In these cases, short-termism will not be punished and long-termism will not be rewarded; investors with such knowledge could keep it a secret and use it for greater private profits.[205] Although short-termism is harmful in general both to the company in the long run and society as a whole, individual investors may possibly benefit from such a strategy and thereby earn immense profits.[206] Thus it is difficult to expect the market or sophisticated shareholders to effectively discipline short-termism. The competition among fund managers and other institutional investors would further intensify the lopsided focus on short-termism, as only a better performance on a quarterly basis can attract more clients.

---

203 Only when the strategy becomes sufficiently clear can the market price truly reflect the fundamental value of the company, just like the Enron case. However, it may be too late as is often the case and the disastrous impact cannot be reversed.

204 Namely, a company invests large amounts of money in R&D, and after a significant time the new products become available, which means the company can start to reap the rewards from the initial R&D investment. If an investor can identify such long-term strategies, then it is possible for them to decide to buy shares just before the company starts to reap those rewards.

205 It is worth noting the fact that the vast majority of investors could not be described as sophisticated, namely trained, rational, continent and alike.

206 That is why Professor Greenfield argues "a short-term investment strategy will become even more successful if the investor can control the timing of the investment's withdrawal to capture as many of the short-term gains as possible before the inevitable downgrade in stock price". Greenfield, 'The Puzzle of Short-termism' (n 193) 638.

It is generally accepted that "many successful enterprises weather years of adversity before succeeding".[207] Notwithstanding that short-term profit maximisation is well known to be devastating,[208] it would be almost impossible for directors to resist the pressure from shareholders' short-term focus and pursue short-term profits as long as shareholder value remains the only gauge. Thus, the fundamental basis of short-termism, namely, SWM as the corporate objective, should be changed and the whole business environment should also be moderated accordingly.

2.5 Rethinking shareholder value

The foregoing discussion on the legal and economic aspects of the agency theory, the residual claim and economic efficiency arguments should make it clear that SWM as a corporate objective is untenable. Shareholders are neither the owners of the company nor the principals of directors. They are not the only residual claimants either. Along with the issues of externalisation and short-termism, it should be time to rethink SWM. Further, empirical data shows that increasingly more public companies are going private and fewer companies are having IPOs, as listed companies are usually under more pressure from SWM.[209]

This section therefore first utilises a doctrinal approach to explore whether there is a legal requirement for SWM, as many would argue that shareholder primacy is decreed by law in accordance with *Dodge v. Ford Motor Co.* Following on from this, the highlighted advantage of the singular objective is challenged, and different shareholders' heterogeneous expectations are discussed.

2.5.1 Is there any legal requirement for SWM?

Neither the US nor UK laws explicitly require public companies to be run for SWM. To begin with, let us first examine the classic US case *Dodge v. Ford*

---

207 Leo Strine, 'One Fundamental Corporate Governance Question We Face: Can Corporations Be Managed for the Long Term Unless Their Powerful Electorates Also Act and Think Long Term?' (2010) 66 *Business Law* 1, 3.

208 For instance, managing according to share market prices may encourage directors to take excessive risks. Also, see Jensen, 'Value Maximisation, Stakeholder Theory, and the Corporate Objective Function' (n 70) 8.

209 For example, in the US, since 1991 the number of listed companies is down by more than 22 per cent and down a startling 53 per cent when allowing for real (namely, inflation-adjusted) GDP growth. David Weild and Edward Kim, 'A Wake-Up Call for America' (November 2009) *Grant Thornton Capital Market Series* 1, 1; also see David Weild and Edward Kim, 'Market Structure Is Causing the IPO Crisis – and More' (June 2010) *Grant Thornton Capital Market Series* 1, 9. Professor Stout also proves the lack of investors' demand for SWM by referring to the recent examples of Google and LinkedIn's dual-class equity structures when going public for weakening outside shareholder power. Stout, *The Shareholder Value Myth* (n 71) 55–56.

Motor Co.,[210] which is thought by shareholder primacists to give a legal requirement for SWM. The Michigan Supreme Court opined that:

> There should be no confusion (of which there is evidence) of the duties which Mr. Ford conceives that he and the stockholders owe to the general public and the duties which in law he and his codirectors owe to protesting, minority stockholders. A business corporation is organized and carried on primarily for the profit of the stockholders. The powers of the directors are to be employed for that end. The discretion of directors is to be exercised in the choice of means to attain that end, and does not extend to change in the end itself, to the reduction of profits, or to nondistribution of profits among stockholders in order to devote them to other purposes.[211]

However, after a close examination, it could be found that this case mainly dealt with the relationship between the controlling shareholder (i.e. Mr Ford) and the minority shareholders (i.e. the Dodge brothers) in a closely held company.[212]

The opinion that pursuing shareholder profits as the primary corporate purpose (i.e. a business corporation is organised and carried on primarily for the profit of the stockholders) is merely judicial dicta;[213] the actual holding is that Mr Ford as the controlling shareholder and CEO cannot stop the Dodge brothers as the minority shareholders from "demand[ing] proper dividends upon the stock they own".[214] As Professor Stout points out, the court thought this case was mainly about the controlling shareholder breaching his fiduciary duty to the minority shareholders.[215] This is not inconsistent with Professor D Gordon Smith's argument that this case is best regarded as "a minority oppression case".[216]

---

210 Mr Ford, as the CEO and controlling shareholder of the Ford Motor Co., announced a plan to stop paying out special dividends to shareholders, and instead take the profits and reinvest them in order to employ more workers and build more factories, which was aimed at employing more people and cutting the costs of the cars to make them affordable to more people. Dodge Brothers as minority shareholders sued to stop Ford's plans as they thought the purpose of the company was to maximise shareholder wealth. *Dodge v. Ford Motor Co* [1919] 170 NW 668 (US).

211 Ibid. 684.

212 In addition, there are two other reasons why Mr Ford stopped paying dividends. First, Ford knew that Dodge wished to use the dividend money to build a rival car company and he probably wanted to bankrupt such potential competition by depriving them of liquid funds. Second, Ford wanted to buy out Dodge brothers' stocks at the lowest possible price. Stout, 'Why We Should Stop Teaching *Dodge v. Ford*' (n 98) 167. And, as known, shareholders in public companies are not entitled to demand dividends.

213 Furthermore, it is argued that Michigan state corporate case law is not an influential source. Ibid.

214 *Dodge v. Ford Motor Co* [1919] 170 NW 668, 685 (US).

215 Stout, 'Why We Should Stop Teaching *Dodge v. Ford*' (n 98) 167.

216 Professor Smith argues that "the court thought it was merely deciding a dispute between majority and minority shareholders in a closely held corporation in the same way courts had decided such disputes for nearly a century". Smith (n 22) 320.

Moreover, the *Dodge* case is rarely cited;[217] indeed, the only citation as authority in the Delaware courts of the last 30 years is on the subject of minority shareholder oppression instead of on corporate objectives.[218]

Instead, in *Shlensky v. Wrigley*,[219] the court upheld the directors' decision to protect the interests of the community (i.e. to keep the neighbourhood from deteriorating) by not installing lights for night baseball games in Wrigley Field. Although night games would make the club, and arguably its shareholders, earn more profits by increasing attendance, the court in *Shlensky* refused to hold the directors liable simply because they failed to pursue additional revenues (i.e. maximising shareholder wealth), and by contrast, supported the directors' consideration for the interests of local residents.

With regard to statutes, another important source for law, company law codes in the US do not require SWM either. Under the *Delaware General Corporate Law* (DGCL), the most representative and important corporate law in the US,[220] any lawful business or purposes are allowed. More importantly, a large number of states enact a "constituency statute" which explicitly authorises "corporate boards of directors to consider the interest of constituencies other than stockholders";[221] in other words, the interests of customers, suppliers, employees and creditors should also be taken into consideration during the decision-making process. The business judgement rule as a shield provides extra ground for directors to act in the best interests of the company, even if doing so may sacrifice shareholders' profits such as rejecting a lucrative hostile takeover offer.[222]

Although both case law and statutes do not require directors to only focus on the interests of shareholders, a company's charter or articles of association may still explicitly set out the purpose of the company to be SWM if incorporators see fit. However, it is hard to imagine any large public company including such a provision in their company's constitution.[223]

217 It has been cited only once by Delaware courts in the past thirty years. Even the shareholder primacist Professor Macey concedes "there are no cases other than Dodge v. Ford that actually operationalize the rule that corporations must maximize profits". Jonathan Macey, 'A Close Read of An Excellent Commentary on Dodge v Ford' (2008) 3 *Virginia Law Business Review* 177, 180.
218 Stout, 'Why We Should Stop Teaching *Dodge v. Ford*' (n 98) 166 and 169.
219 (1968) 237 NE 2d 776 (US).
220 See *infra* Chapter 3, section 3.2.1.
221 Lawrence Mitchell, 'A Theoretical and Practical Framework for Enforcing Corporate Constituency Statutes' (1992) 70 *Texas Law Review* 579, 579–580. In other states, including Delaware, takeover case law takes into account the impact on non-shareholding stakeholders. Martin Gelter, 'The Dark Side of Shareholder Influence: Managerial Autonomy and Stakeholder Orientation in Comparative Corporate Governance' (2009) 50 *Harvard International Law Journal* 129, 145 (footnotes omitted).
222 For example, in *Air Products Inc. v. Airgas, Inc*, Airgas' board of directors rejected a profitable takeover offered by Air Products. The business judgement rule provides directors with the shield for pursuing goals other than SWM (as long as no self-interest is involved). Stout, *The Shareholder Value Myth* (n 71) 30.
223 In many Continental countries, the power of the board stems from the law not the shareholders. For instance, section 119 of *German Stock Corporation Act* specifies: "The shareholders' meeting may decide on matters concerning the management of the company only if required by the management board".

In the UK, partly for historical reasons,[224] the situation is more complicated. Despite the fact that the company as an independent legal person has long been recognised since the *Salomon* case in common law, it is still difficult for the interests of the company to become completely independent from the interests of the shareholders. Under common law, a company is usually seen as an artificial person, and therefore it is difficult to argue that it has independent interests without referring to any human groups. For example, according to Professor Davies, the interest of a company is too vague a guidance for corporate directors to follow, and accordingly, the dominant view under common law is that shareholders are the "primary object of the directors' efforts".[225]

However, it is difficult to find a case directly stating that shareholders' interests are the company's interests, or that the purpose of the company is to maximise shareholder value under case law. In fact, shareholder interest is different from corporate interest: the company is vulnerable to both idiosyncratic and systematic risks, whilst shareholders can be insulated from idiosyncratic risk by adopting diversified portfolios.[226] Therefore, when acting in the interests of shareholders, directors only have to take systematic risk into account, which may hurt corporate interests. Corporate interests are indeed more than shareholder interests.[227] On the other hand, Professor Ireland insists the interest of company is "an interest in the productive utilization of industrial capital", which is oriented towards "long term [sic] prosperity and security of a block of industrial capital assets". The interests of the shareholders, meanwhile, are "a money capital interest in the revenue generated by . . . industrial capital" which aims at "short-term maximisation of the return on a money capital investment".[228] The Canadian case *People's Department Stores v. Wise* may also shed light on the distinction between the two types of interests. The Canadian Supreme Court held that the interests of the company should not be confused with the interests of the shareholders or any other individual stakeholder groups; the interests of shareholders, employees, suppliers, creditors, consumers, governments and the environment, etc. should all be considered when acting in the best interests of the company.[229]

---

224 For example, the partnership origins of UK company law. *Infra* Chapter 3, section 3.2.2.
225 Paul Davies and Sarah Worthington, *Principles of Modern Company Law* (10th edn Sweet & Maxwell, London 2016) 502.
226 For example, see Armour and Gordon (n 114) 36.
227 There is also some support in case law, for example Lord Templeman pointed out in *Winkworth v. Edward Baron Development Co Ltd* [1987] 1 ALL ER 114, 118: "a company owes a duty to its creditors, present and future. The company is not bound to pay off every debt as soon as it is incurred and the company is not obliged to avoid all ventures which involve an element of risk, but the company owes a duty to its creditors to keep its property inviolate and available for the repayment of its debts . . . A duty is owed by the directors to the company and to the creditors of the company to ensure that the affairs of the company are properly administered and that its property is not dissipated or exploited for the benefit of the directors themselves to the prejudice of the creditors".
   Similarly, per Lord Diplock in *Lonrho Ltd v. Shell Petroleum Co Ltd* [1980] 1 WLR 627, 634: "the best interests of the company . . . are not exclusively those of its shareholders but may include those of its creditors".
228 Ireland, 'Corporate Governance, Stakeholding, and the Company' (n 41) 304 and 308.
229 *People's Department Stores v. Wise* [2004] 3 SCR 461 (Canada).

Moreover, as discussed above, through the development of financial derivatives, shareholders may alienate their personal interests from their shares.[230] And after *Percival v. Wright*,[231] it became clear that director's duties are only owed to the company rather than to the shareholders.[232] In *Automatic Self-Cleansing Filter Syndicate Co. Ltd v. Cuninghame*, the court affirmed that directors are not the agents of the shareholders and thereby are not bound to follow shareholders' directions.[233]

In statute, although consideration for other stakeholders is acknowledged by linking it to the success of the company, in section 172 of the *Companies Act 2006*, the so-called enlightened shareholder value (hereafter, ESV) approach is thought by many shareholder primacists to express shareholder primacy or a means to achieve the fundamental ends of SWM. It is argued that the shareholder-centred perspective remains unchanged. Whilst directors are required to have regard to stakeholders' interests, when stakeholder consideration is in conflict with shareholder interests, the latter will prevail. In other words, ESV cannot change existing shareholder primacy, as shareholders' interests continue to be the primary concern.[234] Looking back to the *Companies Act 1985*, section 309 states: (1) The matters to which the directors of a company are to have regard in the performance of their functions include the interests of the company's employees in general, as well as the interest of its members; (2) Accordingly, the duty imposed by this section on the directors is owed by them to the company (and the company alone) and is enforceable in the same way as any other fiduciary duty owed to a company by its directors. In the new *Act*, section 172(1) stipulates:

> A director of a company must act in the way he considers, in good faith, would be most likely to promote the success of the company for the benefit of its members as a whole, and in doing so have regard (among other matters) to – (a) the likely consequences of any decision in the long term, (b) the interests of the company's employees, (c) the need to foster the

230 Take hedge funds, for example, they may not care about the decline in share price as it is possible for them to profit from the bad performance. In particular, if they sell the shares short, a decline in the share price rather than an increase is desired.

231 [1902] 2 Ch 421. Also see *Peskin v. Anderson* [2001] BCC 874, 874 where the court holds: "fiduciary duties owed by directors to a company arose from the legal relationship between directors and the company directed and controlled by them. Fiduciary duties owed by directors to shareholders did not arise from that legal relationship but were dependent on establishing a special factual relationship between the directors and the shareholders in the particular case".

232 Now section 170(1) of the *Companies Act 2006* makes it clear by specifying: "The general duties specified in sections 171 to 177 are owed by a director of a company to the company". This will be further discussed in Chapter 3.

233 *Automatic Self-Cleansing Filter Syndicate Co. Ltd v. Cuninghame* [1906] 2 Ch 34.

234 For example, see Deryn Fisher, 'The Enlightened Shareholder – Leaving Stakeholders in the Dark: Will Section 172(1) of the Companies Act 2006 Make Directors Consider the Impact of their Decisions on Third Parties?' (2009) 20 *International Company and Commercial Law Review* 10, 12. This may be why it is argued that the main effect of ESV is more educational than disciplinary. John Birds *et al.*, *Boyle & Birds' Company Law* (6th edn Jordan Publishing, Bristol 2007) 618.

company's business relationships with suppliers, customers and others, (d) the impact of the company's operations on the community and the environment, (e) the desirability of the company maintaining a reputation for high standards of business conduct, and (f) the need to act fairly as between members of the company.

Although directors must have regard for the interests of employees and other stakeholders, the phrase "in doing so" before "have regard to" is interpreted as revealing the priority, namely the interests of stakeholders are subordinated to "the success of the company for the benefit of its members as a whole". Many hold the view that so-called ESV does not change existing shareholder primacy.[235]

Prior to the *Companies Act 2006*, directors were obliged to act in the interests of the company,[236] but the new law makes it more shareholder-focused by adding "for the benefit of its members as a whole". Unlike some implicit flexibility existing in common law regarding the interpretation of company interest, the wording of section 172(1) seems to hint at shareholder primacy.[237] Professor Davies believes that stakeholder interests would not be taken into consideration unless "it is desirable to do so in order to promote the success of the company for the benefit of its members".[238]

However, similar to the case law, statutes never explicitly state that the company should be run solely for the interests of its shareholders, although it is possible to argue that the stakeholder factor under the so-called ESV is more like an instrument. Demanding directors to act in the best interests of the company for the benefit of its members does not deliver SWM or shareholder primacy. As Professor Worthington argues,

> This does not mean that the company, acting via the directors, has to favour the interests of the shareholders. It simply means that discretions cannot be exercised in bad faith or for irrelevant motivations so as to defeat shareholder interests.[239]

---

235 John Birds, 'The Companies Act 2006: Revolution or Evolution?' (2007) 49 *Managerial Law* 13, 14. Similarly, Professor Keay also argues "directors are obliged, in the course of acting in the way that is most likely to promote the success of the company for the benefit of the members, 'to have regard to' matters mentioned in s.172(1)". Andrew Keay, 'Section 172(1) of the Companies Act 2006: An Interpretation and Assessment' (2007) 28 *Company Lawyer* 106, 108.

236 Similarly, the company's interests and the directors' duties in relation to the company in common law, as discussed earlier, also have some room regarding the interpretation of "company".

237 However, it should be noted that the court in *Cobden Investments Ltd v. RWM Langport Ltd, Southern Counties Fresh Foods Limited, Romford Wholesale Meats Limited* [2008] EWHC 2810 (Ch) held that: "the perhaps old-fashioned phrase acting '*bona fide* in the interests of the company' is reflected in the statutory words acting 'in good faith in a way most likely to promote the success of the company for the benefit of its members as a whole'. They come to the same thing with the modern formulation giving a more readily understood definition of the scope of the duty". Such an interpretation shows that the emphasis remains on the interests of the company.

238 Davies and Worthington, *Principles of Modern Company Law* (n 225) 503.

239 Sarah Worthington, 'Shares and Shareholders: Property, Power and Entitlement: Part 2' (2001) 22 *Company Lawyer* 307, 309–310.

Subsequently, due to the fact that the legitimate interests of stakeholders such as employees, creditors or customers are not allowed to be frustrated either, it is not an overstatement to argue that directors should also act in a bona fide way which they consider to be in the interests of these stakeholders.[240]

More importantly, whilst the interests of the company are sometimes interpreted as the financial well-being of shareholders as a whole,[241] according to *Re BSB Holdings Ltd (No. 2)*, "the law does not require the interests of the company to be sacrificed in the particular interests of a group of shareholders".[242] This implies that English law also acknowledges the difference between shareholder interests and corporate interests. If the interests of the company are in conflict with the interests of the members as a whole, the interests of the company should be given preference.[243] In *Fulham Football Club Ltd v. Cabra Estates*, the court also opined that "the duties owned by the directors are to the company and the company is more than just the sum total of its members".[244] It is the view of the court that the interests of creditors, employees and others should also be included.[245]

Even the wording in section 172 of "have regard to" may not necessarily imply the content following it should be subordinated to the content preceding it. To begin, section 172(1)(a), "the likely consequences of any decision in the long term", cannot be deemed to be non-essential or subordinated to other requirements. As already explicitly stated, the undue focus on short-term shareholder interests has been abandoned at the policy level and, instead, a long-term sense of the best corporate interest is clearly required.[246] It is hard to justify the requirement that long-termism considerations should be subject to any preconditions or be less important than the immediate shareholder interests. Given that long-term and short-term interests are in conflict, according to the shareholder primacists' interpretation of "in doing so" and "have regard to", short-term interests would supersede long-term interests. This is certainly problematic.

By the same token, if subsections (b) the interests of the company's employees, (c) the need to foster the company's business relationships with suppliers, customers and others, and (d) the impact of the company's operations on the community and the environment are only secondary responsibilities for directors, as Professors Davies and Keay would argue, what about the duty of subsection (f) to act fairly between the members of the company? Since the fair treatment of all members

---

240 Ibid. 310 (footnote omitted).
241 For example, see Thomas Clarke, *International Corporate Governance: A Comparative Approach* (Routledge, New York 2007) 281.
242 [1996] 1 BCLC 155, 251.
243 Geoffrey Morse (ed), *Palmer's Company Law: Volume 2* (Sweet & Maxwell, London 2014) para 8.2605. Also see *Mutual Life Assurance Co of New York v. Rank Organisation Ltd* [1985] BCLC 11, 21.
244 *Fulham Football Club Ltd v. Cabra Estates* [1994] 1 BCLC 363, 379.
245 Ibid.
246 For example, see CLRSG (n 13) 39.

follows the phrase "in doing so have regard to", the duty before it should be prioritised. In other words, shareholders could be unfairly treated in order to promote the success of the company for the benefit of its members as a whole. It would be an exaggeration to categorise the equitable treatment of shareholders in a company as a subordinate responsibility, as fair treatment is a well-established principle under modern corporate governance.[247] If long-term consideration and equitable treatment are not subordinated to promote the success of the company,[248] it is then difficult to justify the duty to have regard for stakeholder interests as specified in section 172(1)(b), (c) and (d) as being of a subordinate nature.

In addition, Chapter 4A 'Strategic Report' of Part 12 of the *Companies Act 2006*, in replacing section 417 'Directors' Report',[249] requires directors of a company to prepare a strategic report including information relating to environmental matters and employee matters. In the case of listed companies, further information about social, community and human rights issues, as well as any policies of the company in relation to those matters and the effectiveness of those policies is required to be disclosed.[250] The increasing requirement for disclosure of stakeholder-related information has the potential to force directors to consider rather more stakeholders' interests and any possible impacts on them in practice. Though presently stakeholders other than shareholders have no additional rights to be involved in corporate governance or to take action to challenge directors' ignorance of their interests, setting out such a non-exhaustive list of specific factors requiring consideration can "expand the grounds for judicial review of directors' decision-making".[251]

2.5.2 Heterogeneous expectations of shareholders

Despite it being recognised that the preferences of different shareholders may not be identical, Professors Easterbrook and Fischel have argued that they do not tend to be too dissimilar, and in a given company at a given time most shareholders are a reasonably homogeneous group with an analogous objective.[252]

---

247 For example, the third principle of OECD *Principle of Corporate Governance (2004)* specifies: "The corporate governance framework should ensure the equitable treatment of all shareholders, including minority and foreign shareholders. All shareholders should have the opportunity to obtain effective redress for violation of their rights".

248 Section 172(1)(e) "maintaining a reputation for high standards of business conduct" is also by no means a non-essential duty for directors of the board; it should be one of the primary concerns for the directors.

249 Part 2 of The Companies Act 2006 (Strategic Report and Directors' Report) Regulations 2013 No. 1970.

250 Section 414C (7)(b)(ii) of *Companies Act 2006*.

251 Geoffrey Morse (ed), *Palmer's Company Law* (n 243) para 8.2613. It should also be noted that shareholders could not enforce s.172 against the directors, as this duty is owed to the company rather than shareholders.

252 For more discussion, see Easterbrook and Fischel, *The Economic Structure of Corporate Law* (n 110) 70.

Similarly, it has been argued that those investors of pecuniary capital have been, or at least are able to be, induced to have exceptionally homogeneous interests.[253] In Professor Anabtawi's words: "most observers of corporate governance law nevertheless regard divergences in the interests of shareholders as either insignificant or checked by the corporate law voting principle of majority rule".[254]

However, the divergence could be very significant and therefore should not be ignored. First of all, shareholders may have different expected holding periods. Although in theory the current share price should be able to reflect the future value in a perfect market, share price is not completely immune to manipulation owing to the failure of the efficient capital market hypothesis. The foregoing section makes it clear that short-term shareholders tend to focus on immediate profits from fluctuations in the share market by buying and selling shares with high frequency. In contrast, long-term shareholders tend to focus on long-term development by buying and holding shares regardless of the rise and fall of share prices.

Thus, shareholders with different expected holding periods would unavoidably have divergent preferences over corporate decision-making. The former may be more likely to pressure directors to adopt policies which would maximise short-term share prices, such as axing employees, reducing R&D expenses or selling corporate assets,[255] whilst the latter may sacrifice immediate profits for long-term development. Indeed, short-term and long-term interests are quite difficult to reconcile and integrate. Long-term development, by training employees, investing in technology and improving customer service for example, requires an upfront cost. Such an upfront cost could be considered a negative factor under short-termism because the immediate profits would be impaired as a consequence.

Take hedge funds for example. They are typically only concerned with short-term performance and share price instead of long-term success. When a hedge fund invests in a company, it may then force the directors of that company to seize the maximum possible earnings in a short period due to its "relatively short life span".[256] If some other shareholders in that company take a long-term view, for instance a pension fund, then unavoidably they will have fundamentally different opinions on corporate strategies, such as the attitude towards R&D, especially

---

253 For example, see footnote 122 and accompany text above.

254 Anabtawi (n 184) 577–578 (footnote omitted).

255 According to Professor Jensen, it is not impossible for directors to "increase this year's profits at the expense of future year's profits by moving expenses from this year to the future (by delaying purchases, for example) or by moving revenues from future years into this year by booking orders early (by announcing future price increases, or by giving special discounts this year, or guaranteeing to repurchase goods in the future, and so on)". Jensen, 'Paying People to Lie' (n 183) 387.

256 Division of Investment Management, 'Implications of the Growth of Hedge Funds' *Staff Report to United States Securities and Exchange Commission* (September 2003) at www.sec. gov/news/studies/hedgefunds0903.pdf [accessed 1 March 2017].

in an inefficient stock market.[257] A typical setting is takeover; the example of the hedge fund in MCI, Inc. exemplifies "the potential for short-term shareholders to pursue their interests at the cost of long-term shareholder value".[258] In short, the conflicts between shareholders with different expected holding periods are difficult to reconcile.[259]

Second, the level of diversification determines the risk preference. Diversified shareholders care much less about firm-specific risk than undiversified shareholders, but a shareholder who invests in a given company without also diversifying would be very sensitive to such risk. Indeed, undiversified shareholders may normally give up higher returns for reduced risks. For example, say a company is confronted with two projects, A and B. Project A has a 50 per cent chance of earning £100,000 and 50 per cent of losing £50,000, whilst Project B has a 90 per cent of chance of earning £20,000 and a 10 per cent chance of losing £10,000. A diversified shareholder would be indifferent to the firm-specific risk and would choose Project A since its expected return (£100,000 * 50% – £50,000 * 50% = £25,000) is obviously higher than Project B's expected return (£20,000 * 90% – £10,000 * 10% = £17,000). In contrast, an undiversified shareholder would probably choose Project B since they cannot diversify the firm-specific risk of losing, though the former project has a potentially much higher profit margin. In other words, diversified and undiversified shareholders may have contrasting preferences regarding risk and the like.

Furthermore, the differing expectations between inside shareholders and outside shareholders, hedged shareholders and unhedged shareholders also demonstrate shareholders may have very different interests, thereby making it impossible to maximise all of them at the same time.[260] Shareholder interest may also mean substantially different things to different shareholders. Assuming a shareholder is keen on certain environmental principles for example, then increasing share prices and dividends by ignoring or violating these principles is certainly not in accord with the fundamental interest of this very shareholder. Similarly,

---

257 As discussed in the last section, it is hard for the market to tell the long-term from the short-term strategy. Even though sophisticated investors or shareholders may identify which is which, it by no means implies that the market as whole can benefit from such a discovery and thereby it cannot serve as a reliable criterion. Also, see Lynn Stout, 'The Mechanisms of Market Inefficiency: An Introduction to the New Finance' (2003) 28 *Journal of Corporation Law* 635, 667.

258 Anabtawi (n 184) 582.

259 For example, as Professor Anabtawi has argued, "shareholders with a short timeframe will favour the inflation of current share prices at the expense of long-run value. On the other hand, long-term investors will be willing to sacrifice immediate profits for future appreciation". Ibid. 581.

260 For example, inside shareholders like directors with shares may be more concerned about job security and prefer to maintain the status quo when facing a hostile takeover, even though the offer may be in the best interests of the company. Or in the context of golden parachutes, insider shareholders who happen to be directors would have a greater incentive to facilitate the merger even it is not in the best interests of outside shareholders. Ibid. 583–593 (footnote omitted).

certain institutional shareholders such as labour union funds may care more about labour interest than merely economic interests.[261]

Excepting the general idea of increasing shareholder value, there is no clear guidance as to what to do when a balance is needed. An important criticism against the stakeholder theory regarding the issue of balance can be raised here as well. Indeed, the merits of measurability and certainty are debatable, as Chapter 5 will discuss in further detail.

2.6 Concluding remarks

SWM's rationale has been completely challenged in this chapter. Both the traditional and modern proprietary justifications are not convincing, and contractarian theory – including agency theory – also fails to capture the essence of corporate governance relationships. The relationship between shareholders and directors is not equivalent to that of principals and agents. Shareholders are not the only residual claimants. As demonstrated, other stakeholders can become claimants for residual value and bearers of residual risks. In large public companies (the subject of this book), the equity and physical capital are not as important as they once were.[262] In fact, most shareholder investment nowadays is just the sale and purchase of shares from one shareholder to another, with no new capital being supplied to the company. Companies are more likely to finance themselves through accumulated corporate profits from years of operations, or via debt funds. By contrast, the role and function of non-shareholding stakeholders are increasingly becoming more important than shareholders in many aspects. This chapter also rebuts the so-called economic efficiency argument, a principal basis for most SWM proponents.

SWM not only discourages various stakeholders from making firm-specific investments, but also causes significant negative externalisation as well as short-termism. Pressure from shareholders, the current incentive mechanism in the form of share options, and the value judgement standard including conventional accounting practice, make the above problems to a large extent unavoidable under SWM.

After re-examining SWM, it can be found that the laws in both the UK and the US do not oblige directors to run the company solely for the interests of shareholders. It should be borne in mind that corporate interests are distinguished from shareholder interests. If directors are only required to focus on increasing shareholder value, they only have to take systematic risk into account;

---

261 After a comprehensive review of recent literature, Goranova and Ryan have summarised shareholders' investment horizons, business relationships with the firm, portfolio considerations and discrepancies between cash flow and voting rights may cause different preferences. Maria Goranova and Lori Ryan, 'Shareholder Activism: A Multidisciplinary Review' (2014) 40 *Journal of Management* 1230, 1249.

262 John Kay, 'The Kay Review of UK Equity Markets and Long-term Decision Making' (2012) 25. And the net contribution of new equity to the corporate sector has become negative. Deakin, 'The Coming Transformation of Shareholder Value' (n 131) 15.

this may hurt the company, as the latter is also vulnerable to idiosyncratic risk, which is firm-specific. Meanwhile, it is not impossible for shareholders to be completely alienated from corporate performance by borrowing shares or profit from poorly performing companies by selling shares short or using other modern financial arrangements. In fact, the expectations of shareholders within a company can be diverse. Whether shareholders are diversified or undiversified, inside or outside, hedged or unhedged, among others, could determine different expected holding periods and risk preferences. Thus, SWM is not a singular objective, and there is no guideline for balancing different interests, except the quarterly share price. Along with the indispensable role and function of stakeholders, it is safe to conclude that large public companies at least should look beyond maximising shareholder wealth.

3 Shareholder power and shareholder empowerment

3.1 An overview

Corporate governance is generally regarded as responsible for preventing corporate scandal and failures.[1] Accordingly, there is an increasing trend of believing corporate governance should be more focused on constraining the so-called principal-agent problems in public companies, as discussed in the last chapter. Due to the separation of ownership and control, shareholders regarded as principals in fact cannot control their directors in large companies with dispersed shareholdings. The actual control of the company is generally conferred upon the board of directors, who normally delegate the day-to-day management to the corporate executives. The shareholders' powerlessness is thought by SWM proponents to be a main source of directors' lack of accountability and the recent global financial crises due to ineffective monitoring of directors' unfettered discretionary power. Consequently, shareholder empowerment is seen by professionals, lawyers and policy-makers in the UK and US alike as being the best solution for overcoming the so-called agency problem caused by unaccountable agents in general.[2] In the words of Professor Bainbridge, "virtually all of the reforms mandated after the crisis were designed to empower shareholders".[3]

---

1 It is nevertheless worthwhile to note that some scholars do think corporate governance is not a solution but a problem in itself. For example, see Andrew Johnston, 'Corporate Governance is the Problem, Not the Solution: A Critical Appraisal of the European Regulation on Credit Rating Agencies' (2011) 11 *Journal of Corporate Law Studies* 395, 406.
2 However, some argue that shareholders might be part of the problem rather than the solution. For example, see European Commission, 'Communication on Corporate Governance in Financial Institutions' at http://ec.europa.eu/internal_market/company/modern/corporate_governance_in_financial_institutions_en.htm [accessed 1 March 2017]. Moreover, shareholders' short-termism as discussed in the last chapter further confirms such an argument. Just as summarised by Professor Hill, "lack of shareholder power caused neither Enron nor the global financial crisis, and that enhancing shareholder power will not prevent, and may even provoke, future crisis". Jennifer Hill, 'The Rising Tension between Shareholder and Director Power in the Common Law World' (2010) 18 *Corporate Governance: An International Review* 344, 350 (footnote omitted). This viewpoint will be developed in the following sections.
3 Stephen Bainbridge, *Corporate Governance after the Financial Crisis* (OUP, Oxford 2012) 13. Similarly, Daniel Attenborough observes that both the European Commission and the US have

In the US, shareholder approval is gradually being required in the area of executive compensation. The new proxy access rule could entitle shareholders to nominate directors and put forward their nominees on the company proxy statement for the sake of challenging the control of the incumbent board.[4] The proxy contest becomes an effective threat often used by activists such as labour union funds and hedge funds. In addition, the proposed majority voting for director election and shareholders' say-on-pay will make directors more vulnerable. For example, in the opinion of the Committee on Capital Markets Regulation, granting shareholders more power is generally seen as an effective means of enhancing accountability to increase shareholder value.[5] The situation is similar in the UK. The *Companies (Shareholders' Rights) Regulations*,[6] the *Stewardship Code*, the new *UK Corporate Governance Code*[7] and various government consultations all aim to encourage shareholders to be more active and play a more important role in corporate governance, as it is believed that shareholder engagement could improve managerial accountability, including controlling excessive risk-taking.[8]

The general Anglo-American response to the financial crisis with respect to corporate failures is to empower shareholders and make it easier to involve them in corporate governance, such as board elections and decision-making. This chapter discusses shareholder empowerment, which can be seen as a product of SWM, and assesses its effects. The chapter's conclusion is important for the following chapters. The discussion of Anglo-American shareholder power can serve as a reference when studying shareholder rights in China. Moreover, if shareholder empowerment cannot effectively maximise shareholder wealth – even assuming SWM is the corporate objective – then it will be helpful for the construction of the stakeholder model. Furthermore, it will aid in responding to doubts on how to keep it consistent with the current legal system; namely, ensuring there is no need to empower stakeholders in order to improve stakeholder value.

taken steps to empower shareholders to address the governance problems in the post-crisis error. In short, shareholder empowerment is seen as the alternative to a more stringent rules-based approach. Daniel Attenborough, 'The Various Concept of Shareholder Voting Rights' (2013) 14 *European Business Organization Law Review* 147, 154–155.

4 When it is time to elect directors, the incumbent board nominates a slate, which it puts forward on the company's proxy statement. There is no mechanism for a shareholder to put a nominee on the ballot. Instead, a shareholder who wishes to nominate directors is obliged to incur the considerable expense of conducting a proxy contest to attempt to elect a slate in opposition to that put forward by the incumbents. Ibid. 224.

5 William Bratton and Michael Wachter, 'The Case Against Shareholder Empowerment' (2010) 158 *University of Pennsylvanian Law Review* 653, 655.

6 SI 2009/1632. The Regulations implements the *EC Shareholder Rights Directive* (2007) and aims to strengthen shareholder voices, especially those cross-board ones.

7 The *Combined Code* was renamed the UK *Corporate Governance Code* in 2010.

8 For example, see European Commission, 'Green Paper: Corporate Governance in Financial Institutions and Remuneration Policies' COM (2010) 284 final, 24; European Commission, 'Green Paper: The EU Corporate Governance Framework' COM (2011) 164 final, 3.

3.2 Increasing shareholder power

Before examining shareholder empowerment, it is essential to spend some time exploring shareholder power under US and UK law, as they are normally insulated from corporate management. This section first discusses shareholder rights in both jurisdictions respectively and then analyses their main approaches to increasing shareholder power.

3.2.1 Shareholder rights in US law

The US corporate law statutes are state law, and most major US corporations including the majority of Fortune 500 corporations are incorporated under the law of the State of Delaware.[9] Under *Delaware General Corporate Law* (hereafter, DGCL), the most representative and important corporate law in the US, shareholders' rights are largely limited. Section 141(a) of DGCL explicitly stipulates "the business and affairs of every corporation . . . shall be managed by or under the direction of a board of directors".[10] Shareholders have a right to vote only in matters of (1) director election,[11] (2) fundamental corporate changes such as by-law or charter amendments,[12] mergers,[13] sales of all or substantially all of the corporate assets[14] and voluntary dissolution.[15] This means shareholders are largely restrained from interfering with the managerial authority of the board.

By and large, shareholders can only indirectly influence corporate affairs by influencing the board of directors. In practice, nevertheless, unless an insurgent shareholder appears to conduct an expensive and strenuous proxy contest, the election of directors is in practice controlled by the incumbent board as well, as Berle and Means observed in the 1930s:

> In the election of the board the stockholder ordinarily has three alternatives. He can refrain from voting, he can attend the annual meeting and personally vote his stock, or he can sign a proxy transferring his voting power to certain individuals selected by the management of the corporation, the proxy committee. As his personal vote will count for little or nothing at the meeting unless he has a very large block of stock, the stockholder is practically reduced to the alternative of not voting at all or else of handing over his vote to individuals over whom he has no control and in whose selection he

---

9 According to the State of Delaware's Division of Corporations, more than 1 million business entities have their legal home in Delaware including more than 50 per cent of all the US publicly traded companies and 64 per cent of the Fortune 500. Available at http://corp.delaware.gov/ [accessed 30 October 2015].

10 *Model Business Corporation Act*, which is followed by 24 states, also explicitly forbids public companies from providing shareholders with any powers of intervention. See section 7.32(d).

11 Section 141(k) of DGCL.

12 Sections 109(a) and 242(b) of DGCL.

13 Section 251(c) of DGCL.

14 Section 271(a) of DGCL.

15 Section 275(b) of DGCL.

did not participate. In neither case will he be able to exercise any measure of control. Rather, control will tend to be in the hands of those who select the proxy committee by whom, in turn, the election of directors for the ensuing period may be made. Since the proxy committee is appointed by the existing management, the latter can virtually dictate their own successors. Where ownership is sufficiently sub-divided, the management can thus become a self-perpetuating body even though its share in the ownership is negligible.[16]

If the board is classified or say staggered,[17] it is even more difficult to replace a majority of incumbent directors since this cannot be completed in one annual election circle.[18] Shareholders then have to wait for two years to gain control of the board by replacing directors at two consecutive annual general meetings. The route to changing the company's charter or by-laws to declassify the board is also not straightforward. Even assuming there is provision that directors can be removed without cause, an interim meeting is required to remove a director between annual general meetings, but shareholders do not have such right unless explicitly granted by the certificate of incorporation or the by-laws, which is not the case in many companies.[19] For this reason, Professors Blair and Stout state "shareholders in public corporations do not in any realistic sense elect boards. Rather, boards elect themselves".[20] All suggest shareholders normally have negligible influence in a typical US public company.

Moreover, the *Securities Exchange Act* along with the corresponding Securities and Exchange Commission (SEC) rules discourage individual shareholders or groups from owning shareholdings over 5 per cent by enforcing an extensive disclosure obligation on those who achieve that threshold. These rules indirectly impede shareholders owning or forming a large block to effectively challenge incumbent directors. As one scholar argues:

> By both discouraging the formation of groups of insurgents and the acquisition of large blocks by individual activists, these laws have the (presumably unintended) consequence of indirectly insulating incumbent directors from proxy challenges.[21]

16 Adolf Berle and Gardiner Means, *The Modern Corporation and Private Property* (Transaction Publishers, New Brunswick 1991, originally published 1932) 82.
17 According to section 141(k) of DGCL, a board of directors may be classified into "1, 2 or 3 classes; the term of office of those of the first class to expire at the first annual meeting held after such classification becomes effective; of the second class 1 year thereafter; of the third class 2 years thereafter; and at each annual election held after such classification becomes effective, directors shall be chosen for a full term, as the case may be, to succeed those whose terms expire".
18 Moreover, shareholders cannot call special shareholders' meeting for doing so. Only the board of directors or the authorised person(s) can call such meetings. See section 211(d) of DGCL.
19 Attenborough (n 3) 166.
20 Margaret Blair and Lynn Stout, 'A Team Production Theory of Corporate Law' (1999) 85 *Virginia Law Review* 247, 311; Stephen Bainbridge, 'The Case for Limited Shareholder Voting Rights' (2006) 53 *UCLA Law Review* 601, 603.
21 Bainbridge, *Corporate Governance* (n 3) 205–206. Until recently, federal rules were in place to support state corporate law by discouraging the "formation of large stock blocks" as well

The federal proxy rules and shareholder proposal rules provide further restraints. Apart from the strict disclosure requirement, shareholders cannot include some significant types of proposal such as director nomination and solicitations opposing director proposals in the company proxy statement. Directors can spend company's money to support their proposals by including them in the company proxy statement, but shareholders' ability to communicate and act together is also restricted.[22]

Conversely, the board of directors has almost absolute control. Indeed, the power of the board is generally considered as provided by law rather than shareholders. The essence of US corporate law is to prevent shareholders from exerting a material role in corporate management, as the Delaware Supreme Court states:

> One of the most basic tenets of Delaware corporate law is that the board of directors has the ultimate responsibility for managing the business and affairs of a corporation.[23]

Corporate law in the US allows the board to make significant mergers and acquisitions;[24] only the board can initiate charter amendment[25] and other previously mentioned shareholder rights, except director election, are frequently premised on board initiation or approval.[26] As Professor Bebchuk, the most well-known advocate of shareholder empowerment, points out, these rights can only be seen as a *veto* power for shareholders since they cannot initiate such decisions.[27] According to section 242(b) of DGCL, for example, unless the board of directors first adopts a resolution setting forth the amendment, any charter amendment cannot be put up for consideration at the general meeting. Although shareholders have powers over by-law amendments, they must be consistent with law

---

as "communication and coordination among shareholders". Specifically, there were disclosure requirements for shareholders who held large blocks, there were rules on shareholder voting and communication as well as rules on insider trading and short swing profits, which largely restrained shareholders from acquiring a significant minority shareholding. Ibid. 204–205.

22 For instance, "[a] shareholder who contacts more than ten other shareholders on a voting proposal must have a 'proxy statement' precleared by the SEC's vigorous censors". Bernard Black, 'Agents Watching Agents: The Promise of Institutional Investor Voice' (1992) 39 *University of California Law Review* 811, 824.

23 *Quickturn Design System, Inc. v. Shapiro* (1998) 721 A 2d 1281, 1291 (Delaware, US). As will be discussed in the following paragraphs, even these limited voting rights are weaker than they appear. In the meanwhile, as Leo Strine, the Vice Chancellor of the Delaware Court of Chancery, has pointed out: "corporate law clearly vests the power to manage the corporation in its directors, and not in the stockholders". Leo Strine, 'One Fundamental Corporate Governance Question We Face: Can Corporations Be Managed for the Long Term Unless Their Powerful Electorates Also Act and Think Long Term?' (2010) 66 *Business Law* 1, 4 (footnote omitted).

24 Section 251(f) of DGCL.

25 Section 242(b)(1) of DGCL.

26 For example, sections 109 and 211 of DGCL.

27 Lucian Bebchuk, 'The Case for Increasing Shareholder Power' (2005) 118 *Harvard Law Review* 833, 846–847; Bainbridge, 'The Case for Limited Shareholder Voting Rights' (n 20) 603.

or with the certificate of incorporation according to section 109(b) of DGCL. Considering that the authority of management is normally vested in the hands of boards by law,[28] shareholders in practice cannot interfere with corporate decisions by amending by-laws.[29] Whilst in theory shareholders are able to alter the corporate constitution on power allocation, it is very rare to see such an amendment in practice.[30] Consequently, as summarised by Professors Cahn and Donald, even if shareholders have a right to vote on certain issues, as long as the board has the sole right to initiate a proposal, the voting right turns out to be useless as the board could refrain from initiating such a proposal.[31] That is to say, shareholders are precluded from initiating changes not only to the corporate charter but also to the by-law to the extent of altering managerial power.

Meanwhile, it is not impossible for directors to *evade* the requirement of shareholder approval. Take a merger for example: a director can restructure it as an asset purchase which could circumvent the very procedure.[32] Directors could even achieve the effect of charter amendment by including an amendment in the terms of the merger agreement; as Professor Velasco aptly observes, shareholders would usually accept the change to ensure the success of the merger in order to obtain the benefits.[33] Even when shareholders' approval is required, directors could easily bypass it and achieve an identical result. Put simply, the managerial powers of the company are assigned to the board of directors rather than to the shareholders. Shareholders accordingly have no right to instruct the board on what to do, or not do – even though directors of the board are in theory elected by them.[34] They only have limited veto powers on limited issues as explained earlier. The board of directors controls the issuance of shares[35] and can issue new classes of shares if authorised by the certificate of incorporation.[36] Even the right to make payment of dividends, which is generally thought of as justification for shareholders' residual claims, is controlled by the board.[37] It will be perfectly possible and legitimate for the board to decide not to make payment of dividends, and instead use the profits for other ends, such as improving employees' welfare or customer service, investing in R&D or otherwise.

---

28 For example see section 142(a) of DGCL.
29 Similar to the classic Catch-22 twist. Joseph Heller, *Catch-22* (Simon & Schuster, New York 1961).
30 David Kershaw, *Company Law in Context: Texts and Materials* (2nd edn OUP, Oxford 2012) 213.
31 Unless the incumbent directors can be replaced by new directors who wish to make such a proposal. Andreas Cahn and David Donald, *Comparative Company Law* (CUP, Cambridge 2010) 483. However, as discussed shortly below, shareholders' removal power is also limited.
32 Julian Velasco, 'The Fundamental Rights of the Shareholder' (2006) 40 *University of California Davis Law Review* 407, 419.
33 Ibid. 419.
34 The decision-making power in the US, unlike the situation in the UK which will be discussed below, is generally not through shareholders' delegation.
35 Section 152 of DGCL.
36 Section 161 of DGCL. And in practice the certificate of incorporation often does authorise the board to do so. Cahn and Donald (n 31) 482.
37 Section 170(a) of DGCL.

The business judgement rule gives directors an extra shield which makes their decisions almost unchallengeable. Excepting situations of self-serving and gross negligence, it will be in effect extremely difficult to hold directors liable no matter how suboptimal the decision-making is.[38] Just by making a reasonable effort to be informed, directors' actions will be presumed as proper, and courts will rarely second-guess their decision.[39] In other words, an honest mistake will be protected as long as directors of board honestly, though mistakenly, believed such decision-making was in the company's best interests.[40] Preserving directors' authority may be the most appropriate interpretation of the business judgement rule here.[41] All these reflect the basic stance of US corporate law: shareholders are essentially insulated from corporate decision-making, their power is very limited and it is also very difficult for them to interfere with the directors in a material way.[42]

3.2.2 Shareholder rights in UK law

Unlike US law, where the power of the board is regarded as *original and undelegated*,[43] in the UK the power of the board is largely delegated from the shareholders' meetings through their private ordering. A significant feature of UK company law is to leave internal governance issues to the company itself. UK company law does not stipulate the allocation of powers between shareholders and boards of directors; the division of powers is rather a matter for private ordering represented by the articles of association of each company.[44] Professor Paul Davies argues that this may reflect the partnership origins of UK company law. If directors' power was derived from shareholders "through a process of delegation via articles and not from a separate and free-standing grant of authority from the State", this would undoubtedly underline the shareholder-centred nature in Britain.[45]

---

38 Even conflicts of interest are usually dealt with by board approval rather than shareholder approval.
39 When reviewing business judgements, the Delaware courts create "a presumption that in making a business decision the directors of a corporation acted on an informed basis, in good faith and in the honest belief that the action taken was in the best interests of the company". *Aronson, et al. v. Lewis* (1984) 473 A 2d 805, 814 (US).
40 For example, see *Re the Walt Disney Company Derivative Litigation* (2005) 907 A 2d 693 (US).
41 It should be noted that there are many other interpretations of business judgement rules, such as those for protecting legitimate entrepreneurial risk-taking or due to judicial incompetence (namely, judges are not commercial experts, therefore they may not be competent to judge specific corporate decisions).
42 Just as Professor Bainbridge comments, "shareholder control rights in fact are so weak that they scarcely qualify as part of corporate governance" in the US. Bainbridge, 'The Case for Limited Shareholder Voting Rights' (n 20) 616.
43 In other words, such power is directly from the "organizational form provided by the law". Bratton and Wachter, 'The Case Against Shareholder Empowerment' (n 5) 662 (footnote omitted).
44 Richard Nolan, 'The Continuing Evolution of Shareholder Governance' (2006) 65 *Cambridge Law Journal* 92, 98–99, 105 and 109.
45 Paul Davies and Sarah Worthington, *Principles of Modern Company Law* (10th edn Sweet & Maxwell, London 2016) 356. That is also why shareholders are considered to retain a residual power and have more freedom to participate.

Nevertheless, as article 3 of Schedules 1–3 in *The Companies (Model Articles) Regulations 2008* specifies, "subject to the articles, the directors are responsible for the management of the company's business, for which purpose they may exercise all the powers of the company". In practice, the *Model Articles* are generally adopted with only slight amendments, and their almost universal adoption has meant that they form the core organisational structure of UK registered companies, which means the board of directors in a typical UK company has adequate managerial power.[46] Whilst it is not impossible to substantially modify *Model Articles*, because most shareholders buy into companies, especially large public companies which are already mature, it would be very hard for them to remove some or all of the board's managerial power from the articles of association.[47] That is to say the board is still responsible for management in the UK, though the statute does not directly specify that a company has to be managed "by or under" the board like in US law.

According to the first *Principle* of the latest *UK Corporate Governance Code* (2014), which remains largely unchanged from the previous combined codes, albeit with a newly added word *long-term*, "every company should be headed by an effective board for the long-term success of the company". The *Supporting Principles* to this *Main Principle* further explain:

> The board's role is to provide entrepreneurial leadership of the company within a framework of prudent and effective controls which enables risk to be assessed and managed. The board should set the company's strategic aims, ensure that the necessary financial and human resources are in place for the company to meet its objectives and review management performance. The board should set the company's values and standards and ensure that its obligations to its shareholders and others are understood and met.

The second question concerns the division of powers. Considering that the board obtains powers from shareholders' initial arrangement (e.g. articles of association), do shareholders still retain such power? In other words, after conferring authorities upon the board of directors, do shareholders still have a say in these delegated areas? If the answer is no, such power transference can be deemed irreversible and therefore the effect of such conferring is similar to that of obtaining authority from laws in the US, at least from the perspective of shareholders' ability to influence the board's decisions. For example, after transferring certain

---

46 Ibid. 59. And it is agreed that directors rather than shareholders manage the business in the UK. Sarah Worthington, *Sealy and Worthington's Text, Cases and Materials in Company Law* (11th edn OUP, Oxford 2016) 189–190.

47 Attenborough observed: "under the corporations legislation, and standard articles of association (as interpreted by the courts in the twentieth century), the board of directors is the most important day-to-day organ in the corporation. The board is given the power to manage the business of the corporation, and the general meeting is not permitted to interfere with exercise". Attenborough (n 3) 164.

rights to the board of directors, if such a right only belongs to the board, then shareholders will find it difficult to interfere with corporate decision-making in that particular area. Nevertheless, in contrast to the US approach, there is a possibility that shareholders could retain managerial powers as they are regarded as "the ultimate source of managerial authority within the company" and thereby "conferring authority on an agent does not normally restrict its own authority to act".[48] In fact, prior to the end of the nineteenth century, it was thought that shareholders could give the board binding instructions by ordinary resolution.[49]

But from the twentieth century, the courts had begun to recognise that directors should no longer be seen as mere agents. After a series of cases including *Automatic Self-Cleansing Filter Syndicate Co v. Cuninghame*,[50] *Quin & Axtens v. Salmon*[51] and *Shaw & Sons (Salford) Ltd v. Shaw*,[52] it generally became clear that directors were not bound to follow shareholders' direction, rather they had the authority to run the company. Just as Buckley LJ in *Gramophone and Typewriter Ltd* pointed out: "the directors are not servants to obey directions given by the shareholder as individuals; they are not agents appointed by and bound to serve the shareholders as their principals".[53] Moreover, as Greer LJ opined in *Shaw*:

> If powers of management are vested in the directors, they and they alone can exercise these powers … *[Shareholders] cannot themselves usurp the powers* which by the articles are vested in the directors any more than the directors can usurp the powers vested by the articles in the general body of shareholders.[54]

In other words, if managerial power is conferred on the board of directors, shareholders cannot usurp the power and have no power to dictate to directors what to do or not do. This is more clearly explained in *Ashburton Oil NL v. Alpha Minerals NL* as the court held that:

> Directors who are minded to do something which in their honest view is for the benefit of the company are not to be restrained because a majority shareholder or shareholders holding a majority of shares in the company do not want the directors so to act.[55]

---

48 Davies and Worthington, *Principles of Modern Company Law* (n 45) 59, 358–359.
49 This means the directors of the company had to act strictly in accordance with the general meeting's decisions. For example, per Cotton LJ in *Isle of Wight Railway Company v. Tahourdin* (1883) 25 Ch D 320, 331–332: "[the general meeting] having undoubtedly a power to direct and control the board in the management of the affairs of the company".
50 [1906] 2 Ch 34.
51 [1909] AC 442, HL.
52 [1935] 2 KB 113.
53 "Rather, [directors] are the persons who may by the regulations [articles of association] be entrusted with control of the business". *Gramophone and Typewriter Ltd v. Stanley* [1908] 2 KB 89, 105–106.
54 *Shaw & Sons (Salford) Ltd v. Shaw* [1935] 2 KB 113, 134 (emphasis added).
55 (1971) 123 CLR 614, 620 (Australia).

Now article 4 of *Model Articles*[56] specifies shareholders may direct the directors to take or not take any specified action only by special resolution, i.e. a 75 per cent majority is required. This is not inconsistent with Greer LJ's statement that altering the articles of association is a way for shareholders to "control the exercise of the power vested" and a special resolution is enough for the threshold of article amendment.[57] Although less evident than in the US, shareholders in the UK are also essentially isolated from control in terms of managerial powers due to such high thresholds, which are difficult to meet in practice, especially in large public companies with dispersed shareholdings.[58] More importantly, shareholders' instruction by such special resolution cannot invalidate anything directors have made before the passing of the resolution. This implies directors are able to make genuinely independent decision-making and its effects are irreversible.

Shareholders' approval rights may be regarded as another potentially effective device for restraining directors, since they are often required when the board decision would significantly impact shareholder interests, such as amendments to articles,[59] allotment of shares,[60] disapplication of pre-emption rights,[61] variation of class rights[62] and voluntary winding up.[63] Furthermore, transactions with directors including long-term service contracts,[64] substantial property transactions,[65] loans and quasi-loans to directors,[66] credit transactions[67] and related arrangements[68] also require shareholder approval.[69] These mandatory requirements for shareholder approval for certain corporate activities may potentially foster the shareholders' role in corporate decision-making. Though some of them are raised mainly to deal with conflicts of interests between directors and their company, the rest could be seen as checks against directors' managerial power. Take the amendment of the company's constitution for example: unlike US law, shareholders under UK law can initiate changes without the board's help.

---

56 The Companies (Model Articles) Regulations (SI 2008 No.3329).
57 "The only way in which the general body of the shareholders can control the exercise of the power vested by the articles in the directors" is, according to Greer LJ, through amending the articles of association or refusing to re-elect the directors when an opportunity arises. *Shaw & Sons (Salford) Ltd v. Shaw* [1935] 2 KB 113, 134. Of course, shareholders in the general meeting could also seek to remove the directors if they disapprove of their actions.
58 As discussed later in this chapter, most institutional shareholders would also prefer to be apathetic due to high costs, collective action problems and rival competition among others.
59 Section 21 of *CA 2006*.
60 Section 549 of *CA 2006*.
61 Section 569 of *CA 2006*.
62 Section 630 of *CA 2006*.
63 Section 84 of *Insolvency Act 1986*
64 Section 188 of *CA 2006*.
65 Section 190 of *CA 2006*.
66 Sections 190 and 198 of *CA 2006*.
67 Section 201 of *CA 2006*.
68 Section 203 of *CA 2006*.
69 In addition, the *Listing Rules* stipulate that transactions exceeding a quarter of a company's existing assets also require shareholder approval.

However, the same problems of collective action and expensive costs of action may effectively deter these attempts.[70] As Harry Hutchinson argues:

> The capacity of shareholders (as a disparate group) to manage relatively large corporations is hindered by collective action problems tied to disparate preferences, different persuasive abilities, different time horizons, as well as differing capabilities to digest in pertinent financial, microeconomic and macroeconomic information (even when widely available).[71]

In addition, as discussed in the last subsection, it is not impossible for directors to find ways around shareholder approval requirements.[72]

Although UK law does not specify the appointment of directors and they can be appointed by the board itself, according to section 168 shareholders have the right to remove them.[73] Proponents may then argue that even if shareholders in general meetings cannot interfere or override the board's decision-making, the removal power entitles shareholders to remove disobedient directors without reason by ordinary resolution at a meeting before the expiration of their period of office, which could possibly reveal shareholders' ultimate control. Although the right to remove a director without cause at any time is not identical to the right to give binding instructions, it is still a powerful weapon for shareholders to induce directors to follow their preferred action, as they can remove directors only by ordinary majority rather than supermajority. Therefore if a shareholder cannot get a 75 per cent vote to give directors instructions, they can choose to remove the disobedient director by ordinary majority, which might be a little easier to achieve.

Nevertheless, there are significant practical hurdles for exercising such a right.[74] Directors will be given special notice for extraordinary meetings for their

---

70 The shareholder has to invest in researching particular problems and communicating with others in order to take effective action, and the gain from a successful action will be shared by all shareholders regardless whether contribute or not. Therefore, shareholders would choose to be rationally apathetic and to free ride on others' efforts. For further discussion, see Lynn Stout, 'Investor's Choices – The Shareholder as Ulysses: Some Empirical Evidence on Why Investors in Public Corporations Tolerate Board Governance' (2003) 152 *University of Pennsylvania Law Review* 667, 673; Bainbridge, 'The Case for Limited Shareholder Voting Rights' (n 20) 606–607.

71 In contrast, "directors are generally seen to be less likely to be blinkered by such collective action problems". Harry Hutchinson, 'Director Primacy and Corporate Governance: Shareholder Voting Rights Captured by the Accountability/Authority Paradigm' (2005) 36 *Loyola University Chicago Law Journal* 1111, 1201.

72 Indeed, it is argued that there is a 'certain artificiality' of the shareholder power in modern large companies. For more discussion, see John Birds *et al.*, *Boyle and Birds' Company Law* (7th edn Jordan Publishing, Bristol 2009) 421.

73 What should be noticed is that the *Companies Act* does not say the directors must be appointed by the shareholders. According to the *Model Articles*, it can be by ordinary resolution or by the directors themselves.

74 For example, Professor Keay points out that the right of removal is "not viable, too costly or risky or all of these". Andrew Keay, 'Company Directors Behaving Poorly: Disciplinary Options for Shareholders' [2007] *Journal of Business Law* 656, 673–675.

removals and have the chance to make representations.[75] Apart from the costs of lobbying shareholders to support the removal, among other expenditures, a director can usually claim for compensation or damages regarding the removal which would not be insignificant. Consequently, the costs of exercising this right and the collective action problems determine such a right may not be a cost-effective approach. In practice, even in the case of clear wrongdoing, the wrong-doer is usually paid and leaves quietly instead of being removed without notice.[76] After all, the removal power is not intended to control or direct directors, rather it is more a remedy or deterrence.[77]

Judges in the UK, like their US counterparts, would not like to second-guess directors' decisions in order to prevent the danger of judging with hindsight. In *Regentcrest Plc v. Cohen*, the court opined:

> The question is not whether, viewed objectively by the court, the particular act or omission which is challenged was in fact in the interests of the company; still less is the question whether the court, had it been in the position of the director at the relevant time, might have acted differently. Rather, the question is whether the director honestly believed that his act or omission was in the interests of the company. The issue is as to the director's state of mind.[78]

As long as directors act in a bona fide manner, courts will not interfere with the business decision made by directors. Directors only owe fiduciary duties to the company, not to shareholders.[79] Meanwhile, general meetings as discussed earlier are in principle not permitted to interfere with the board of directors either. In fact, *independent* judgement and decision-making is not only permitted but is also required in both the US and the UK.

Despite the fact that shareholder power in the UK is less restrained than in the US for historical reasons concerning partnership, shareholders are also generally prohibited from being involved in directors' managerial decisions. Lord Wedderburn commented as early as the late 1980s that "any idea of *shareholder control as a counter to managerial power is baseless* (except, at any rate, in small companies)".[80] From this aspect, directors' managerial prerogative as a general rule does not need shareholders' assent, which is not substantially different from the US.

---

75 Section 169 of *CA 2006*.
76 The reluctance is partly due to the worry about the impairment of corporate reputation, i.e. highlighting its own problems.
77 The right to elect or re-elect directors is no different from the right to remove from this aspect.
78 [2001] 2 BCLC 80, 105. Similarly, as Lord Greene put it in *Re Smith and Fawcett Ltd* [1942] Ch 304, 306: "the principles to be applied in cases where the articles of a company confer a discretion on directors . . . are, for present purposes, free from doubt. They must exercise their discretion bona fide in *what they consider – not what a court may consider –* is in the interests of the company, and not for any collateral purpose". Courts admit that they are ill-equipped to take corporate or commercial decisions.
79 *Supra* Chapter 2, section 2.3.1.
80 Bill Wedderburn, 'Control of Corporate Actions' (1989) 52 *Modern Law Review* 401, 401–402.

3.2.3 Shareholder empowerment

As shown, shareholders are insulated from the decision-making process and directors are free to make their independent judgement in both jurisdictions. Unfortunately, this is thought by some to be the main culprit for governance failures during the financial crisis.[81] On the one hand, directors are criticised for not adopting all value-enhancing changes especially when some changes were disfavouring directors themselves. On the other, shareholders are not able to prevent corporate failure as their role is limited to voting on selected issues in the general meeting. It is argued that the insulation of shareholders from management is inadequate for ensuring an optimal corporate governance arrangement, because shareholders' limited veto power cannot help to effect changes. Shareholders' removal power is also criticised as insufficient since it can hardly take effect if the board is staggered, for example. This "bundling problem"[82] seems to further strengthen the case for increasing shareholder power. Not surprisingly, therefore, increasing shareholder power and/or reducing limitations on shareholder power is believed to be a good way to improve corporate governance, overcome many current problems and at the same time reduce external regulatory intervention.[83] The recent global financial crisis intensifies such demand for greater shareholder empowerment, which is expected to ensure better monitoring in both the US

81 It is worth noting that there are different views regarding the cause of this financial crisis. One view is that the financial crisis is largely attributed to the "failures and weaknesses in corporate governance arraignments". For example, see Grant Kirkpatrick, 'The Corporate Governance Lessons from the Financial Crisis' [2009] 1 *Financial Market Trends* 61, 62. The other view is that corporate governance did not fail in the financial crisis. For example, Professor Coffee argues "the 2008 financial crisis stands above all as testimony to the error of excessive reliance on broad principles and self-regulation". John Coffee, 'What Went Wrong? An Initial Inquiry into the Causes of the 2008 Financial Crisis' (2009) 9 *Journal of Corporate Law Studies* 1, 22. Similarly, Professor Cheffins also agrees that the financial crisis is irrelevant to corporate governance failure. Brian Cheffins, 'Did Corporate Governance "Fail" During the 2008 Stock Market Meltdown? The Case of the S&P 500' (2009) 65 *Business Lawyer* 1, 61.

 As noted in the introduction to this chapter (n 3), there is another viewpoint that shareholders themselves might be part of the problem even if there is also something wrong with the corporate governance. For example, as Professor Robert Clark addressed in the opening comments of the *Sixth Annual Law and Business Conference* in Vanderbilt University, corporate law shifts the focus from protection of shareholders to protection of the company from shareholders.

82 Put simply, when shareholders are forced to replace the incumbents with a rival team that follows shareholders' willingness to initiate a change, it bundles together the change and the replacement of the board. For more discussion and examples, see Bebchuk, 'The Case for Increasing Shareholder Power' (n 27) 857–861.

83 For instance, Professor Bebchuk argued that shareholder empowerment is a benefit to increasing shareholder value by overcoming agency problems between shareholders and directors. Ibid. 836; Lucian Bebchuk, 'Letting Shareholders Set the Rules' (2006) 119 *Harvard Law Review* 1784, 1784. For a more recent review of support, see Maria Goranova and Lori Ryan, 'Shareholder Activism: A Multidisciplinary Review' (2014) 40 *Journal of Management* 1230, 1246. In short, it is generally agreed by proponents that managerial deficiencies could be addressed by shareholder empowerment and activism.

and the UK.[84] US Senator Chuck Schumer commented in a news conference introducing the *Shareholder Bill of Rights Act of 2009*:

> During this recession, the leadership at some of the nation's most renowned companies took too many risks and too much in salary, while their shareholders had too little say. This legislation will give stockholders the ability to apply the emergency brakes the next time the company management appears to be heading off a cliff.[85]

Changes happened as a result. The SEC adopted new measures to facilitate director nominations by shareholders under which companies are required to "include in their proxy materials, under certain circumstances, shareholder proposals that seek to establish a procedure in the company's governing documents for the inclusion of one or more shareholder director nominees in the company's proxy materials".[86] In other words, the new rules, contrary to the restraints on shareholder proposal and proxy rules, require companies to include the nominees of shareholders in their proxy materials alongside the nominees of the existing board. This "proxy access" helps to facilitate the ability of shareholders to nominate and elect their nominees, as traditionally the director election is usually dominated by the incumbent board without a proxy contest.[87]

---

84 For example, see John Coffee, 'Financial Crisis 101: What Can We Learn from Scandals and Meltdowns – from Enron to Subprime' in Robert Austin (ed), *The Credit Crunch and the Law* (Ross Parsons Centre of Commercial, Corporate and Taxation Law, Sydney 2008) 37 referred to by Jennifer Hill, 'The Rising Tension between Shareholder and Director Power in the Common Law World' (2010) 18 *Corporate Governance: An International Review* 344, 344. It follows that "any response to the financial crisis by an incoming president will be incomplete if it fails to address this basic issue of shareholder rights". See John Plender, 'Shout Out' *Financial Times* (London, 18 October 2008) at www.ft.com/cms/s/0/b63025ca-9cad-11dd-a42e-000077b07658. html#axzz3eRwkb5h3 [accessed 1 March 2017].

85 Karey Wutkowski, 'U.S. Sen. Schumer Unveils Shareholder Bill of Rights' *Reuters* (Washington, 19 May 2009) at www.reuters.com/article/2009/05/19/us-financial-shareholders-schumer-idUS TRE54I4PF20090519 [accessed 1 March 2017].

86 The US Securities and Exchange Commission, 'Facilitating Shareholder Director Nominations' at www.sec.gov/info/smallbus/secg/14a-8-secg.htm [accessed 1 March 2017].

87 Moreover, in June 2010, the SEC voted in favour of adopting Rule 14a-11 which disallows restrictions on shareholder nominating power. It was seen as a victory for shareholder empowerment as shareholders who had owned 3 per cent or more of the voting power of the company's securities for at least three years could nominate directors by using the companies' proxy material directly. Although this rule was finally stuck down by the US Circuit Court of Appeals in July 2011 after being challenged by the Business Roundtable and US Chamber of Commerce, the trend itself could be seen as another powerful case of the shareholder empowerment movement. For example, the former SEC Chairman commented after the Rule 14a-11 was struck down that "I firmly believe that providing a meaningful opportunity for shareholders to exercise their right to nominate directors at their companies is in the best interest of investors and our markets. It is a process that helps make boards more accountable for the risks undertaken by the companies they manage". For more discussion, see George Drymiotes and Haijin Lin, 'Shareholder Empowerment and Board of Directors Effectiveness' (AAA 2015 Management Accounting Section (MAS) Meeting, California, November 2014) at http://papers. ssrn.com/sol3/papers.cfm?abstract_id=2462984 [accessed 1 March 2017] 2–3.

Campaigns are also launched for adopting the majority vote for electing directors. Until recently, merely a plurality shareholder vote sufficed for the election of directors,[88] which means the candidate who receives more votes than any other but does not exceed an absolute majority could still be elected. This is the image described by Professor Grundfest:

> Plurality means that if a million shares count as a quorum, and if 999,999 ballots strike your name out and say no, you, as the director, owning only one share, and you vote for yourself, congratulations, you win. You have the plurality.[89]

Under such a context, the power to nominate director candidates amounts to the right of appointment. Recent trends towards majority voting would undoubtedly enhance shareholders' voice regarding the election. As Professor Bainbridge observes: "many states have amended their corporation laws to allow firms to use a majority vote . . . to elect directors".[90] This is mainly to prevent situations similar to the *Walt Disney* case,[91] where even though a majority of shareholders declined to vote for certain candidates they were still able to be elected or re-elected.

It is similar in the UK. According to provision B.7.1 of the *UK Corporate Governance Code*,[92] all directors of FTSE 350 companies should be submitted for annual re-election by shareholders. The frequency of director re-election increased from at least every three years to every year. As discussed above, although shareholders have the right to remove directors, in practice such a right is costly. More frequent re-election makes it less costly to remove directors, since the potential compensation or damage would be much lower if the service contract were shorter. Indeed, the Financial Reporting Council points out such change "would provide greater accountability and give shareholders a further opportunity to send a signal to the board if they have concerns".[93]

Apart from facilitating the replacement of incumbent directors, shareholders' say on directors' remuneration also increases shareholders' impact. Both the US Department of the Treasury's *Troubled Assets Relief Program*[94] and

---

88 For example, section 216(3) of *Delaware General Corporate Law* formally specifies: "[d]irectors shall be elected by a plurality of the votes of the shares present in person or represented by proxy at the meeting and entitled to vote on the election of directors".

89 Lucian Bebchuk (ed), 'Symposium on Corporate Election' (2003) *Harvard John M. Olin Discussion Paper Series No. 448*, 99–100.

90 Bainbridge, *Corporate Governance* (n 3) 203.

91 In this case shareholder activists opposed the election of CEO Michael Eisner among others. Although 43 per cent of Disney shares had withheld authority to vote for Eisner, he was still re-elected as the CEO. For more details, see Bainbridge, *Corporate Governance* (n 3) 217.

92 From this time on, the re-election at regular intervals becomes a main principal.

93 Financial Reporting Council, '2009 Review of the Combined Code: Final Report' (December 2009) para 3.24.

94 For more details, see the website of the US department of the Treasury, available at www.treasury.gov/initiatives/financial-stability/TARP-Programs/Pages/default.aspx [accessed 1 March 2017].

the UK Department for Business Innovation & Skills' *Shareholder Voting Rights Consultation*[95] show a trend towards increasing shareholders' influence on deciding directors' compensation. Binding say-on-pay is proposed not only by shareholder activists but also by policy-makers.[96] A greater say-on-pay would undoubtedly increase shareholders' influence on directors both directly and indirectly.

What is more, the *Walker Review* recommends an engagement model which requires (institutional) shareholders to engage more effectively.[97] Similarly, the *UK Stewardship Code 2010* also aims to enhance shareholder involvement by requiring (institutional) shareholders to: 1) publicly disclose their policy on how they will discharge their stewardship responsibilities; 2) have a robust and publicly disclosed policy on managing conflicts of interest in relation to stewardship; 3) monitor their investee companies; 4) establish clear guidelines on when and how they will escalate their activities as a method of protecting and enhancing shareholder value; 5) be willing to act collectively with other investors where appropriate; 6) have a clear policy on voting and disclosure of voting activity; and 7) report periodically on their stewardship and voting activities.

In addition, *The Companies (Shareholders' Rights) Regulations 2009* lowers the minimum threshold for shareholder votes to require directors to call a meeting. The original 10 per cent contained in section 303 is now lowered to 5 per cent. The change to the minimum percentage shareholding qualification makes it easier for insurgent shareholders to act. Besides, it is also argued that it adds more shareholder approval requirements and facilitates their rejection power.[98]

Not surprisingly, all these recent reforms aim to empower shareholders (by removing previous limitations and giving them a greater say) and encourage shareholders to be more active.[99] In consequence, directors become comparatively more dependent and more vulnerable to shareholders under the enhanced shareholder pressure. Although most shareholders remain rationally apathetic – meaning

95 UK Department for Business Innovation & Skills, 'Executive Pay: Shareholder Voting Rights Consultation (March 2012) at www.gov.uk/government/uploads/system/uploads/attachment data/file/31372/12–639-executive-pay-shareholder-voting-rights-consultation.pdf [accessed 1 March 2017].

96 UK Department for Business Innovation & Skills, 'Directors' Pay: Consultation on Revised Remuneration Reporting Regulations' (June 2012) at www.gov.uk/government/uploads/system/uploads/attachment_data/file/31358/12–888-directors-pay-consultation-remuneration-reporting.pdf [accessed 1 March 2017].

97 David Walker, 'A Review of Corporate Governance in UK Banks and Other Financial Industry Entities: Final Recommendations' (26 November 2009) para 5.1.

98 For example, Professor Bebchuk goes further and argues that shareholders should be able to make the rules-of-the-game changes, namely constitution amendments and other very important corporate decisions. Bebchuk, 'Letting Shareholders Set the Rules' (n 83) 1784.

99 Such empowerment and activism are described as 'shareholder spring'. And it starts to exert a material influence upon management. For example, see Erika Morphy, 'Yahoo CEO Succumbs to Shareholders' Spring' Forbes (Jersey City, 3 May 2012) at www.forbes.com/sites/erikamorphy/2012/05/13/yahoo-ceo-succumbs-to-shareholders-spring/ [accessed 1 March 2017].

shareholder empowerment or the proposed empowerment may not cause a major difference in practice – it is not infrequent for those few activist shareholder groups with a special political or social agenda to blackmail the board to promote their own interests at the expense of the company, and become the real beneficiaries of such enhanced power.[100] It might be argued that if the interests of activist shareholders are not aligned with those of others, gaining access to a company's proxy material, for instance, may not have a real effect since enough support from other shareholders is still needed for a resolution. But it is exactly such generally rational apathy which makes it possible for special interest groups who are usually minority shareholders to exert a significant effect. Activists do not suffer from rational apathy, which makes them able to exert disproportionate power to influence the board.[101] In a nutshell, the groups that would take advantage of shareholder empowerment are usually those special interest groups which are most likely to abuse the increased power.[102]

3.3 Reassessing shareholder empowerment

Shareholder empowerment is indeed shifting decision-making power from the board of directors to shareholders. That is to say, it places constraints on directors' authority over corporate management and decision-making. In order to fully discuss both the positive and negative aspects of shareholder empowerment, this section starts by exploring the benefits of authority which could be seen as the conventional rationale for limiting shareholders' power.

3.3.1 Value of authority

In 1974, the Nobel Laureate Professor Kenneth Arrow aptly pointed out the value of authority in the context of organisations by developing Hobbes's classic statement in the case of government.[103] Arrow argues that "authority is needed to

---

100 Bainbridge, *Corporate Governance* (n 3) 247. At least, the possibility for shareholders to successfully engage in opportunism or self-interest behaviour is significantly increased. Due to the fact that most shareholders are rationally apathetic, an activist shareholder with only fractional shares may utilise the increased power to exert a material influence on directors to pursue their sectional interests.

101 Apart from proxy battles, activist shareholders could make various non-legal methods to exert pressure on the directors of the board, for example a publicity campaign by creating embarrassing news stories.

102 For example, employee welfare, corporate social performance or environmental goals could be emphasised by particular special interest groups or activist shareholder groups, and it will be easier for them to pursue their own interests as a result of the increased power. Goranova and Ryan (n 83) 1249; Joseph Grundfest, 'The SEC's Proposed Proxy Access Rules: Politics, Economics, and the Law' (2010) 65 *Business Lawyer* 361, 378–383. Hedge funds are also activists in particular during a bull market. But again, they may not care about the interests of the company as it is possible for them to profit from the decline in the share price as discussed in the last chapter. *Supra* Chapter 2, section 2.4.2.

103 Thomas Hobbes, *Leviathan* (1651) at www.gutenberg.org/files/3207/3207-h/3207-h.htm#link2H_4_0001 [accessed 1 March 2017].

achieve a coordination of the activities of the member of the organization".[104] In Arrow's view, the centralised decision-making in organisations "serves to economize on the transmission and handling of information":

1   Since the activities of individuals interact with each other, being sometimes substitutes, sometimes complements, and frequently compete for limited resources, joint decision on the choice of individuals' activities will be superior to separate decisions.
2   The optimum joint decision depends on information which is dispersed among the individuals in the society.
3   Since transmission of information is costly, in the sense of using resources, especially the time of the individuals, it is cheaper and more efficient to transmit all the pieces of information once to a central place than to disseminate each of them to everyone.
4   For the same reasons of efficiency, it may be cheaper for a central individual or office to make the collective decision and transmit it rather than retransmit all the information on which the decision is based.[105]

It is not difficult to see that allocating the decision-making to the hands of a *central place* is the only optimal choice when information is widely dispersed and speed is needed. Consequently, a typical large public company with scattered information must also require a centralised authority to deal with the information in order to make informed decisions for the sake of organisational efficiency.[106]

Even leaving efficiency or productivity aside (i.e. assuming all members of an organisation have at least substantially identical information as the foundation for decision-making or information could be virtually exchanged without cost and in a timely manner), without an authority-based decision-making structure, dilemmas will frequently arise. As long as the interests of members of a given organisation differ, it would obviously become impracticable to expect all members to achieve a consensus. Due to the disparities of interests and self-utility maximisation, involving all participants in the decision-making process will not result in the best decisions.

In the context of public corporations,[107] different shareholders may possibly have different investment time horizons from short-term buy-and-sell speculation to long-term buy-and-hold strategies. Similarly, some may prefer risky investment

---

104 Kenneth Arrow, *The Limits of Organization* (Norton, New York 1974) 68.
105 Ibid. 68–69.
106 Lynn Stout, 'The Mythical Benefits of Shareholder Control' (2007) 93 *Virginia Law Review* 789, 792–793.
107 In contrast, in closed companies where the number of shareholders is usually limited and the relationship between shareholders is closer, a consensus is easier to achieve, thereby the role played by the board as a centralised decision-making organ may be less remarkable. This is why shareholders in such companies could have a larger role to play.

schemes whilst others may prefer less risky programmes according to their respective risk preferences.[108] Or as the heterogeneous expectations model goes, investors tend to overweigh their own estimate of corporate value whilst under-valuing other inventors' estimates, giving rise to the situation that pessimists sell shares to optimists and then to even more optimistic investors.[109] Besides, in view of the fact that the information can never be exchanged for free in the real world, the information inevitably differs among individual participants. A consensus is then extremely difficult, if not impossible, to achieve even if all shareholders have an identical interest. Tax consideration should be taken into account as well. For instance, shareholders in different tax brackets may have different views on divi-dends, reinvestment and the like.[110]

Dispersed information, costly transmission of information as well as col-lective action problems are almost insurmountable especially in large public companies where the shares are usually dispersed. Shareholders lack both infor-mation and incentive to actively participate in corporate decision-making. Even institutional investors are likely to be rationally apathetic.[111] As Professors Cahn and Donald argue:

> Power is delegated (to a central authority) both because effective decision-making requires concentration of authority in a relatively agile group of persons and because shareholders either do not want to manage the com-pany or do not have the necessary skill to do so.[112]

Centralised management can effectively eliminate "redundancy and waste in decision-making and facilitate the coordination of the multitude of activities that are carried out by a large, complex business".[113] Along with Professor Arrow's efficiency argument, it is not difficult to identify the necessity and benefits of authority.[114]

3.3.2 Assessment in context

Generally speaking, increasing shareholder power or reducing restraints on shareholder power are aimed at limiting directors' authority and ensuring the

---

108 For instance, a fully diversified shareholder is more likely to ignore the firm-specific risk and prefer a high-risk strategy.
109 Bratton and Wachter, 'The Case Against Shareholder Empowerment' (n 5) 706–707. Also see *supra* Chapter 2, section 2.5.2.
110 Stephen Bainbridge, 'Director Primacy and Shareholder Disempowerment' (2006) 119 *Harvard Law Review* 1735, 1745.
111 Bainbridge, *Corporate Governance* (n 3) 243–244. More discussion will be provided in the next sub-section.
112 Cahn and Donald (n 31) 299.
113 Robert Clark, *Corporate Law* (Little, Brown 1986) 781.
114 By the word of Professor Arrow, "authority is undoubtedly a necessity for successful achievement of an organization's goal". Arrow (n 104) 79.

accountability of directors.[115] Such accountability is essential on the grounds that if individual participants in organisations with centralised authority are not required to be accountable, other participants would never agree to form such a team or coalition in the first place. In other words, all the benefits brought by the centralised authority will be offset by the fear of potential abuse of such power if no constraints are put on those decision-makers. More importantly, a central-ised authority cannot avoid making errors from time to time. The limitation of dealing with information and decision-making among others as summarised by Professor Arrow suggests that it is of significance and value to hold a centralised authority responsible to an organisation.[116]

In the corporate context, various corporate stakeholders would be afraid to make firm-specific contributions if they feared the resources they contribute may be misused or that they might be unfairly treated ex post. There is obviously no reason to preserve directors' authority when self-interest is involved. It is argued that directors may "divert resources through excessive pay, self-dealing, or other means; reject beneficial acquisition offers to maintain its independence and private benefits of control . . . engage in empire-building and so forth".[117] Thus, author-ity cannot exist without any constraint. Indeed, in the words of Michael Dooley, "it should be readily apparent that neither Model [authority model or account-ability model] exists in pristine form in the real world . . . any feasible governance system must and does contain elements of both Models".[118] He continues:

> Standing alone, neither Model could provide a sensible guide to the govern-ance of firm-organized economic activity because each seeks to achieve a distinct and separate value that is essential to the survival of any firm.[119]

Consequently, both authority and accountability should be valued for the sake of good corporate governance. By virtue of their antithetical relationship, however, it is impossible to increase director accountability whilst maintaining their author-ity at the same time. This begs the question: which of them should predominate for a more efficient and effective governance system? If authority accounts for a more important role in corporate governance, i.e. the costs of decreasing author-ity outweigh the expected benefits of increasing accountability, then shareholder empowerment may not be the helpful solution originally supposed.[120]

---

115 The shareholder approval requirement and the rights to remove directors, for example, do not belong to the "corporate decision-making process". Rather, they are designed to promote director accountability. For more discussion, see Michael Dooley, 'Two Models of Corporate Governance' (1992) 47 *Business Lawyer* 461, 468.
116 Arrow (n 104) 74–75.
117 Bebchuk, 'The Case for Increasing Shareholder Power' (n 27) 850.
118 Dooley (n 115) 463.
119 Ibid.
120 This is because the efficiency would dictate that equilibrium is achieved where the marginal costs of decreasing authority equal the marginal expected benefits of increased accountability.

To begin with, directors, along with their appointed managers, are better informed and positioned. Because of the inadequate information and incentive for most shareholders to make an optimal corporate decision, ceding authority to the board of directors and its delegations is generally the rule for modern public companies. Informed decision-making requires full disclosure in addition to specific skills. But completely full disclosure is, if not impossible, very costly. Costs including increased regulation and sharing information with competing companies will effectively deter the enforcement of full disclosure, no matter what the benefits. Therefore, even if directors make all the required disclosures, they are still undoubtedly better informed.[121] Furthermore, the cost of surmounting the problem is more expensive than identifying it. On the other hand, rational shareholders in effect have no incentive to be fully informed regarding corporate affairs. Obviously, the cost for shareholders to make informed decisions is not insignificant considering the complexity of disclosure among other corporate documents, whilst the benefits for doing this may be limited due to diversification of shareholdings.

Nevertheless, supporters of shareholder empowerment argue that "effective centralized management does not require boards to retain absolute power".[122] This may be generally true; however, the crux is that the majority of shareholders, if any, are not only passive but also solely focus on short-term profits.[123]

First of all, shareholders are normally not active participants in the corporate governance system;[124] they may either lack the resources, skills or willingness to be involved. Institutional shareholders, who manage a large pool of assets and become the major part of shareholder classes nowadays, may still prefer to be apathetic except for a few activist shareholder groups. Even assuming the proportionate share of expected benefits would increase after institutional shareholders' active participation in corporate decision-making and exceed all costs, institutional shareholders may still prefer to remain passive. It should not be ignored that any gains generated after active institutional shareholders' efforts would be shared by all shareholders, including other passive institutional investors, but only the activist bears the costs. In other words, rival institutional investors may free

---

121 Just as Professor Bratton and Wachter have pointed out: "[a]s between directors and shareholders, it is the directors who have the best access to information and are best able to serve as the monitors of the managers, increasing the likelihood of compliance with continuing and emerging regulations. As between managers and shareholders, the managers are the ones who have the day-to-day knowledge of the company, its history, policies, opportunities, vulnerabilities, and challenges. The managers are likely to have the information and institutional perspective suited to anticipate points of conflict with the outside political economy and to formulate a responsive strategy". Bratton and Wachter, 'The Case Against Shareholder Empowerment' (n 5) 659–660.

122 For example, see Bebchuk, 'Letting Shareholders Set the Rules' (n 83) 1792.

123 European Commission (n 8) 3. It will be discussed in some detail shortly below.

124 *Supra* Chapter 3, sections 3.2.1 and 3.2.2.

ride and benefit from the activist's successful intervention.[125] When institutional investors are evaluated on their relative performance (namely better than their competitors), it is no surprise that they remain passive even if the expected gain is larger than the expected cost of engagement.

On the other hand, choosing alternative courses of action, for example exiting by selling shares rather than active engagement, may avoid the collective action problem and have a larger gain which cannot be shared by competitors.[126] In addition to the collective action problem, the demand for liquidity may further impede (institutional) shareholders from being active, as they prefer not to be "locked in". To become an active actor requires (institutional) shareholders to put in sufficient time and effort into investigating the investee companies, which means they would be locked in since the "voice" takes a significantly longer period than simply "exit".[127] They have to obtain and analyse all the necessary information first and then, even more difficult and costly, challenge the incumbent board to effect a change. This is longer and more complicated than the exit strategy, which may deter investors who value liquidity highly. Indeed, the average holding period of shares has considerably reduced.[128] In particular, high trading frequency implies that institutional investors may hold shares for only seconds before selling them. In such cases, it is not optimistic to expect shareholders to effectively engage in corporate governance.

We can also see that insurance companies and investment banks, including bank trust departments in commercial banks, as important institutional investors provide or are willing to provide other financial services to investee companies,[129] which suggests they cannot be a serious monitor.[130] As previously discussed, the

---

125 Take fund managers, for example, passive fund managers can share the benefits from an active fund manager's successful intervention but not share any costs, so the activist's relative performance will not overcome his "free riding" rivals, indeed his position may be worse under the competitive environment due to the cost of activism. For more discussion, see Bernard Black and John Coffee, 'Hail Britannia?: Institutional Investor Behavior under Limited Regulation' (1994) 92 *Michigan Law Review* 1997, 2058–2059.

126 As a result, institutional shareholders prefer to address the problem by seeking private benefits not those shared with others. For example, see Bainbridge, 'Director Primacy and Shareholder Disempowerment' (n 110) 1754–1756.

127 Therefore, they may not freely liquidate their shares at least immediately due to being "locked in". And this is opposite to the current high frequency trading practice in the real business world.

128 European Commission (n 8) 12.

129 For example, it is not uncommon for a bank to invest in a company and provide credit at the same time, though there is increasingly more restriction to separate the different or even potentially competing activities. See Margaret Blair, *Ownership and Control: Rethinking Corporate Governance for the Twenty-First Century* (The Brookings Institution, Washington 1995) 149–152. In other words, the incentives to please investee companies and provide other services to them may dominate the incentive to actively monitor.

130 Namely, it is not optimistic to say empowering shareholders will induce the institutional investors to be more active.

result will be a few activist shareholders exploiting the increased power to pursue their own interests more easily. Directors may be pressured to accommodate these activist shareholders by taking value-decreasing actions. Second, shareholder empowerment intensifies the pressure from shareholders' short-termism.[131] In fact, short-termism or excessive risk-taking may be beneficial to shareholders, or at least shareholders may think them worthwhile, since they "would fully benefit from the upside of such a strategy, whilst they participate in losses only until the value of shareholder equity reaches zero, after which further losses would be borne by the creditors".[132]

Prior to the financial crisis in 2008, "investor culture had shifted from long-term to short-term orientation", which can contribute to creating much-needed liquidity in order to remain solvent.[133] Professor Blanaid Clarke observes:

> The behaviour of shareholders in financial institutions in the run-up to the Global Financial Crisis demonstrated not only "a lack of appropriate share-holder interest" in management accountability but also a short-termism approach to the company's operation.[134]

The financial crisis did little to change this short-term culture.[135] Increased pressure on directors to meet short-term targets can only make the situation worse.

Shareholder empowerment, according to Professors Bratton and Wachter, will then cause directors to "manage to the market"[136] and pursue a short-term strategy under shareholder pressure. Directors who have informational superiority and expertise are thereby less able to make optimal decisions independently, since shareholder empowerment itself means disempowering directors' authority. In other words, making directors more vulnerable and dependent delivers to directors and their delegated managers a signal to increase observable earnings. Such pressure forces directors to continuously show good corporate performance. The asset management world exemplifies this vivid image: they gain new clients if investment results are good and lose clients if the investment results are disap-

---

131 Chapter 2 discussed the issue of shareholder short-termism and its negative consequences in detail, in order to avoid reiteration, this part just re-emphasises the main effects of the increased pressure from shareholders' short-termism. *Supra* Chapter 2, section 2.4.2.

132 European Commission (n 8) 11.

133 Jonathan Mukwiri and Mathias Siems, 'The Financial Crisis: A Reason to Improve Shareholder Protection in the EU' (2014) 41 *Journal of Law and Society* 51, 60 (footnote omitted).

134 Blanaid Clarke, 'The EU's Shareholder Empowerment Model in the Context of the Sustainable Companies Agenda' (2014) 11 *European Company Law* 103, 104.

135 Mukwiri and Siems (n 133) 60; Andrea Ginevri, 'The Rise of Long-term Minority Shareholders' Rights in Publicly Held Corporations and Its Effect on Corporate Governance' (2011) 12 *European Business Organization Law Review* 587, 602.

136 Bratton and Wachter, 'The Case Against Shareholder Empowerment' (n 5) 690. Managing to the stock market would possibly lead to a decrease in expenditure on R&D, employee welfare or improving customer service in order to increase the near-term earnings – namely, the stock price.

pointing. Instead of focusing on an actual understanding of individual companies, these investors more or less follow the market, which has become standard practice in the investment industry.[137] As Professor Coffee notes, "short-term results are therefore essential".[138]

Not surprisingly, the *Kay Review* reveals that much of the bad corporate decisions, especially for failed companies, "were supported or even encouraged by a majority of the company's shareholders".[139] Shareholders did not stop or even encourage excessive managerial risk-taking. As a result, insufficient directors' accountability or insufficient shareholder engagement may not be the culprits at all.

Another direct consequence of shareholder empowerment is "intershareholder opportunism".[140] Due to the heterogeneous expectation of different shareholder groups, it is "rational for them to engage in rent-seeking activities" which are socially costly and adverse to the interests of shareholders as whole.[141] Increasing shareholder power will only make such rent-seeking activity worse, since it becomes easier and less costly for shareholders with private interests to engage in rent-seeking activities. A typical example is shareholders holding corporate voting rights whilst having no corresponding economic interests in them. This is not uncommon through modern derivative and hedge techniques. The well-known case of hedge fund Perry Capital shows the private interests of such institutional investors may be opposed to the interests of shareholders collectively as well as the company.[142]

More importantly, unlike directors, shareholders do not owe mandatory fiduciary duties to companies. Neither the law nor the market will condemn the self-interested behaviour of shareholders unless they are controlling shareholders. Investors' *profit-centric ideology* is not regarded as abnormal and is usually accepted by most people in the context of private property.

---

137 Jaap Winter, 'Shareholder Engagement and Stewardship: The Realities and Illusions of Institutional Share Ownership' 6, Working Paper (2011) at http://papers.ssrn.com/sol3/papers.cfm?abstract_id=1867564 [accessed 1 March 2017].

138 Ibid. Some more general discussion on short-termism can be found in Chapter 2, section 2.4.2.

139 'The Kay Review of UK Equity Markets and Long-Term Decision Making, Final Report' (July 2012) Para 1.28.

140 Stout, 'The Mythical Benefits of Shareholder Control' (n 106) 794. *Supra* Chapter 2, section 2.5.2.

141 Iman Anabtawi, 'Some Skepticism About Increasing Shareholder Power' (2006) 53 *University of California Los Angeles Law Review* 561, 575.

142 In this case, Perry Corp owned 7 million shares of King Pharmaceuticals which Mylan Laboratories agreed to purchase at a premium. In order to ensure the success of the merger, Perry purchased a block of Mylan's shares but fully hedged them through a derivative contract with a brokerage firm. Then Perry used its voting power in Mylan to influence and push the merger through at a premium over market price. Stout, 'The Mythical Benefits of Shareholder Control' (n 106) 794; Theodore Mirvis, Paul Rowe and William Savitt, 'Bebchus's "Case for Increasing Shareholder Power": An Opposition' (2007) *Harvard Law School John M Olin Center for Law, Economics and Business Discussion Paper Series Paper No. 586* at www.law.harvard.edu/programs/olin_center/papers/pdf/586.pdf [accessed 1 March 2017].

Thus, Professor Talbot writes: "shareholders have no inherent commitment to one particular company".[143] Accordingly, it is not difficult to imagine that shareholders speculate on the rise and fall of stock prices at the expense of long-term benefits; or worse, pursue private benefits as they are not constrained by fiduciary duties. This is consistent with the argument that "a weak and uniformed decision-maker may be better than a conflicted one".[144]

There is then little sense in empowering shareholders as a class as they may be either inactive or irresponsible. Most shareholders will remain rationally apathetic, and those who can ultimately benefit from the empowerment initiatives are shareholder activists who frequently have a "private purpose". The interests of activists and other shareholders can be misaligned. It is not impossible for certain shareholder activists such as union pension funds to use proxy access, for example, as leverage to extract private gains at the expense of others by abusing such empowerment. Unfortunately, the evidence confirms this.[145]

Findings by Professor Ferreira and others once again prove that the banks in which directors enjoy a higher degree of insulation from shareholder pressure are more likely to weather the recent financial crisis without government support.[146] In other words, shareholder empowerment negatively affects corporate decision-making and ultimately makes banks weaker and less able to survive. Though the situations of banks or other financial institutions are different from non-financial companies due to implicit and explicit state guarantees for avoiding consequent realisation of systemic harms,[147] shareholders in general are well-known for reducing risks by holding diversified portfolios and even shifting risk, owing to the characteristic of the limited liability rule as discussed in the last chapter. By the same token, diversified shareholders in non-financial companies can also be insulated from firm-specific risks and prefer excessive risk-taking beyond a socially optimal level.[148] Along with the fact that the increase in shareholder power makes directors of those companies less independent and less able to resist pressure from

143 Lorraine Talbot, 'Why Shareholders Shouldn't Vote: A Marxist-progressive Critique of Shareholder Empowerment' (2013) 76 *Modern Law Review* 791, 813. Professor Talbot continues to argue: "if they do stay with a company for a period it is because they have organised their investment around a diverse portfolio so as to spread the risk of lower performing shares. In serving their self-interest, few focused on monitoring a particular company but on information provided by the market, such as indexing and share prices". Ibid.

144 Attenborough (n 3) 154.

145 For example, the activism by CalPERS for political reasons. For more details, see Bainbridge, 'Director Primacy and Shareholder Disempowerment' (n 110) 1754–1756.

146 Daniel Ferreira *et al.*, 'Shareholder Empowerment and Bank Bailouts' (2013) *European Corporate Governance Institute – Financial Research Paper No. 345/2013* at http://ssrn.com/abstract=2170392 [accessed 30 October 2015] 28.

147 For examples, see Bryan Kelly, Hanno Lustig and Stijn Van Nieuwerburgh, 'Too-Systemic-To-Fail: What Option Markets Imply About Sector-Wide Government Guarantees' (2012) *Chicago Booth Research Paper No. 11–12.*

148 At least, shareholders who can diversify idiosyncratic risk can force directors to ignore such risk during decision-making.

shareholders,[149] there are strong reasons to believe that this finding could extend to non-financial companies.

Directors' accountability is of course important – without it all the value of centralised authority would vanish. Although much still needs to be done in order to effectively balance the authority and accountability/responsibility aspects, as Professor Arrow correctly explains, "responsibility must be capable of correcting errors but should not be such as to destroy the genuine values of authority. Clearly, a sufficient strict and continuous organ of responsibility can easily amount to a denial of authority".[150] If every single decision made by the board as the centralised authority were to be scrutinised by the shareholders, it would be no different from entitling shareholders to make all decisions. Granting shareholders the power to review all (major) decisions made by directors would amount to giving them the power to make (major) corporate decisions. However, the cost would undoubtedly exceed any expected benefits. Just as the American Bar Association states:

> If corporations were directly managed by shareholders, and the actions of management were the subject of frequent shareholder review and decision-making, the ability to rely on management teams would be diluted and the time and attention of managers could, in many cases, be diverted from activities designed to pursue sustainable economic benefit for the corporation. For example, valuable board time might have to be diverted to address referenda items propounded by particular shareholders who may have interests that diverge from those of other shareholders or interests other than sustainable economic benefit. In addition, since shareholders generally do not owe fiduciary duties to each other or the corporation, such power would not be accompanied by corresponding accountability.[151]

Indeed, fiduciary duties for directors and the requirement for shareholder approval for major corporate issues under current company law are the exact tools required to ensure accountability and prohibit the pursuit of self-interest. It is hard to imagine a wise director daring to pursue self-serving behaviour by utilising their position. Besides, as Professor Bainbridge aptly observes, "a pervasive web of accountability mechanisms" including various disciplines from capital, product and labour markets and the constraint of professional reputation may effectively ensure

---

149 It is not surprising that, in the context of shareholder empowerment, directors become more obedient and defer to shareholders' risk preference even at the expense of the long-term success of the company.

150 He continues with an example which makes it more straightforward: "If every decision of A is to be reviewed by B, then all we have really is a shift in the locus if authority from A to B and hence no solution to the original problem". Arrow (n 104) 78.

151 Committee on Corporate Laws of the American Bar Association Section of Business Law, 'Report on the Roles of Boards of Directors and Shareholders of Publicly Owned Corporations' (2010) at www.hunton.com/media/SEC_Proxy/PDF/SEC_Agenda_Section2.PDF [accessed 30 October 2015] 5.

directors' accountability.[152] The threat of being removed in a takeover or proxy contest will also constrain the self-serving or shirking of directors. Professor Stout confirms that other corporate stakeholders who fear the "hold-up" problem have more faith in companies run by boards than in companies run by powerful shareholders.[153] This external check along with legal constraints implies it is not that easy for directors to seize private interests at the expense of shareholders and the company. Rather, it is in directors' best interests to keep the company alive and prosperous as they can keep their position and avoid a career-threatening dismissal.

Of course, there is certainly room for improving director accountability. Shareholders' limited powers could be seen as a means of checking non-accountability.[154] It may be difficult in practice to find exactly where the balance between authority and accountability sits; shifting the decision-making rights from the board to shareholders may not be an optimal solution. Shareholder empowerment is not the only available way.[155] In fact, the cost is much greater than the potential benefits.[156] Increasing shareholder power is, according to its strongest advocate, only a means to an end.[157] Nevertheless, as exhibited earlier, shareholder empowerment is by no means *the* approach to increasing shareholder value since it cannot ensure better corporate performance.[158] Consequently, its value should not be taken for granted.

---

152 Bainbridge, 'Director Primacy and Shareholder Disempowerment' (n 110) 1746–1747; Stephen Bainbridge, *The New Corporate Governance in Theory and Practice* (OUP, New York 2008) 112.

153 Professor Stout also argues that, unlike activist shareholders, directors cannot benefit financially from making similar threats. Stout, 'The Mythical Benefits of Shareholder Control' (n 106) 797. This is also why Theodore Mirvis *et al.* argue: "it is reasonable to expect shareholders to promote their private interests in the same circumstances where experience shows directors will act for the good of shareholders and the corporation". Mirvis, Rowe and Savitt (n 142).

154 For example, Professor Bainbridge argues "shareholder voting is properly understood not as an integral aspect of the corporate decisionmaking structure, but rather as an accountability device of last resort to be used sparingly, at best". Bainbridge, 'The Case for Limited Shareholder Voting Rights' (n 20) 627.

155 Legal devices, a mature competitive market system and such like are all available approaches. However, it is beyond the purpose of this chapter to tackle this century-long problem, though the author notices that a combination of different methods or even new techniques might be needed since none of above measures can be a perfect solution to ensure accountability alone.

156 Even under the context of shareholder wealth maximisation, any potential benefit brought by increasing shareholder power may be offset by the cost. As pointed out by Strine, "its structure must be designed with efficiency in mind, lest it destroy more value than it protects". Leo Strine, 'Toward a True Corporate Republic: A Traditionalist Response to Bebchuk's Solution for Improving Corporate America' (2006) 119 *Harvard Law Review* 1759, 1777.

157 For example, see Bebchuk, 'The Case for Increasing Shareholder Power' (n 27) 842–843. But it should also be noted that some scholars regard shareholder empowerment not as a derivative goal, but an end in and of itself. They see that shareholder empowerment can enhance the happiness of shareholders. James McConvill, 'Shareholder Empowerment as an End in Itself: A New Perspective on Allocation of Power in the Modern Corporation' (2007) 33 *Ohio Northern University Law Review* 1013, 1015 and 1057.

158 In contrast, the empirical study confirms that investors reveal a preference for companies where they have almost no powers during the period of an IPO. For example, see Stout, 'The Mythical Benefits of Shareholder Control' (n 106) 802–803; Bainbridge, 'Director Primacy and Shareholder Disempowerment' (n 110) 1743–1744.

In fact, shareholders themselves may prefer weak shareholder rights in order to avoid shareholder activism.[159] If investors prefer greater shareholder control, then IPO companies have the incentive to offer shareholders more control by raising more money at a cheaper cost. However, studies of recent IPOs indicate that shareholders generally prefer a governance structure with weak shareholder control.[160] This is strongly exemplified by the case of an Australian company, Boral Ltd., which passed an amendment to restrain shareholders' rights to requisition a meeting to alter the company's constitution.[161]

Last but not least, empirical evidence also shows "high levels of mistrust and suspicion" of increasing sovereign wealth funds from some emerging economies;[162] however, the fact that the majority of shares in UK listed companies are now held by overseas investors[163] may add extra doubt about the effects of enhanced shareholder power and engagement.

3.4 Concluding remarks

A hierarchical decision-making structure has been identified as the most important economic virtue of large public companies.[164] The concern is that active investor involvement made by shareholder empowerment will disrupt the very mechanism of modern public companies. As the foregoing discussion shows, increasing shareholder power may not change the status quo of shareholder apathy. Or worse still, such empowerment may encourage certain shareholders to abuse their enhanced power to advance their private benefits instead of pursuing common interests.

Recent initiatives could be regarded as an attempt to encourage passive shareholders to exert a more active role and institutional investors to be more responsible. However, "cultural change does not come easy".[165] Take the minimum percentage shareholding qualification for example: the reduction in the minimum threshold for requiring a meeting has not seen a significant impact.

---

159 Leo Strine, 'Toward a True Corporate Republic: A Traditionalist Response to Bebchuk's Solution for Improving Corporate America' (2006) 119 *Harvard Law Review* 1759, 1766.
160 The Google's IPO in 2004 is a typical example. It was oversubscribed although it adopted a dual-class charter which meant that outside investors were almost powerless. Stout, 'The Mythical Benefits of Shareholder Control' (n 106) 802–803.
161 For more discussion, see Jennifer Hill, 'The Rising Tension between Shareholder and Director Power in the Common Law World' (2010) 18 *Corporate Governance: An International Review* 344, 355.
162 Javier Jimenez and Antonio Urena, 'Sovereign Wealth Fund (SWF) Global Regulation and Transparency: A Preliminary Private-Investment Law Approach' (2010) 25 *Journal of International Banking Law and Regulation* 441, 446.
163 See *supra* Chapter 2 footnote 57 and accompanying text.
164 Professor Bainbridge has argued: "the chief economic virtue of the public corporation is . . . that it provides a hierarchical decisionmaking structure well-suited to the problem of operating a large business enterprise with numerous employees, managers, shareholders, creditors, and other constituencies". Bainbridge, 'Director Primacy and Shareholder Disempowerment' (n 110) 1749.
165 David Milman, 'Ascertaining Shareholder Wishes in UK Company Law in the 21st Century' (2010) 280 *Company Law Newsletter* 1, 5.

There is little evidence to suggest that shareholders prefer to convene a meeting to ensure or improve directors' accountability.[166] Shareholder apathy, according to Professor Milman, is not easy to change. Given that they have been empowered, it is unlikely to foster substantial shareholder involvement,[167] not to mention improving overall corporate welfare. Even assuming shareholders could properly use their increased power to more effectively discipline directors, the result of short-termism is difficult to avoid. Institutional shareholders' short-term focus, along with the characteristic that short-term results are more predictable and less risky, will affect directors' decision-making. Empowering shareholders and giving them a greater "say" means directors will be less independent and thereby less able to resist pressure to adopt a short-term strategy.

The question thus remains: why is shareholder empowerment still so appealing if it has more negative impacts than benefits? Shareholder wealth maximisation, or say shareholder primacy, may partly explain the trend. Given the focus on shareholder interests, support for increasing shareholder power is not surprising even if it is more likely an emotional response.[168] Giving shareholders more rights accords with the view of the superior position of shareholders in corporate governance. This is also why even the benefits of shareholder empowerment are not convincing; they are popular among academics and policy-makers. However, as shown in Chapter 2, shareholders do not own the company they invest in – they are not the principals of directors, nor the only residual claimants. Trust between various stakeholders including shareholders, long-term sustainable development and the unignorable drawbacks of SWM among others all suggest a broader aim is needed.[169]

The benefits of centralised board decision-making and the harm of intershareholder opportunism, as well as the potential for abuse, show that shareholder empowerment is not *the* effective means by which to improve shareholder value, let alone enhance social wealth.

---

166 Especially when the factor of shareholders' apathy is taken into account.

167 Even Professor Bebchuk, the most prominent shareholder empowerment advocator, also admits that the evidence for shareholder empowerment is weakly backed in his earlier draft of 'The Myth of the Shareholder Franchise'. In other words, there is a lack of direct evidence that shareholder empowerment can improve corporate performance. Stout, 'The Mythical Benefits of Shareholder Control' (n 106) 799.

168 Professor Stout argues, the misleading metaphor of shareholder ownership, ex post shareholder calls for shareholder democracy and the Enron Effect, are three sources of such emotional appeal. Stout, 'The Mythical Benefits of Shareholder Control' (n 106) 803–807. And it is also argued that proponents of SWM are inclined to support shareholder empowerment. McConvill (n 157) 1029.

169 If the stakeholder model can be proved to be valid in Chapter 5, there will be even less foundation for shareholder empowerment.

4 Shareholder rights and corporate objective in China

Past and present

4.1 An overview of corporate evolution and shareholder rights in China

Whilst it seems that China's corporate system lags far behind Western developed countries such as the UK, the US and Germany, as early as 1904, China's first corporate law[1] was promulgated by the imperial government, the Qing government. It included the rule of limited liability and equal treatment of shares among others.[2] Why then did it take another century for a mature corporate law system or governance structure to be established? The past is essential to understanding the current status of shareholder rights and corporate objectives in China. Therefore, the first section of this chapter focuses on the historical development of corporate forms and shareholder rights in China, and their respective features as well as the main causes and effects.

Modern and contemporary history is divided into three distinctive periods: the Late Qing Dynasty from 1860 to 1911, the Republican Period from 1912 to 1948 and the People's Republic of China since its establishment in 1949; each distinctive period can be further divided into different phases. This evolution is traced as an important background and evidence for the following discussion on shareholders' role, rights and corporate objectives.

4.1.1 Late Qing Dynasty

Prior to 1860

The Qing Dynasty (1616–1911), like most of the previous ruling dynasties, strongly suppressed the production and distribution of commercial goods

---

1 It was called "*gong si lü*" dissimilar to the current company law which is called "*gong si fa*". For example, see Mingxin Zhang and Yujie Wang, 'A Brief Analysis of the Birth and Features of the Company Regulation At the End of the Qing Dynasty' (2003) 119 *Law Review* 148, 149–150.
2 Ibid. 150–151. Also see *Hundred-Year History of China's Corporate Law* at www.civillaw.com.cn/Article/default.asp?id=36171 [accessed 1 October 2014]. It was argued that shareholding was not an unfamiliar concept to Chinese businessmen, the more meaningful innovation for the *Company Law 1904* was to establish the rule of limited liability which could facilitate the raising of capital and attract public investors, as previously discussed.

in order to maintain the agrarian economy and its centralisation of authority. The role of businessmen was intentionally underestimated and despised in its long history: no matter how rich they were their social status was very low in accordance with traditional Confucianism, the dominant political ideology in ancient China. Despite the existence of some examples of successful family-run firms, private businesses were strictly constrained in certain fields[3] and not allowed to be independently involved in large-scale production. This meant that even though private businesses operated by big families could be quite prosperous, they were first and foremost rigidly limited in certain domains, and second, they were premised on obtaining commercial licences for trading. More importantly, virtually all of these large-scale private businesses were under some form of state sponsorship or government patronage.[4] Such a situation not only led to the slow development of a private-sector economy, but also resulted in family-run firms being hardly independent from the state.[5]

1861–1894: Self-Strengthening Movement

Directly influenced by the serious defeats in the *First Opium War* (1840–1842) and *Second Opium War* (1856–1860), the Qing government (to be more precise, a group of progressive officials) launched the *Self-Strengthening Movement*. After the Opium Wars, the Qing government was forced to open several port cities to foreign companies and individuals and permit them to carry on business, which had been strictly constrained or even forbidden in the past. By virtue of the fast growth of foreign companies in these treaty ports, the imperial Qing government had to encourage the development of domestic enterprises to compete with overseas ones. On the other hand, of great significance, the study and adoption of advanced military technology and armaments from the West for the sake of enhancing national defence became essential for the regime.

Three main types of enterprise evolved during this period.[6] The first was *guan ban* (government management), namely the enterprises that were completely funded and managed by the government. This was not a new type. For example, original salt production and imperial porcelain production belonged

---

3 For example, salt and steel production were virtually completely controlled by the imperial governments during Ming Dynasty (1368–1644) and Qing Dynasty.

4 Such as deferred treatment of tax payments. William Goetzmann and Elisabeth Köll, 'The History of Corporate Ownership in China' in Randall Morck (ed), *A History of Corporate Governance around the World: Family Business Groups to Professional Managers* (University of Chicago Press, Chicago 2005) 152. And this situation lasted until 1900, after when the Qing imperial government openly encouraged private businesses and industrial enterprises. Ibid. 160.

5 They are frequently compelled to donate large sums of money to the government in order to maintain a good relationship with it and they would be easily affected by the political factors since there was no legal protection. Man Bun Kwan, *The Salt Merchants of Tianjin: State-Making and Civil Society in Late Imperial China* (University of Hawai'i Press, Honolulu 2001) 37–45.

6 See Yu Li, *Development of Corporate System during Late Qing Dynasty* (People Press, Beijing 2002) 7.

to this category.[7] However, the *guan ban* did not include projects like railroads, telegraphs and mining; these required a great amount of capital and a larger base of investors, something the Qing government, who confronting a variety of domestic and international problems, could not afford. The second type of enterprises, *guan du shang ban* (government supervision and merchant management), appeared as a consequence. Under this model, merchants – a preferred term at that moment – and public investors (namely, ordinary people) subscribed to the entire share capital of firms and took risks, although in reality government officials controlled the firms. Despite being called *merchant management*, the merchants as shareholders in fact had no practical control rights. They might be responsible for daily operations, but were only allowed to act with the sanction and permission of the government. Even though occasionally the government did not directly administer the personnel, operational and financial affairs, these sorts of issues remained under its close supervision.

Notwithstanding the fact that progress made in the form of *guan du shang ban* was remarkable during that period – for the first time it officially attracted private capital to support giant, costly projects and indirectly allowed private actors to engage in large industrial sectors – there were some obvious disadvantages. Among public investors, merchants as shareholders were not able to enjoy so-called ownership rights: first, they had to surrender part of the profits to the government,[8] and second, they had no control over the firms they invested in to any great extent. Moreover, increasingly severe conflicts, including differing agendas between merchants and government officials, the bureaucracy, and the resulting low efficiency made investors less willing to invest in firms controlled and supervised by the government.

To further attract private investment, the Qing government set up a third form of enterprise – *guan shang he ban* (joint government-merchant management). There were several new features under this model: first, government and merchants would both subscribe to business's share capital and undertake the risks of the business together; second, merchants and public investors had more rights since they could send their own representatives to engage in management; third, both government and merchants were required to make explicit contracts or arrangements specifying the rights and obligations of each group, the respective proportion of profits, and measures to distribute the profits. This form of *guan shang he ban* was supposed to provide more flexibility for drawing capital from the general public, particularly merchants who were generally wealthier, to develop domestic enterprises.[9]

Unfortunately, managerial power still largely rested with government officials, whilst merchants' representatives were practically powerless. This ultimately failed

---

7 Indeed, private businesses are strictly restrained to participate in these areas.
8 The government had the power to decide the profit allocation despite merchants contributing the entire equity capital. John Fairbank and Kwang-Ching Liu (eds), *The Cambridge History of China: Volume 11, Late Ch'ing, 1800–1911* (CUP, Cambridge 1980) 434–435.
9 It should be noticed that exclusively private industrial firms were still not allowed to be independently established without the involvement of the government until the end of the nineteenth century.

to attract enough private funds as expected. The contradiction and dilemma here was apparent. For one thing, the Qing government wished to study the military weaponry and advanced technology of Western countries and then compete with them. For another, the imperial government did not expect to carry out a complete reform – even in the economic field – for fear of losing its controlling position as well as the potential incompatible clash with traditional morality. In short, there was no intention to reform the old institutions of the Qing government.[10] Government-dominated corporate forms in the late Qing Dynasty with corruption and ineffective political systems were doomed to failure in attracting desperately demanded capital. Without enough funds to establish and develop companies, and with severe restraints upon private firms, the overall development of both public and private firms during this period was disappointing and the *Self-Strengthening Movement* was finally aborted.

1895–1911: late Qing reform period

Defeat in the *First Sino-Japanese War* (*jia wu zhan zheng*) was a difficult blow for the Qing government. It was compelled to pay an enormous compensation, much as it had after the two *Opium Wars*, but of a much larger amount.[11] Pursuant to article 6 of the *Treaty of Shimonoseki*, the post-war treaty between the Qing and Japanese government in 1895, the former was also forced to permit foreigners, viz. Japanese citizens, to build factories. It should be noted that though that foreigners could do business in certain port cities after the *First Opium War*, they were not allowed to build factories to engage in the manufacturing industry. After signing the *Shimonoseki Treaty*, the policy of forbidding Chinese citizens to engage in industrial firms whilst allowing foreigners to do so became senseless. Thus from 1895 onwards, restrictions were eliminated and private firms in light industry as well as the consumer goods industry developed very quickly, especially in the original *guan du shang ban* and *guan shang he ban* enterprises.[12]

In order to further facilitate commerce and help industry, the Qing government established the Ministry of Commerce and enacted China's first company law, *gong si lü* in 1904,[13] aiming to establish a shareholder-friendly environment

10 The strategy is "*zhong xue wei ti, xi xue wei yong*" (Chinese learning for fundamental principles and Western learning for practical uses). The political status quo of the conservative imperial monarchy was forbidden from being touched.

11 The Qing Government was forced to pay an indemnity of 230 million *silver kuping taels* to Japan in total according to articles 2 and 4 of Treaty of Shimonoseki. Available at http://china.usc.edu/treaty-shimonoseki-1895 [accessed 1 March 2017]. Since one *kuping (treasury) tael* was about 37.3 grams in weight, it meant China had to pay approximately 8.56 million kilograms of silver.

12 Goetzmann and Köll (n 4) 160.

13 As was commented by Professor Kirby: "[t]he Company Law was the first modern law drafted by the Imperial Law Codification Commission, whose work was part of the Qing government's reformist 'new policies' in the wake of China's recent humiliations at the hands of Japan and the Western powers". William Kirby, 'China Unincorporated: Company Law and Business Enterprise in Twentieth-Century China' (1995) 54 *Journal of Asian Studies* 43, 43.

for encouraging private investment. It is worth mentioning that during the late nineteenth and early twentieth centuries, cotton-spinning mills and other industries involved a high level of risk. The rule of limited liability introduced by the *Company Law 1904* substantially facilitated investors, who in the past might have feared unlimited liability when the business failed, to put money into the company. Purchasing stocks from a specific company or the public market would only risk the corresponding value instead of the entire personal wealth, because the liability had been limited to the value of the shares to which they subscribed.[14] Consequently, fears that once largely restricted the size and scope of companies could be removed by the new law, whilst raising large amounts of capital turned out to be feasible at least from a technical point of view. A more important factor for China's political and economic environment, as some scholars aptly note, was the "hands-off" effect of the *Company Law 1904*, i.e. replacing state patronage and government interference with a set of explicit legal rules to enhance shareholder rights.[15] Put simply, shareholders were destined to become the central players for substituting the traditional role of government in corporate activities.

Optimistic readers might think that with a series of economic reforms and the appearance of modern company laws, China seemed to possess the conditions for developing modern corporations. However, this did not happen in the eight decades following the promulgation of the first modern company law in 1904. Even after eliminating government interference and enacting the rule of limited liability, without an accessible capital market, the difficulty of raising capital remained a huge problem and obstacle for the development of private companies. In the absence of an accessible capital market, it was hard to raise money from the public. One often-mentioned reason for weak shareholder rights or unfettered managerial power was the lack of an active stock market for domestic companies. Although the first securities market emerged in Shanghai as early as the 1870s, after a string of booms it became an ineffective capital market for domestic companies.[16] In particular, the mid-1880s stock market crisis (China's first stock market bubble), principally a result of price manipulation and insider trading,[17] heavily dampened investors' confidence.

In addition, government withdrawal from direct involvement did not necessarily mean that the controlling right would return to shareholders as a

---

14 For the detailed positive effect of 'Limited Liability', see Henry Hansmann and Reinier Kraakman, 'The Essential Role of Organizational Law' (2000) 110 *Yale Law Journal* 387, 398–405 and 423–427; Henry Hansmann, Reinier Kraakman and Richard Squire, 'Law and the Rise of the Firm' (2006) 119 *Harvard Law Review* 1333, 1343–1350.

15 Goetzmann and Köll (n 4) 163.

16 However, the Shanghai Stock Exchange worked quite well for the foreign-domiciled companies, indeed it became one of the most active stock markets around the world at the time. Ibid. 151.

17 As Professors Goetzmann and Köll interestingly point out: "at about the time that robber barons Gould and Fisk were manipulating [the] prices of railroad securities on the New York Stock Exchange, the Shanghai market suffered from the same problems of insider trading". Ibid. 155–156.

whole – they could potentially be transferred to a blockholder or a small group of large shareholders. In the case of China, the founder/managing director took control. There were two main reasons: first, founders or managing directors would establish "institutional structures of control in combination with social networks";[18] second, the legal enforcement mechanism did not work well, thus it would be difficult to expect the court to effectively implement the existing legal institutions and safeguard shareholders' legitimate rights.[19]

Further, there was inadequate legal protection for minority shareholders. After the government's withdrawal, companies were firmly controlled by the founders or managing directors and it was almost impossible for disgruntled minority shareholders to effectively express their opinions. Some institutions introduced by the 1904 law, such as the requirement for an *auditor*, became rubber-stamps owing to the fact that founders or managing directors usually dominated the board. This in turn resulted in, or at least enhanced the tradition of, raising capital from kinship and interpersonal networks. As Gary Hamilton astutely observes,

> Kinship and native place collegiality constitute an *institutional medium* out of which people create organized networks. In this regard, kinship and collegiality in China played a role analogous to those played by law and individuality in the West.[20]

Family ties and interpersonal networks remained the only reliable source of capital since such relationships could provide certain protections and guarantees. People did not dare risk their money under the management of someone they did not know.

> The idea that members of the public would be invited to join one's business and share in its control and profits was indeed repugnant. On the other hand, the notion that one's money be put into the pocket of some strangers for them to run a business was just as unthinkable.[21]

Such imbedded distrust and problematic legal enforcement mechanisms, along with an inaccessible public market, substantially restricted the development of corporate form.

18 Ibid. 171.
19 As observed by Dwight Perkins, businessmen are not prepared to go to the local magistrate which is responsible for dealing with disputes including commercial ones, as they believe the officials in the magistrates office are neither competent nor impartial. This means that even though *Company Law 1904* stipulates certain types of shareholder rights, when they are infringed, no effective legal enforcement mechanism exists to protect these rights. Ibid. 183.
20 Gary Hamilton, 'The Organizational Foundations of Western and Chinese Commerce: A Historical and Comparative Analysis' in Gary Hamilton (ed) *Asian Business Networks* (De Gruyter, Berlin 1996) 43.
21 Jun Li, 'The Kung-ssu-lu of 1904 and Modernization of Chinese Company Law' (1974) 11 *Chengchi University Legal Review* 171, 205 quoted in Kirby (n 13) 50.

4.1.2 Republican period

With the collapse of the Qing Dynasty, the previous centralised authority was substantially weakened. As Professor Perkins illustrates, the governments of the first few decades of the twentieth century "had little capacity to do much of anything other than to mobilize an army to fight the government's political opponents".[22] Along with the decline of state authority, the political stimulus to boycott foreign commodities and enthusiasm for developing domestic companies, this period was seen as the golden age of Chinese capitalism.[23] Nonetheless, the difficulty of raising capital persisted. Although more businesses and commercial activities were conducted between strangers, rent and mortgage remained the paramount method of financing, rather than equity purchasing.[24] Preferring debt investment to equity was undoubtedly influenced by traditional views. More crucially, the prevalence of controlling shareholders, as well as inadequate protection for minority shareholders, may also have contributed to the above situation.

After 1927, the newly established *Kuomingtang* (KMT or Nationalist Party of China) Nanjing government led by Chiang Kai-shek gradually acquired the ruling position over the entire nation, argued by some historians as an indication of "the bureaucracy's return in force and the decline of the bourgeoisie".[25] This was followed by an era of nationalisation of many companies, wherein the state again dominated the development of all fundamental heavy industries and infrastructure. The start of the Sino-Japanese war in 1937 indisputably accelerated the scope and pace of such nationalisation. As statistics show, by 1942 the state controlled 70 per cent of the total capital of China's industry.[26] Take the National Resource Commission (NRC), the largest state industrial agency, as an example: some of NRC's over 100 organisations either operated as "purely administrative units" or completely NRC-owned companies, whilst others took a public-private form whereby NRC accounted for the majority of shares without exception.[27]

In the meantime, the Nanjing government had already drafted Five-Year and Ten-Year Plans for the post-war period which focused on state-dominated development.[28] Given that the *Kuomingtang* could preserve the regime for a longer period, it logically predicated the further centralisation of economic power in the hands of the state and continuous contraction of non-governmental companies soon thereafter.

---

22 Randall Morck (ed), *A History of Corporate Governance around the World: Family Business Groups to Professional Managers* (University of Chicago Press, Chicago 2005) 183.
23 Kirby (n 13) 48–49.
24 Ibid. 49 and 50.
25 Marie-Claire Bergère, *The Golden Age of the Chinese Bourgeoisie* (CUP, Cambridge 1990) 272.
26 Jian Sun, *Economic History of China 1840–1949* (China People's University Press, Beijing 2000) 1237–1240.
27 Some other organisations, mostly mining firms, were organised as limited joint-stock companies between provincial governments and the NRC. Kirby (n 13) 53.
28 Ibid. 54.

4.1.3 People's Republic of China

1949–1983: socialist transformation and state-owned enterprises

Subsequent to a lengthy civil war against the KMT, the *Communist Party of China* (hereafter, CPC) took over full control of Mainland China and established the *People's Republic of China* (hereafter, PRC) in 1949. Communist or socialist ideology then determined the ownership structure in society. Articles 5, 6 and 7 of the 1954 *Constitution of the People's Republic of China* – the first constitution of PRC – specified two main categories of ownership: state ownership, i.e. ownership by the whole people; and co-operative ownership, i.e. collective ownership by the masses of working people.[29]

Private ownership was not allowed and entirely abolished during the socialist transformation period. Apart from a small fraction of co-operative-owned enterprises, the vast majority of corporations in the first three decades after 1949 were state-owned. Though state-owned property belonged to every Chinese person in name, as criticised by many contemporary scholars, belonging to *the whole people* equals belonging to nobody.[30] It is simply impossible for every citizen to engage in corporate activities in spite of the fact that he or she theoretically has a stake in them. Inevitably, the government represents *the whole people* in holding and exercising ownership rights. The state utilised its finances to fund state-owned enterprises (hereafter, SOEs), and then completely controlled the management and operation of those companies.

More importantly, under the system of planned economy, everything from resource allocation to operation, production and distribution was totally planned by the state in advance. The SOEs during this period functioned not materially

---

29 Beyond these two principal ownership forms, there were two other forms, namely ownership by individual working people and capitalist ownership. The first type was strictly restrained in terms of scale, which implied it could not develop and play an important role; indeed during the following two decades, private trading was suspended under the planned economy system. For the second type, though such capitalist ownership patterns contributed dramatically to the overall economy and national prosperity during the past half century, it became insignificant after 1949. Articles 4 and 10 of the PRC *Constitution* explicitly specified that the system of exploitation, which principally meant capitalism, should be abolished. Such capitalist industry among others was indeed strictly restrained and transformed into various forms of state-capitalism in the following periods until they were replaced by a structure of ownership by the whole people.

Moreover, compared with state-owned enterprises, which were defined as the leading force in the national economy and the material basis on which the state undertook the socialist transformation according to article 6 of the *Constitution*, co-operative owned enterprises were comparatively smaller in scale. In fact, co-operative ownership mainly referred to ownership types of land in rural areas of China by aggregates of peasants. As a result, during this period, the state ownership structure became the focus.

30 For example, see Lee Joyce, 'From Non-tradable to Tradable Shares: Split Share Structure Reform of China's Listed Companies' (2008) 8 *Journal of Corporate Law Studies* 57, 76; Jun Lin, Linming Liu and Xu Zhang, 'The Development of Corporate Governance in China' (2007) 28 *Company Lawyer* 195, 199; Shumo Cai and Yingxia Deng, 'Corporate Governance in China – Obstacles and New Development' (2001) 29 *International Business Lawyer* 455, 456.

differently from government affiliates: their almost sole objective was to complete the task assigned by the state or government. Accumulating profits never necessarily became a priority for the official-like managers of SOEs. Even though continuous losses for a particular company appeared, as long as the assignment allocated by the state was fulfilled, then the government would usually subsidise such companies instead of blaming them.[31] Both ownership rights and control lay in the hands of the state. To speak of corporate governance, which is most likely to be derived from a free market economy, became ironic under such a centralised, planned economy on the grounds that any governance mechanism was replaced by bureaucratic administration. Enterprises functioned no differently from government affiliates or government-like organisations.

1984–1992: enterprise reform

In 1984, the *Third Plenum of the Twelfth CPC National Congress* announced economic structural reform (*jing ji ti zhi gai ge*), and the development of a socialist commodity economy (*she hui zhu yi shang pin jing ji*) relying on the *law of value* within the system of the planned economy. This marked the first official recognition of the role of the market in PRC. More excitingly, it enabled enterprises to become the focal issue of this reform as expressed by the *Central Committee of CPC's Decision of Economic Structural Reform*. As a consequence, the obligations of government and SOEs had to be explicitly divided – the responsibility to manage SOEs had to be given back to companies *as such*. The government, as stipulated by the *Decision*, was requested not to interfere with the management of SOEs.

The government believed the problems of SOEs were attributable to the lack of managerial autonomy and a proper performance-based reward system. Subsequently, SOEs were granted more autonomy in order to be enabled to make operational decisions independently and to be responsible for their own operation; to this end, incentive mechanisms based on managerial performance were gradually established. The management contract responsibility system (*jing ying cheng bao ze ren zhi*) was another direct product of the *1984 Economic Structural Reform*. A typical management contract would contain the arrangements of an agreed amount of profits among other fees paid to government as the contracted responsibility, as well as the allocated measure of excess profits between the government and the SOE management team. Its essence, following the guideline of the *Reform*, was to separate the management from the so-called ownership. Managers of SOEs certainly did not have ownership rights because virtually all shares belonged to the state. However, the *Reform* entitled managers

---

31 In fact, during most of this period, no real market existed, so it is less meaningful to discuss "profits" while everything was planned. And even if it suffered a constant loss, due to there being no exit mechanism a particular SOE would not be forced into bankruptcy; instead, the state would keep injecting capital into that SOE.

to possess relatively autonomous managerial power and independent discretion over operations, which they had not had in the past. Moreover, SOEs were permitted to retain additional profits as long as the returns exceeded a fixed amount specified by the state, and managers could also be correspondingly rewarded for a proportional bonus. These new designs were supposed to motivate managers to make optimal decisions and work more effectively.[32]

In the latter half of the 1980s, an increasing number of SOEs started to securitise, and stocks began to be tradable over-the-counter.[33] The Shanghai Stock Exchange and Shenzhen Stock Exchange were established at the end of 1990. The following year, the China Securities Regulatory Commission (hereafter, CSRC) was set up as the national watchdog of securities exchanges. The emergence of the stockholding system constituted the foundations for raising capital to support the development of large companies. As reminded by the lessons from the Qing and Republican periods, active and accessible securities markets are an essential base for the growth of private-sector companies in contrast to government-sponsored ones.

Notwithstanding the material improvement achieved, there are three fatal limits of the reform in this period. First, as the state controlled the power of appointment and removal with respect to the management, it was possible for the government to remove a non-obedient manager. Interestingly, the managers in SOEs would usually have certain administrative ranks and could be interchanged directly with officials in central or local governments.[34] Managers were consequently more loyal to the government than the company they ran. Second, whilst the profitable SOEs were able to enjoy the additional profits, unprofitable or losing SOEs could not afford the fixed amount committed to the state. Because there was no exit mechanism, managers of unsuccessful SOEs did not feel valid competitive pressure. Third, myopic decision-making could hardly be avoided due to the short-term nature of management contracts. This short-termism resulted in many serious problems including pursuing immediate income maximisation at the expense of long-term benefits.[35] In the end, high debt-to-asset ratios became a strong impetus for further ownership reform, since turning SOEs into true corporations without thoroughly reforming ownership structures turned out to be impossible to achieve.[36]

---

32 According to a management responsibility contract, when a loss occurs, the SOE has to offset the deficit.

33 Michael Ellman, 'China's OTC Markets' (1988) 30 *Comparative Economic Studies* 9–64 quoted in Yong Kang, Lu Shi and Elizabeth Brown, *Chinese Corporate Governance: History and Institutional Framework* (Rand Corporation, Santa Monica 2008) 6.

34 Min Yan, 'Obstacles to China's Corporate Governance' (2011) 34 *Company Lawyer* 311, 318.

35 For example, the R&D department is most likely to be overlooked as it cannot contribute a fast return. Meanwhile, because those SOEs are still owned by the state, such short-term behaviour would ultimately hurt the state interest.

36 Yong Kang, Lu Shi and Elizabeth Brown, *Chinese Corporate Governance: History and Institutional Framework* (Rand Corporation, Santa Monica 2008) 7. In fact, according to the statistics, more than two-thirds of SOEs were operating at a loss at the start of the 1990s. Yingyi Qian, *Reforming Corporate Governance and Finance in China* (Economic Development Institute of the World Bank, 1994).

1993–2005: socialist market economy

In 1992, the *Fourteenth CPC National Congress* first expressly introduced the policy of establishing a socialist market economy (*she hui zhu yi shi chang jing ji*).[37] This implies China entered a new economic era, with a market economy replacing its initial centrally planned one. The following year, the first company law in PRC was promulgated, granting SOEs independent status. Pursuant to article 3 of the *Company Law of People's Republic of China 1993* (hereafter, *Company Law 1993*), all incorporated companies are legal persons with an independent personality in law and are responsible for their own behaviour. Furthermore, the *Fifteenth CPC National Congress* in 1997 and its *Fourth Plenum* in 1999 made a series of theoretical innovations to overcome the ideological obstacles for SOE reforms. Private ownership,[38] initially eliminated and prohibited in the beginning, was gradually permitted in the late 1980s and recognised as beneficial supplement to public ownership after the *Thirteenth CPC National Congress*. Since the *Fourteenth CPC National Congress*, and especially the *Fifteenth*, private ownership started to be seen as an important part of the whole economy, indicating that such an ownership pattern would be continuously encouraged. The subsequent amendment to the *Constitution* in 1999 clarified that non-public sectors of the economy, including the individual and private sectors, constituted an important component of the socialist market economy. Thus, multiple forms of ownership structure, particularly private ownership, were developed with great expectations from policy-makers of improving the productivity and efficiency of national industries. All enterprises including SOEs were then required to establish modern corporate governance structures as the kernel of modern enterprise transformation.[39]

This ownership reform, in contrast to the management-oriented reform in the previous period, not only statutorily allowed, but also encouraged investment from private sectors. The percentage of private ownership increased rapidly in the original SOEs. In fact, since the establishment of the securities market, the role of private capital has come to be highly important, because a fundamental reason for having stock markets is to raise capital from numerous individuals and entities. Diversifying types of corporate ownership to change situations in which the state was the sole or controlling shareholder, became the trend. By and large, more structural and organisational autonomy was granted to individual SOEs by virtue of the "corporatisation" process.[40] The implicit

---

37 It is indeed a mixture of state-owned enterprises with an open-market economy and mainly based on the paramount CPC leader Deng Xiaoping's political innovation of *you zhong guo te se de she hui zhu yi* (socialism with Chinese characteristics).

38 This excludes individual economy (i.e. ownership by individual working people such as craftsmen) which is insignificant compared with other forms.

39 In fact, at the same time, the importance of corporate governance also arises under the new business structure.

40 For example, see Stefan Voß and Yiwen Xia, 'Corporate Governance of Listed Companies in China' at https://emnet.univie.ac.at/uploads/media/Vo%C3%9F_Xia_01.pdf [accessed 1 March 2017].

privatisation revitalised the corporate sectors. Meanwhile, the promulgation of the *Securities Law* by the end of 1998 and the more active role taken by CSRC, along with a series of corporate governance codes, greatly improved the shareholder-friendly investment environment.

Nonetheless, subsequent to granting directors/managers more autonomy and discretion, the issue of how to keep the conflict between shareholders and directors in check should not underestimated. The protection of shareholder interests was of growing importance. More crucially, the state was still the controlling shareholder; under such multiple forms of ownership structure, directors of the board and their delegated managers were not infrequently driven to serve majority shareholders' interests at the expense of minority shareholders. As one officer from the Shanghai Stock Exchange summarised, most directors understood the principles of good corporate governance as well as its significance, but more than a few continued to think that their relationship with the government was more important than that with (minority) shareholders in the transition from a centrally planned to market-oriented market.[41] The focal point in corporate structure changed into questions of how to effectively protect public investors as minority shareholders, whereas the state remained the majority shareholder. Even assuming that the influential political factor of the state was removed, minority shareholders remained vulnerable in the context of concentrated ownership structure since managers, blockholders or both could effortlessly exploit them. In addition, state ownership was regarded as having a negative impact on the performance and value of the company from an economic perspective, as many scholars argue.[42] On the contrary, both private and institutional investors, regardless of whether they are domestic or overseas, can generally offer a positive contribution.[43] All of these imply that further reform was necessary.

---

41 Neil Andrews and Roman Tomasic, 'Directing China's Top 100 Listed Companies: Corporate Governance in an Emerging Market Economy' (2006) 2 *Corporate Governance Law Review* 245, 308–309.

42 For example, see Martin Hovey, 'Corporate Governance in China: An Analysis of Ownership Changes after the 1997 Announcement' (2005) at http://papers.ssrn.com/sol3/papers.cfm?abstract_id=811105 [accessed 1 March 2017]; Changyun Wang, 'Ownership and Operating Performance of Chinese IPOs' (2005) 29 *Journal of Banking & Finance* 1835–1856; Zuobao Wei, Feixue Xie and Shaorong Zhang, 'Ownership Structure and Firm Value in China's Privatized Firms: 1991–2001' (2005) 40 *Journal of Financial and Quantitative Analysis* 87–108; Martin Hovey, Larry Li and Tony Naughton, 'The Relationship Between Valuation and Ownership of Listed Firms in China' (2003) 11 *Corporate Governance: An International Review* 112–122; Ferdinand Gul, 'Government Share Ownership, Investment Opportunity Set and Corporate Policy Choices in China' (1999) 7 *Pacific-Basin Finance Journal* 157–172; Jian Chen, 'Ownership Structure as Corporate Governance Mechanism: Evidence from Chinese Listed Companies' (2001) 34 *Economics of Planning* 53–72.

43 Martin Hovey and Tony Naughton, 'A Survey of Enterprise Reforms in China: The Way Forward' (2007) 31 *Economic Systems* 138, 153.

From 2005 onwards: further reform

Further reforms have been pushing ahead since 2005. First of all, the revised *Company Law* in 2005 brought with it many new changes. For instance, it made the independent director system a legal requirement and accorded shareholders more channels to appeal when they find misconduct or feel harmed.[44] Many good corporate governance structures stemming from Western countries have also been introduced and transplanted into China.

Another sweeping and far-reaching reform was in the field of the traditional split-share system. Shares in China's stock market are classified into two main categories, namely tradable and non-tradable shares. The latter category is comprised of state shares[45] and legal person shares.[46] Each class accounted for approximately one-third of all shares until 2005. Therefore, the controlling shareholder (i.e. the state) who owned shares either directly or indirectly through legal persons[47] was entrenched and almost immutable on the grounds that approximately two-thirds of all shares could not be transferred in the stock market.[48] In 2005, the CSRC restarted the project to lower the state's shareholding by converting non-tradable shares to tradable shares after some failed attempts earlier in the the end of twentieth century and beginning of twenty-first century. Following the initial success of *Beijing Tsinghua Tongfang*, as well as three other listed companies' experiments, a second group of 42 listed companies was later requested to join the split-share reform, and finally the reform was extended to all remaining domestic listed companies[49] by the end of 2005.

44 Such as articles 54, 102, 151 of *Company Law 2005*.

45 State shares are defined as *shares legally invested with state funds in a company by officially approved departments or organisations that can represent the State to invest.*

46 Legal person shares are defined as *shares invested in other companies by enterprises that are owned by 'the whole people' and granted operational autonomy*. It should be noticed that the distinction between state shares and legal person shares is questionable; it is said that legal persons could be owned or controlled by the state, which means that their shares also belong to the state to some extent. Donald Clarke, 'Independent Directors in Chinese Corporate Governance' (2006) 31 *Delaware Journal of Corporate Law* 125, 133. However, it is not the purpose of this chapter to discuss the differences between them.

47 "Legal persons" include incorporated companies, non-bank financial institutions and SOEs with at least one non-state shareholder. Most legal persons are ultimately controlled by the state.

48 This means that the minority shareholder or outsiders can never through transactions in the stock market gain control of the company on the grounds that only about one-third of shares are issued to the public, while the other two-thirds are firmly in the hands of the state. Gradually, management understands they will not lose jobs even if they run a company unprofitably since the company would rarely be in danger of takeover. Instead, the paramount job for these directors and senior managers is to satisfy their controlling shareholder in order to preserve their position and receive generous compensation. It has also been argued that because of the nature of non-transferability, the controlling shareholders with non-tradable shares do not care about the fluctuation of share prices in the stock market, a situation exacerbated by the fact that the state as the controlling shareholder usually uses its dominant control for certain political considerations other than maximising profits. Yan (n 34) 314.

49 According to the CSRC statistics, there was a total of 1,377 domestic companies listed on China's A-share and B-share stock markets in 2005, and most of them were state-owned.

The reform of the split-share structure is incontrovertibly beneficial to the further development of the capital market and enables controlling shareholders to be exposed directly to market pressure and supervision. Public investors, both individual and institutional ones, can thereby experience a fairer environment with more accessible protection. And the market for corporate control, hostile takeovers in particular, which is seen as the ultimate disciplinary mechanism by neoclassical economists, now became viable in the light of such split-share reform. At the very least, one fundamental obstacle to the free market was removed.

The continuous economic reforms since have materially metamorphosed and reconstructed China's economic situation, including corporate structures. The free market is not only allowed but encouraged to efficiently perform a resource allocation role, and an effective legal framework has also been set up to ensure that an infringed shareholder can obtain a remedy without unreasonable difficulties. These will definitely foster further development.

4.2 Shareholder rights in contemporary China

4.2.1 Shareholders' extensive powers

Due in part to the unique historical factors explored earlier, when the corporate system was restored after the official acknowledgement of the socialist market economy status, it triggered a huge demand for emphasising shareholder rights and their protection. In this way, shareholder empowerment is considered an important way to protect shareholders' rights against mismanagement and encourage their activism.

First of all, the long absence of private property rights in China has given rise to a lopsided stress on shareholder rights. Even after the establishment of PRC, shareholders had little role to play in corporate governance, but now the advantage of shareholder participation has been recognised, partly due to lessons from history and partly due to Western influence.[50] As Professor Baoshu Wang, a prominent Chinese corporate law scholar opines, shareholders should be entitled to more rights and protection, which could encourage them to exercise their rights, because Chinese corporate practice has only just started in PRC.[51] In other words, adequate shareholder rights are regarded as beneficial to shareholder participation and thereby to good corporate governance.

Second, economic development is regarded as one of the top priorities for the Chinese government at the moment – since the *Third Plenum of the Fourteenth Communist Party of China National Congress* in 1993 the main policy standpoint has been "giving priority to efficiency with due consideration of fairness".[52]

---

50 Unfortunately, such benefits might be overstated as discussed in Chapter 3.
51 Baoshu Wang and Qingzhi Cui, *The Principle of Chinese Company Law (zhong guo gong si fa yuan li)* (Social Science Documents Press, Beijing 1998) 25–26.
52 *xiao lü you xian, jian gu gong ping.*

Economic development requires large amounts of capital among other things. In particular, since the policy aims to stimulate and encourage investment from private sectors, and attract both domestic and overseas capital to develop the economy, the role of shareholders is inevitably a prime focus. Investors might be more concerned about investing in a company if they have few rights, as in the past. Meanwhile, abstention from government intervention and allowing companies to develop independently is also generally regarded as more business friendly and economically efficient. Unlike government agencies or bureaucrats, shareholders are regarded as having the utmost incentive to monitor management to pursue the best interests according to the so-called residual claimant principle, which is largely affected by the West.

Moreover, politically, the Chinese government intends to maintain state control over large companies, which are usually state-owned or dominated. The policy of "keeping to the socialist road" by controlling the management of these "corporatised" SOEs also contributes to the extensive power of shareholders in China.[53] The insulation and autonomy of the board of directors is further reduced and eliminated by the concentrated ownership which prevails in the largest public companies.

All these lead to the tendency to put control into shareholders' hands or grant more powers to the shareholder. Like shareholder empowerment in the Anglo-American sphere – especially after the financial crisis – the revised *Company Law* in 2005 also entrusts extensive power to shareholders in China in order to improve shareholders' position and influence in corporate governance.[54]

Before discussing shareholder power in contemporary China, it should be noted that there are two types of company under the revised company law statute, namely limited liability companies (hereafter, LLC) and joint stock limited companies (hereafter, JSLC).[55] The liability of a shareholder in an LLC is limited to the extent of their capital contributions, while the liability of a shareholder in a JSLC is limited to the extent of the shares subscribed by them. Only a JSLC can issue stocks to the public and trade on stock exchanges, according to the first section of the fifth chapter of *Company Law 2005*. Therefore, an LLC is analogous with private companies and a JSLC is analogous with public companies under common law jurisdictions. Both types of company are regulated by the same law, and the basic rights of shareholders are the same.[56]

---

53 Yan (n 34) 318.
54 The specific reasons behind each are not identical. It should also be noted that *Company Law 2005* was revised slightly in 2013 with some changes to its numbering. The articles cited in this book adopt the original numbering in order to keep the consistency unless the context explicitly indicates.
55 Article 3 of *Company Law 2005* stipulates: "shareholders of a company with limited liability shall assume liability towards the company to the extent of the capital contributions subscribed respectively by them; and the shareholders of a company limited by shares shall assume liability towards the company to the extent of the shares subscribed respectively by them".
56 For example, article 100 of *Company Law 2005* states: "the provisions regarding the authorities of the shareholders' meeting of a limited liability company as prescribed in the first paragraph of Article 38 of this Law shall apply to the shareholders' assembly of a joint stock limited company".

Pursuant to articles 37 and 99, the shareholders' meeting, either in an LLC or a JSLC, is the organ of power of the company, which shall exercise its functions and powers accordingly. That is to say, all the power in the company is exclusively generated from shareholders' meetings, which implies the managerial power of directors is conferred by the shareholders. Shareholders can exercise their governance rights through a shareholders' general meeting as the main platform. The powers of shareholders as a whole are stipulated by article 38, and include: (1) to decide on the operational policy and investment plan of the company; (2) to elect or replace directors and supervisors who are not representatives of the staff and workers, and to decide on matters concerning the remuneration of the directors and supervisors; (3) to examine and approve reports of the board of directors; (4) to examine and approve reports of the board of supervisors or the supervisors; (5) to examine and approve the annual financial budget plan and final accounts plan of the company; (6) to examine and approve the company's plans for profit distribution and for making up losses; (7) to adopt resolutions on the increase or reduction in the registered capital of the company; (8) to adopt resolutions on the issue of corporate bonds; (9) to adopt resolutions on the merger, division, dissolution, liquidation or transformation of the company; (10) to amend the articles of association of the company; and (11) other functions and powers provided for in the company's articles of association.[57] Furthermore, for listed companies, shareholder approval is needed for major asset transactions or certain types of guarantees.[58]

As discussed in the last chapter, only matters of director removal, constitutional changes, substantial property transactions, voluntary winding-up and a few other fundamental changes need shareholders' approval in the Anglo-American company law system.[59] In this regard, except for the power to (2) elect or replace directors, (5) examine and approve corporate annual accounts and (9) approve the merger, division, dissolution, liquidation or transformation of the company, the rest are difficult to match with the Western system.[60] In other words, Chinese company law bestows extensive powers to shareholders. Indeed, it would not be an overstatement to conclude that there are two decision-making organs in a typical Chinese company, namely the board of directors and the shareholders' meeting.

---

57 This also applies to shareholders of JSLC according to article 100 of *Company Law 2005*.
58 Article 122 of *Company Law 2005* states: "where a listed company purchases or sells major assets within one year, or the amount of guarantee exceeds 30 percent of its total assets, the matter shall be subject to resolution by the shareholders' general meeting, which shall be subject to adoption by the shareholders present who hold two-thirds or more of the voting rights".
59 For example, only the merger under the US law and disapplication of pre-emption rights and variation of class rights in UK law need shareholders' approval. Reinier Kraakman *et al.*, *The Anatomy of Corporate Law: A Comparative and Functional Approach* (3rd edn OUP, Oxford 2017) 50–51 and 172–174. Also see *supra* Chapter 3, sections 3.2.1 and 3.2.2.
60 Even as regards the election of directors, it is largely left to the board of directors to decide in the Anglo-American jurisdictions. For example, UK company law does not touch upon the issue of director appointment.

Though the board of directors is able to decide on the operational plans (*ji hua*) and investment programme (*fang an*) of the company,[61] the more important and strategic decisions such as operational policy (*fang zheng*) and the investment plan (*ji hua*) can only be decided by shareholders. It is generally recognised in the UK, the US and many other countries that the company should be managed by, or under the direction of, boards of directors as discussed in the last chapter; shareholders are not entitled to be directly involved in management. However, in contrast with shareholder rights in the UK or US, shareholders in Chinese companies are not only allowed to engage in corporate management, but also have substantial managerial powers.

More precisely, the shareholders' meeting is more than another decision-making organ: it has powers superior to those of the board of directors. If decisions of the shareholders' meeting and the board diverge, the board's decision would be seen as void and cannot go against the shareholders' decision. In fact, shareholders can give binding instructions to the board of directors and the latter is required to implement any resolution adopted by the shareholders' meeting.[62]

Apart from the powers to decide operational policy and investment plans, shareholders in China can also decide on the allocation of profits and dividends, which is exclusively the right of the board in Anglo-American countries and many other jurisdictions. It entitles shareholders to direct claims to cash flow as well as the control of its allocation. Moreover, powers to approve budget plans and decide on issues of corporate bonds, which are normally within the scope of the directors' authority, are again in the hands of shareholders in Chinese companies. Even the directors' remuneration is determined by shareholders instead of the board or its sub-committee in China.

The first clause of article 47 may further reflect the relationship between the shareholders and the board as the latter should report on its work to the former. Shareholders have the right to examine and approve reports of the board of directors apart from giving binding instructions.[63] On the other hand, the board of directors is more like an executive branch of the shareholders' meeting and its primary task is to implement shareholders' resolutions; almost all important managerial issues are dependent either on shareholders' decisions or approval.[64]

---

61 Article 47(3) of *Company Law 2005.*
62 Article 47(2) of *Company Law 2005.* From the wording we can know such a resolution can include both special and ordinary resolutions.
63 Article 34 of *Company Law 2005* also stipulates that shareholders have the right to inspect resolutions of the meetings of the board of directors.
64 Directors under *Company Law 2005* are required: (1) to convene the meeting of the shareholders' meeting, and to report on its work to the shareholders' meeting; (2) to implement the resolutions adopted by the shareholders' meeting; (3) to decide on the operational plans and investment plans of the company; (4) to draw up the annual financial budget plan and final accounts plan of the company; (5) to draw up plans for profit distribution and plans for making up losses of the company; (6) to draw up plans for the increase or reduction in the registered capital and the issue of corporate bonds of the company; (7) to draw up plans for the merger, division, dissolution and transformation of the company; (8) to decide on the establishment of the internal administrative bodies of the company;

Moreover, it is not infrequent for boards of directors to refer issues not speci-fied by the law or company constitutions to shareholders' meetings and to ask them for the final decision in practice. As discussed later, this can cause many serious problems.

Shareholders are entitled to inspect the resolutions of the board meeting in addition to the financial reports and accounting books, which ensures their access to accurate corporate information.[65] They can also ask directors to attend share-holders' meetings as non-voting participants and ask them tough questions.[66] Under certain circumstances, shareholders may request the court to rescind any board resolution.[67]

Shareholders who individually or jointly have more than 3 per cent of shares can make provisional shareholder proposals 10 days prior to the convening of the shareholders' meeting in order to counter directors' control of a meet-ing's agenda and content.[68] Shareholders above a certain threshold are entitled to propose an interim meeting.[69] In the case that a board of directors fails to

(9) to decide on the appointment or dismissal of the manager of the company and the matters concerning his remuneration, and upon recommendation of the manager, decide on the appointment or dismissal of the deputy manager(s) and persons in charge of the financial affairs of the company, and on the matters concerning their remuneration; (10) to formulate the basic management system of the company; and (11) to exercise other functions and powers stipulated by the company's articles of association. See article 47 of *Company Law 2005*. Also according to article 109 which regulates the JSLC, the provisions in article 47 on the functions of the board of directors of a limited liability company shall apply to that of the board of directors of a joint stock limited company.

65 Articles 34 and 98 of *Company Law 2005*. This is a quite extraordinary provision as common law countries usually prohibit shareholders from inspecting board decisions.

66 Article 151 of *Company Law 2005*.

67 Article 22 of *Company Law 2005* provides: "the resolution adopted by the shareholders' meeting or the shareholders' general meeting or the board of directors of a company, which in content violates laws or administrative regulations, shall be invalid. Where the procedures for convening the meet-ing of the shareholders' meeting or the shareholders' general meeting, or the board of directors, or the voting formulas are against laws, administrative regulations or the articles of association of a company, or the content of the resolution adopted is against the company's articles of association, the shareholders may, within 60 days from the date the resolution is adopted, request the people's court to rescind the resolution".

This provision and the provisions mentioned in the following paragraphs of this section are also designed to protect minority shareholders' interests by encouraging them to use their rights. Nevertheless, the insufficient system may impair the remedy mechanism of minority shareholders, which in turn could affect their use of rights. However, only the relationship between the directors and the shareholders would be focused on, as shareholders are considered as a whole.

68 Article 103 of *Company Law 2005* states: "a shareholder individually holding, or the sharehold-ers together holding, more than 3 per cent of the shares of the company may make provisional proposals and submit them in writing to the board of directors 10 days prior to the convening of the meeting of the shareholders' general meeting; and the board of directors shall notify the other shareholders of such proposals within two days from the date it receives the proposals and shall submit them to the shareholders' general meeting for deliberation".

69 In LLC, shareholders should represent 10 per cent or more of the voting rights, while in JSLC shareholders should individually or jointly hold more than 10 per cent of the company's shares. See articles 40 and 101 of *Company Law 2005*.

convene a shareholders' meeting, shareholders can convene and preside over the meeting on their own initiative.[70] If shareholders are not happy with directors, they can remove them in the general meeting or interim meeting before their tenure expires.[71] They can exit the company by selling shares in the open market or request the company to purchase their shares in certain circumstances.[72] Shareholders with more than 10 per cent of voting rights may even request a court to dissolve the company in deadlock according to article 183.

Shareholders can bring lawsuits against directors if their interests are damaged by directors' breach of duty. They can also bring lawsuits when a company's interests are damaged.[73] In practice, the wrongdoers may hold the majority of seats on the board or could influence the majority of the board; therefore they are unlikely to be sued for breach of duty by their own board on behalf of the company. However, under derivative action, a situation where a board refuses to bring a claim against its own board members can be rescued.[74] Directors are liable for compensation if they cause any loss to the company by violating laws, administrative regulations or the articles of association during the course of performing their duties.[75] Moreover, a restitution remedy is defined at the end of article 149, whereby the income of any director from any act in violation of the forbidden matters specified in this article shall be returned to the company.

---

70 In order for shareholders to convene the shareholders' meeting on their own initiative, the shareholders in LLC should represent 10 per cent or more of the voting rights and the shareholders in JSLC should individually or jointly have held more than 10 per cent of the company's shares for 90 or more consecutive days. See article 102 of *Company Law 2005*.

71 There can be many reasons, for example directors do not execute their resolution well, or sometimes shareholders just want the dishonest directors to leave quietly instead of having to sue them. According to article 104 of *Company Law 2005*, as long as more than half of the voting rights held by the shareholders present at the shareholders' meeting agree to do so, they can remove any director.

72 According to article 75 of *Company Law 2005*, under one of the following circumstances, where a shareholder votes against the resolution adopted by the shareholders' meeting, they may request the company to purchase their equity at a reasonable price: (1) the company fails to distribute its profits to the shareholders for five consecutive years, when it has been making profits for five years running and meets the conditions for distributing profits as is provided for by this law; (2) the company is to be merged or divided, or the principal part of its property is to be transferred; or (3) when the period of business stipulated by the company's articles of association expires or other situations originating the dissolution stipulated by the said articles of association arise, a resolution is adopted by the shareholders' meeting to revise the articles of association for the continued existence of the company. Article 143 also states that when a shareholder objects to the shareholder resolution on the merger or division of the company, they may request the company to purchase their shares.

73 In principle, if directors' behaviour is violating laws, administrative regulations or the articles of association, the shareholders of LLC, or the shareholders of JSLC individually or jointly having held 1 per cent or more of its shares for 180 or more consecutive days may request, in writing, that the board of supervisors or the supervisors of the company with limited liability where there is no such board, bring a lawsuit to a people's court. See article 152 of *Company Law 2005*.

74 Similar to the English law, shareholders can use their own name to bring a lawsuit to a court in the interests of the company.

75 Article 149 of *Company Law 2005*.

Last but not least, the widespread concentrated ownership structure means the board is even less autonomous.[76] In addition to the above legal requirements, controlling shareholders are able to impose their will on directors by their influence, *inter alia* threatening to remove them or reduce their remuneration. In short, shareholder approval and decision-making powers are much more widespread and influential in China.

4.2.2 Directors' duties

Apart from shareholder rights, directors' duties are undoubtedly another important way to reflect the position of shareholders. The more restraints on directors, the more powerful shareholders are. As shown in the last chapter, limiting directors' authority is indeed a way of empowering shareholders. For the first time in Chinese law, article 148 of the *Company Law 2005* introduced the duty of loyalty (*zhong shi yi wu*) into company law, stipulating that directors shall comply with laws, administrative regulations and articles of association. Similar to fiduciary duties in the UK and US, directors shall bear the duties of loyalty and diligence to the company.[77]

The law also provides comparatively detailed content on the duty of loyalty. Pursuant to the second half of article 148 and article 149, a director is prohibited from: accepting any bribe or other illegal gains by taking advantage of their position, or encroaching on the property of the company; misappropriating funds of the company; depositing the company's funds into an account in their own name or in any other individual's name; loaning the company's funds to others or providing any guarantee to any other person by using the company's property in violation of the articles of association without the consent of the shareholders' general meeting or board of directors; signing a contract or trading with the company by violating the articles of association or without the consent of the shareholders' general meeting or shareholders' meeting; seeking business opportunities for themselves or any other person by taking advantage of their authority, or operating for themselves or for any other person any similar business of the company they work for without the consent of the shareholders' meeting; taking

---

76 China is characterised with a concentrated ownership structure for both historical and political reasons. Although most large companies have been transformed from the original SOEs, the state still holds the majority of shares after they were changed into corporate form. Yan (n 34) 313. Generally speaking, the concentrated corporate ownership system seen in, for example, Germany, would effectively restrain agency and short-horizon costs among other negative aspects as a result of the dispersed ownership structure. But the potential for conflict between majority and minority shareholders is increased. As a result, the foremost conflict manifested in China as in many other East Asian countries, is between controlling shareholders and other shareholders rather than between managers and shareholders.

77 According to article 148 of *Company Law 2005*, the duty of loyalty also applies to supervisors and senior managers, which reinforces shareholder protection even further by enlarging the scope of application of the fiduciary duty. However, for simplicity and consistency, the duties of directors, supervisors and senior managers are simplified into directors' duties.

commissions on the transactions between others and the company; and disclosing the company's secrets without permission. Furthermore, article 148(8) as a catch-all provision which encompasses all other acts that are inconsistent with the duty of loyalty to the company. This inexhaustible list allows the court to "go beyond the strictures of specified proscription" when deciding whether the duty of loyalty is breached, thereby making it a fundamental duty.[78] In other words, *Company Law 2005* forbids self-dealing, usurpation of corporate opportunities and misappropriation, among other conflicts of interests. Directors are not allowed to pursue any forms of self-interest at the expense of the company and its shareholders.

Article 148 also states that directors have a duty of diligence (*qin mian yi wu*) to the company, but the law fails to specify this duty. Similar to the duty of loyalty, however, *CSRC Guidelines for Articles of Association of Chinese Listed Companies* defines the duty of diligence. Article 98 of the *Guidelines* states:

> A director should comply with the law, administrative regulations, and these articles. He has the following duties of due diligence towards the company: (1) should be careful, serious and diligent in exercising his authorities conferred by the company, in order to ensure that the business activities of the company comply with the nation's law, administrative regulations and various economic policy requirements of the nation. The business activities cannot exceed the scope of activities specified by the business licence; (2) should treat all shareholders fairly; (3) should understand at all times the operation and management circumstances of the company business; (4) should sign confirmation opinions on the periodic reports of the company. He should ensure that the information disclosed by the company is true, accurate, and complete; (5) should truthfully supply relevant circumstances and information to the supervisory board, and not interfere with the exercising of duties by the supervisory board or supervisors; and (6) other due diligence duties specified by the law, administrative regulations, department regulations and these articles.[79]

From a strictly legal perspective, directors owe fiduciary duties to the company. In China, however, it is with unique Chinese characteristics. According to article

---

78 Rebecca Lee, 'Fiduciary Duty without Equity: "Fiduciary Duties" of Directors under the Revised Company Law of the PRC' (2007) 47 *Virginia Journal of International Law* 897, 907. *2014 CSRC Guidelines for Articles of Association of Chinese Listed Companies* equally emphasise the duty of loyalty. The meaning of article 97 of the *Guidelines* is almost exactly the same as articles 148 and 149 of *Company Law 2005*.

79 According to the actual circumstances, companies can increase due diligence duties towards company directors in these articles. Alex Lau, 'The First Complete English Version of the 2006 CSRC Guidelines for Articles of Association of Chinese Listed Companies: Part 2 – Shareholders and Meetings' (2008) 19 *International Company and Commercial Law Review* 119, 128–129. Article 98 of the revised Guidelines in 2014 remains the same.

47 of *Company Law 2005*, the board of directors is required to be accountable to the shareholders' meeting, which implies shareholders enjoy a central and more important position in China's corporate governance system.

4.3 Shareholder wealth maximisation in China

4.3.1 Ascertaining the corporate objective

Historically, private property rights in China were disregarded, not to mention shareholder rights and the like. Even after PRC was established, traditional SOEs were more likely to function as government organisations or their affiliates. This suggests no independent corporate objective was needed because the objectives were almost equivalent to the plans and aims of the government. But the situation changed with the government's gradual withdrawal from traditional SOEs and the introduction of modern enterprise reform – that is, corporatisation of SOEs. The viewpoint then generally evolved to one in which companies should be run for shareholder interests, which is now the prevailing belief in China.

It is argued that the *Company Law 1993* set down "the maximization of owners' interests as the primary goal of corporate practice".[80] But after reading all 230 provisions, there is no explicit expression of pursuing shareholder wealth maximisation. By contrast, its first article clearly states that the law is to protect the legitimate interests of the company, shareholder and creditor in order to maintain economic order and foster the development of the socialist market economy.[81] Even in the 2005 *Company Law*, which is generally believed to improve shareholder protection in substance, the legislative purpose is almost the same as in the previous law.[82] At the very least, the shareholder is not the only priority management should take into account pursuant to the statute.[83]

Nevertheless, it is argued that shareholders of China's companies are able to claim "assets' benefits".[84] Specifically, article 4 of *Company Law 2005* states: "shareholders of a company shall, in accordance with law, enjoy such rights as benefiting from the assets of the company". It is clear that corporate property is distinguished from its members' personal property; corporate assets only belong to the company itself. Given that shareholders are allowed to reap the benefits of those assets, it might suggest that shareholders are the owners of the company

---

80 Kang, Shi and Brown (n 36) 7.
81 As discussed elsewhere, even the interests of shareholders collectively are different from the company's interests.
82 Article 1 of *Company Law 2005* specifies: "this Law is enacted for the purposes of regulating the organization and operation of companies, protecting the legitimate rights and interests of companies, shareholders and creditors, maintaining the socialist economic order, and promoting the development of the socialist market economy".
83 As emphasised in Chapter 2, the interests of the company are different from the interests of shareholders due to the different risk-preference and modern financial derivatives among others.
84 OECD, *Corporate Governance of Listed Companies in China* (OECD Publishing, 2011) 33.

which holds all those assets in its name. In fact, at the moment, most people, including corporate lawyers in China, believe that shareholders should be indisputably the owner of companies and thereby have full control.[85] If shareholders continue to be regarded as the owner in law, the issue of searching for corporate objective would be largely simplified, since proprietors of the property are certainly entitled to maximise the value and utility of their own belongings in the light of the traditional proprietorship justification.[86]

Despite the specification in article 4 of the revised *Company Law* in 2005 that "the shareholders of a company shall be entitled to enjoy the capital proceeds, participate in making important decisions, choose managers and enjoy other rights", it may not necessarily indicate shareholders are the *owners of the company*.[87] Pursuant to the legal person theory, a company, or at least an incorporated company, is an independent person in law distinct from any of its members who establish it, and the corporate property is also distinct from the property of any of its members or the aggregate of its members.[88] Shareholders are entitled to the *assets' benefits* under China's company law, and thus, at least as a whole, may be seen to continue to have some ownership right to the company. However, in reality, it should be the shares possessed by shareholders which enable them to reap the profits of the increased value of the company. If any ownership right exists, it should be rigidly limited to ownership of shares, which are an independent item of financial property and autonomous from corporate assets. Shareholders are only owners of shares and have no direct proprietary rights against the property of the company.[89] Indeed, the separate legal personality has become the foundation of modern company law. Corporate separate personality suggests a company is both the legal and the beneficial owner of its property. In short, a company as an independent legal person *as such* is completely free to have its own objectives.[90]

Among the rules in company law, directors' fiduciary duties could be viewed as the most direct expression of the behavioural norm of directors, which specify

85 Chapter 2 has proved that the traditional ownership concept of the company in academia is no longer the justification for shareholder primacy as companies have independent legal personality under modern company law. However, for the general public including professionals, shareholders are still regarded as the owners of the company, therefore the company should be run for their interests. Investors may also feel that they are the owners and that they are thereby entitled to control rights, which may also contribute to the problem.

86 *Supra* Chapter 2, section 2.2.1.

87 However, it should be noticed that shareholders are recognised by the *Code of Corporate Governance for Listed Companies in China* (2002) as the owner of the company. Although, this *Code* is just a departmental regulation and cannot override the law, it is not difficult to see the embedded viewpoint of the position of shareholders in contemporary China. This will be discussed in detail.

88 *Supra* Chapter 2 footnotes 34–44 and accompanying text.

89 Ibid.

90 The company is able to have a will and this is recognised by law. For example, a company can be held criminally liable where *mens rea* is required. Section 30 of *Criminal Law of the People's Republic of China* states: "any company . . . that commits an act that endangers society, which is prescribed by law as a crime committed by an institution, shall bear criminal responsibility".

what they should and should not do. Of greater significance is the underlying legislative purpose of the corporate objective, namely for whose interests should the directors serve those duties. Take the UK, for example: section 172(1) of the *Companies Act 2006* expressly requires directors to act in good faith and to try their best to promote the success of the company for the benefits of its members. Thus, in order to act in the best interests of the company, the directors must avoid conflicts of interest and abide by fiduciary obligations. From a strictly legal perspective, directors only owe duties to the company, not to shareholders as individuals.[91] As discussed earlier, the revised *Company Law* in 2005 raised a similar provision in China for the first time. Article 148 stipulates that directors of a company shall assume the duties of loyalty and diligence to the company. Apparently, according to this provision, such *duty of loyalty* is aimed at the company rather than the shareholders, neither individually nor collectively. However, the board of directors in China is required to be accountable to the shareholders' body. CSRC interprets this duty into the design to mainly protect the interests of the company as well as its shareholders.[92] The *Listed Company Director Selection and Conduction Guidance* and *Guidelines on Conduct of Corporate Directors of SME Board Listed Companies* by the Shenzhen Stock Exchange goes further by stating that directors shall be loyal to their company and shareholders' interests.[93]

The interests of a company are nevertheless different from the collective interests of shareholders, as the latter can diversify idiosyncratic risk whilst the former cannot. If directors are required to act solely in the interests of shareholders, then only systematic risks would be considered, leaving the company vulnerable to idiosyncratic risks. Furthermore, Professor Ireland explains that the interest of company is "an interest in the productive utilization of industrial capital" oriented towards "[long-term] prosperity and security of a block of industrial capital assets", whilst the interests of shareholders are "a money capital interest in the revenue generated by . . . industrial capital" aimed at "short-term maximisation of the return on a money capital investment".[94] Not to mention the fact that through modern financial arrangements, it is not impossible for shareholders to alienate their personal interests from their shares.[95] Therefore, even though directors are required to run a company for the best interests of the company and shareholders, it is not equivalent to the statement that a company should only or primarily serve shareholder wealth maximisation.

---

91 *Percival v. Wright* [1902] 2 Ch 421 clearly shows directors' duties are not owed to the shareholders individually. Also see Simon Goulding, *Principles of Company Law* (Routledge, Oxford 1996) 223; Geoffrey Morse, *Charlesworth's Company Law* (17th edn Sweet & Maxwell, London 2005) 297–298.

92 OECD, *Corporate Governance of Listed Companies in China* (OECD Publishing, 2011) 77.

93 See article 4 of *Guidelines on Conduct of Corporate Directors of SME Board Listed Companies.*

94 Paddy Ireland, 'Corporate Governance, Stakeholding, and the Company: Toward a Less Degenerate Capitalism' (1996) 23 *Journal of Law and Society* 287, 304 and 308. For more discussion see *supra* Chapter 2, section 2.4.1.

95 Take hedge funds, for example, they may not care about the decline in share price as it is possible for them to profit from the bad performance. Especially when they sell the shares short, a decline in the share price rather than an increase is desired. *Supra* Chapter 2, section 2.3.2.

However, the fact that the shareholders' general meeting is regarded as the power organ with extensive managerial rights, could be a strong indication of shareholders' superior position, although it is not possible to identify SWM directly from the law per se. In other words, as long as the board is subordinated to the shareholders' body, it is difficult to imagine the board impartially making an optimal corporate decision after balancing various corporate stakeholders' interests.[96]

Leaving aside company law for a moment, the most direct evidence of the objective of *Corporate China* can be found in China's first corporate governance code – the *Code of Corporate Governance for Listed Companies in China 2002* (hereafter, *Code*). Article 86 of the *Code* states:

> While maintaining the listed company's development and maximising the benefits of shareholders, the company shall be concerned with the welfare, environmental protection and public interests of the community in which it resides, and shall pay attention to the company's social responsibility.

Although this provision is under the chapter entitled "stakeholder", the term "maximising the benefits of shareholders" strongly shows what the corporate objective is considered to be. Besides, article 8 of *Measures for the Administration of the Takeover of Listed Companies* provides that the decisions made and the measures taken by the board of directors of the target company for takeover shall be beneficial for maintaining the interests of the company and shareholders. Furthermore, shareholders continue to be deemed to be the owners of companies in China, as opposed to the legal person theory among general modern corporate law principles. As previously discussed, according to the *Code*, "as the owner of a company, the shareholder shall enjoy the legal rights stipulated by laws, administrative regulations and the company's articles of association".[97] So although they are only departmental regulations promulgated and implemented by CSRC to focus on listed companies and cannot override statutory law and governmental rules,[98] the predominant position of the shareholder in contemporary China can be easily identified in spite of the fact that the laws do not expressly indicate that the company should be managed for shareholder wealth maximisation.

The shareholders' general meeting is regarded as the organ of power of a company and shareholders have extensive powers such as the right to give binding instructions; it is therefore a straightforward matter to identify the primary position of shareholders in the corporate governance system. Inasmuch as the

---

96 Compared with the board of directors in the UK and US who has a more independent status as discussed in Chapter 3, the dependent board in a typical Chinese company is more likely to have a lopsided focus on shareholders' interests even at the expense of other stakeholders or the interests of the company as a whole.

97 Article 1 of *Code of Corporate Governance for Listed Companies in China*.

98 Articles 79 of *Legislation Law of PRC*.

shareholders' body has powers superior to the board of directors,[99] directors' decision-making will inevitably depend upon either shareholders' final say or approval. In other words, shareholders as a whole are able to tell directors of boards what to do or not do, which certainly includes maximising their interests. It is difficult to resist the pressure of maximising shareholder interests in such a situation. As a result, the objective of China's companies could be defined as a practical shareholder-centred approach.[100]

The general opinion of corporate participants can also largely influence directors' ultimate decision-making. For instance, during a period when shareholder status or rights are not recognised by most corporate participants or the general public, directors may not be confronted with the trouble of maximising shareholder interests at all. In contrast, if the general opinion is dominated by the shareholder-centred ideology, then any directors' behaviour that deviates from such a general standpoint will not be tolerated, at least from a moral perspective. Consequently, directors who usually prefer a peaceful life and avoiding troubles may be affected by such a general opinion.[101] In fact, the concept of shareholders and their role has been gradually accepted after continuous enterprise reform and study of Western best corporate governance practice. The general opinion at present is shareholder-centred. As Professors Tomasic and Andrews's empirical work shows, a prevailing answer to the question of the dominant stakeholder in the company is the majority shareholder.[102] The controlling or majority shareholders are viewed as most important, which means priority is usually given to this group and its demands should be satisfied first. Though the state (i.e. government) remains a significant factor in most large companies, it is now due in an increasingly large part to its majority shareholdings rather than its administrative/political influence as before. Furthermore, the frequent practice by the government, as the controlling shareholder, of pursuing goals differing from other shareholders is generally believed to be a corporate governance problem which is not compliant with modern governance theories. Collectivism is no longer an indisputable belief in China. Neither is it difficult to find many senior executives or directors expressing the view of shareholder wealth maximisation.

Corporate participants and even the majority of ordinary people in China nowadays would agree that the company is established by shareholders and hence should be run for their interests. It would become morally correct for

---

99 *Supra* Chapter 4, section 4.2.

100 It becomes more obvious when considering the relationship between the body of shareholders and the board of directors. Ibid.

101 Marianne Bertrand and Sendhil Mullainathan 'Enjoying the Quiet Life Corporate Governance and Managerial Preference' (2003) 111 *Journal of Political Economy* 1043, 1043. In particular, the concept of harmony in China plays a significant role.

102 However, it should be noted that the state is most likely to be a majority shareholder in those transforming SOEs and consequently needs to be emphasised. Roman Tomasic and Neil Andrews, 'Minority Shareholder Protection in China's Top 100 Listed Companies'(2007) 9 *Australian Journal of Asian Law* 88, 96–97.

individuals to make corporate decisions only for the maximisation of shareholder wealth even at the expense of others. The general public would also accept that the first priority of the company is for the benefit of shareholders. For instance, a redundancy simply for immediately boosting share prices would likely not garner much criticism. Under such circumstances, it would be hard for directors to resist the pressure to maximise shareholder wealth; in other words, directors are encouraged to do so even by externalising negative costs to other corporate stakeholders.[103]

In short, although company law itself does not expressly tell us what the corporate objective is, many subordinated regulations show a bias towards shareholders. More importantly, the power allocation and relationship between shareholders and directors, departmental regulation and the general opinion of corporate participants more directly show an inclination towards shareholder wealth maximisation. It is not difficult to conclude that directors place shareholders' interests in a central position when making corporate decisions.

4.3.2 The rationale behind

The question remains: why is SWM appealing in contemporary China? The tradition of ignoring shareholder rights and the influence of SWM in the UK and US precipitates the increasingly urgent demand for shareholder-centred corporate law and governance structures in China. Individual property rights have long been unacknowledged. Until the 2004 amendment to the *Constitution of the People's Republic of China* stipulating that the legal private property of citizens is inviolable and China's first *Property Law* in 2007, the private property rights of individuals were not statutorily recognised or admitted.[104] The absence of effective shareholder protection, as well as the increasingly significant role of investment from private sectors for overall economic growth, has led both academics[105] and policy-makers – including legislators – to emphasise investor protection in the corporate law field. Accordingly, the following paragraphs focus on real situations of ownership rights and control at various stages in order to ascertain their effect on the corporate objective in China. In addition to the very important historical influence, political, legal, economic and other factors are each discussed.

---

103 *Supra* Chapter 2, section 2.4.2.
104 However, it should be noted that according to article 11 of China's first *Constitution* in 1954, "the state protects the right of citizens to own lawfully earned income, savings, houses and other means of subsistence". Ironically, article 12 even mentioned that the state protects the rights of citizens to inherit private property, but the private property *as such* was not legally recognised until the twenty-first century.
105 For example, it is argued that the majority of academic research in the field of corporate law and corporate governance in China focuses on shareholder protection, either from the shareholder-management perspective or the majority-minority shareholder perspective. Kang, Shi and Brown (n 36) 2.

Historical influences

The development of corporate forms, as discussed in the first section of this chapter, described the role of shareholders and different types of control over firms in different stages. Accordingly, bureaucratic control, managing director's control and state control can be identified. Their advantages and disadvantages are discussed here in order to determine their effect on shareholder-centred ideology.

(1) *Bureaucratic control.* A remarkable feature of the companies in the late Qing Dynasty was government interference. From the *guan ban* (government management) to *guan du shang ban* (government supervision and merchant management) and *guan shang he ban* (joint government-merchant management), government prevailed everywhere in corporate activities. Regarding non-government investors, whilst they could obtain certain privileges and sponsorship from government, such as customs exemption or tax deferment, individual investors including their representatives were powerless in practice. Under the structure of *guan du shang ban*, government was able to control the firm. It was impossible for individual investors, or say merchants, to claim any rights against government officials in the company, despite the fact that capital for funding the firm was completely contributed by those individual investors. Under the structure of *guan shang he ban*, although individual shareholder rights were supposed to be explicitly written in the agreement with the government beforehand, such an arrangement never practically worked and the managerial power remained in the hands of governmental representatives. It was recorded that for the non-government shareholders, fighting for rights against government was just like "striking rocks with eggs".[106]

Notwithstanding that government involvement can bring benefits from direct financial subsides to indirect policy support, the disadvantages were apparently greater without a set of mature institutions to curb the government's power. Corruption, limited managerial autonomy by private investors and more fatally the potentially different agendas between the government and merchants could definitely impede or even destroy the incentive to invest. Shareholders as a whole could not control the company they invested in.[107] In short, there were neither managerial autonomy nor shareholder rights during this period.

(2) *Managing director's control.* The failure of the above three models demonstrated that bureaucratic involvement could not succeed and a new form – *shang ban* (merchant management) occurred. This time the company was mainly managed by the private "owners" or their representatives. The *Company Law 1904* (*gong si lü*) and other related regulations for incorporation of private companies

---

106 Fairbank and Liu (n 8) 434.

107 Shareholders were seen as the owners of the company. In this regard, shareholders cannot control the company they "own".

facilitated individual investors, for the first time, to realise they could claim rights and obtain legal protection in accordance with the law, although in practice the law did not function well. The weak position of minority shareholders and the conflicts between founder-directors and their fellow shareholders then substituted the old problem of government interference. First, shareholders without leverage could not challenge the founder/managing directors. Second, even if a managing director did not possess majority ownership, he could utilise the institutional structure and interpersonal relationships to retain control.

A common practice for private business then became to receive fixed and guaranteed interest payments for equity investment. Despite the lack of a concept of dual-class shares or preferred shares at the time, such creditor-like rights for investors were very popular.[108] *Dasheng Corporation*, one of the most successful companies during its time, had to pay shareholders 8 per cent interest on their share investment.[109] This phenomenon is easier to understand after examining the unfavourable situation for shareholders. Though the government gradually relinquished control, managerial power ultimately dropped into the hands of company founders rather than shareholders as a whole. The founder would usually be a managing director and exert substantial control and influence even without possessing a majority of shareholdings. Pursuant to historical documents from the local archives, even after introducing the annual shareholder general meeting by promulgating the *Company Law 1904*, the original corporate governance structure, which was characterised by the dominance of managing directors, remained the same to a great extent.[110] Logically, due to the inability of minority shareholders and incoming investors to practically participate in corporate management by utilising their voting power, they could anticipate obtaining dividends, without which investing in a company would be senseless. Therefore, the significance of having a fixed and high dividend was self-evident. Meanwhile, such a design could partly constrain the behaviour of controlling shareholders, who were usually managing directors at the same time, since the risks of failing to satisfy the fixed dividend always existed if they deviated too much from enhancing corporate values. The high debt-equity ratio might then have been the only effective deterrent against managerial unaccountability because of the paralysis of the market for corporate control[111] and inadequate minority shareholder protection.

The situation of ownership rights in this second stage was distinguished by the managing directors' control; non-founder shareholders or minority shareholders were unable to effectively play a role in corporate governance.

108 Goetzmann and Köll (n 4) 168.

109 Elisabeth Köll, *From Cotton Mill to Business Empire: The Emergence of Regional Enterprises in Modern China* (Harvard University Asia Center, Harvard 2003) 130.

110 Nantong Municipal Archives (*nan tong shi dang an guan*) quoted in Goetzmann and Köll (n 4) 167.

111 This is largely because no active securities market existed during that time.

Although the fixed and comparatively high dividends were to a certain degree a remedy for powerless shareholder rights, the founder entrepreneur, controlling shareholder and managing director, who often overlapped, dominated the management of the company.

(3) *State control.* Since the establishment of PRC, there have been two stages of state control. The first was that the state gradually obtained the entire ownership of all the major industrial companies around the country along with the so-called socialist transformation after 1949. Private sectors of the economy were almost eliminated during this stage. The state directly ran SOEs with highly centralised planning and control, and people became accustomed to a system without clear-cut boundaries between the government and enterprises.[112] The second stage was the reforming period, in which former SOEs started to recruit capital from private investors, leading to the co-existence of public and private ownership. The state as the majority owner or through its political influence other than usual voting power dominated companies with multiple ownership structures. By virtue of the different or even competing agendas from time to time, private or minority shareholders were doomed to be expropriated.

In general, similar to the above discussed bureaucratic control, no meaningful shareholder rights existed in the first stage. After traditional SOEs began to recruit private capital, the expropriation of minority shareholders was highlighted. The crucial role of shareholders, especially investors from private sectors, and their protection became prominent.

(4) *Analysis.* Since private investors were allowed to take part in industrial companies in the late Qing Dynasty, government either directly controlled or closely interfered in corporate management. As demonstrated, in both forms of *guan du shang ban* and *guan shang he ban*, ownership and control were separated. The situation whereby "ownership of wealth without appreciable control and control of wealth without appreciable ownership", as Berle and Means characterised American corporations in the early twentieth century, was only partly true here, because it was not led by the rapid and extensive concentration of economic power of the modern corporate form and the subsequently increasing dispersion of shareholdings in those companies. Although investors, principally merchants at the time, subscribed to the shares of the company, they could not gain control owing to the fact that the control right was usurped by the government. This situation can be termed *mandatory separation of ownership and control.* Not surprisingly, the most urgent needs under this context were that shareholders could effectively exert their shareholder rights based on their equity rights without interference from the government and its representatives.

Subsequent to government withdrawal from companies, control rights of the company returned to shareholders. In particular, the *Company Law 1904* set up the shareholder general meeting and other related rules, providing an

---

112 For example, see Jinglian Wu, 'China's Economic Reform: Past, Present and Future' (2000) 1 *Perspectives* at www.oycf.org/Perspectives2/5_043000/china.htm [accessed 1 November 2012].

opportunity for China's corporate forms to develop in a way similar to those of the UK or US. Nevertheless, not all shareholders could enjoy such rights; the control relinquished by the government was transferred to majority shareholders, or to be more precise the founder/managing director. These founders/ managing directors usually held a large proportion of shareholdings, but did not necessarily account for the majority. In *Dasheng No.1 Mill* for example, 553 shareholders subscribed to the outstanding stocks, among which Zhang Jian, the founder and managing director, as well as his family only held 6.4 per cent of total equity; the largest single shareholder held 4 per cent and the shareholdings of the next 17 shareholders varied from 2.4 per cent to 1.3 per cent.[113] It clearly exhibits that dispersed shareholdings did exist in some measure at that time.

Again, it can hardly be categorised into the classic separation of ownership and control as the founder/managing director normally possesses a not insignificant percentage of shareholdings. Even as far as Berle and Means's classification of control[114] is concerned, by virtue of the complexity of control by the founder/managing director there is no one single type suited for such control. The founder/managing director may have almost complete ownership or majority ownership, but he could also retain control by means of a particular institutional structure and social network when he becomes a minority shareholder. In the latter situation, legal devices such as pyramiding of holding companies, non-voting stock or voting trusts are not necessarily used to obtain or maintain control. Instead, inefficient, and usually intentionally designed, corporate structures could lead to the outcome that other shareholders' voices cannot be effectively expressed or heard. Furthermore, the enormous influence of the founder/managing director and their family plays a more decisive role. Manifestly, the chief desire of all shareholders except the controlling one – most likely the founder or managing director or both simultaneously – is equitable shareholder rights. At the same time, it is clear that the founder/managing director's control is distinct from the foregoing where the control is seized by government which has no ownership at all; this situation can be called *unclassifiable separation of ownership and control* because the ownership and control is partly separated and partly unified.

Separation of ownership and control may not be the magic solution to corporate governance problems that many Chinese scholars believe it to be.[115]

---

113 Goetzmann and Köll (n 4) 173.
114 In their classic book *The Modern Corporation and Private Property*, Berle and Means classify the control into five major types, including: 1) control through almost complete ownership, 2) majority control, 3) control through legal device without majority control, 4) minority control and 5) management control. Adolf Berle and Gardiner Means, *The Modern Corporation and Private Property* (Transaction Publishers, New Brunswick 1991, originally published 1932) 67–84.
115 Professor Donald Clarke aptly points out: "much Chinese commentary continues to view the separation of ownership from control not as a regrettable concomitant of the division of labor between suppliers and managers of capital, but as a positive good to be pursed for its own sake because it appears to be a necessary feature of the modern enterprise system". Donald Clarke, 'Corporate Governance in China: An Overview' (2003) 14 *China Economic Review* 494, 498.

In fact, by and large, the dispersed ownership structure is also regarded as superior to the concentrated one not only in China but globally.[116] However, its absence is not necessarily a bad thing or doomed to be associated with negative corporate performance. For instance, large shareholdings under the concentrated ownership structure are often deemed helpful in lowering so-called agency costs between shareholders and management because of the added incentive and effectiveness to monitor; this could help ensure managerial accountability and constrain potential divergence of interests. The frequent controlling block in countries with good quality laws like Germany and Sweden implies the vitality of the concentrated ownership structure. In contrast, the *mandatory and unclassifiable separation of ownership and control* cannot be said to be having a generally positive effect on corporate performance, as examined earlier.

However, it is not impossible that China's companies would develop a West-style structure naturally during this period, since the expansion and further development of a company requires more money from the wider public. Take the above-mentioned *Dasheng Corporation* for example: the founder/managing director was finally forced to give up control and alter the original institutional structure in order to acquire the urgently needed capital to overcome the crisis in the 1920s. But the nationalisation initiated in the late 1920s checked and suppressed such a possibility. The government gradually acquired vast majority ownership of industrial companies and, of course, their control. Once again, the arena for private investors was restricted.

Similarly, the first three decades of the post-1949 period repeated the history of both the beginning of the Late Qing Dynasty as well as the late Republican era, in which the state acquired almost complete control over the national economy through large-scale socialist transformation. The decision-making powers of enterprises were entirely in the hands of the state, enterprises were run no differently from government units, and thus there was no incentive or even necessity for a corporate governance system to exist. The state was the sole shareholder and controlled every aspect of the operation of companies. Even when private-sector actors were allowed to enter into traditional SOEs following a series of reforms, they were in the minority and were without question powerless. By virtue of divergence and lack of legal protection, among other things, the yearning to improve the status of shareholders is not surprising at all.

This distinct corporate evolution boosts the current focus on shareholders' roles and their power. As a result of being dismissed and ignored historically, to the detriment of corporate development, these rights have now become more valuable and shareholders are expected to play a larger role.

116 For example, see Ronald Gilson, 'Controlling Shareholders and Corporate Governance: Complicating the Comparative Taxonomy' (2006) 119 *Harvard Law Review* 1641, 1647–1648.

Legal factors and enforcement problems

Law and associated institutions always have a material impact which cannot be ignored. Though shareholders in China nowadays have extensive managerial power, as the above section shows, the rights, including many remedies, often lack specific guidelines. For example, with regard to the restitution remedy, there are no details specifying how such a right should be exercised or who can exercise it.[117] The vagueness of provisions on the remedy is easy to identify.[118] In a civil-law-based jurisdiction, without any case law tradition, many uncertainties exist. A general principle may not solve a practical problem, and a loophole can easily be found by potentially unaccountable directors.[119]

Setting aside the historic lack of an effective legal system for shareholder protection, from a legal perspective in present-day China, courts and judges are criticised for a lack of independence as they are appointed by corresponding levels of governments. Chinese judges generally lack competence and most are not trained to interpret the law broadly or innovatively in order to fill the gap left by incomplete laws. In addition, judges have limited powers in legal interpretation.[120] As a civil law country, Chinese legislators prefer a generally rigid and unequivocal standard to a vague and open one.[121] So, from the outset, judges are not expected to play an innovative role in filling the gaps. Indeed, judges in China are inclined to adopt a more restrictive approach and strictly follow the legislation. Meanwhile, if about to face difficult or sensitive cases, courts often refuse to accept them from the start.[122] Therefore, it is difficult to expect judges to remain impartial when the government is involved as one party. The courts, as Professor Donald Clarke argues, are not powerful enough from the political perspective and as a result are "reluctant to take cases involving large sums of money and powerful defendants".[123]

The Supreme Court even forbade lower courts from accepting securities-related claims as class actions.[124] Whilst there was a number of securities frauds

---

117 Guangdong Xu *et al.*, 'Directors' Duties in China' (2013) 14 *European Business Organization Law Review* 57, 61. In fact, apart from the question of whether there are effective ways to remedy the damages caused by the directors or their executives, the enforcement system also substantially determines the level of shareholders' status in reality.

118 Ibid. 73.

119 Even though a shareholder could win the case in due course, the cost of uncertainty alone may deter an aggrieved shareholder from using a formal means of litigation to remedy directors' breach of duty.

120 Randall Peerenboom, *China's Long March toward Rule of Law* (CUP, Cambridge 2002) 317.

121 There is no case law or precedents to be followed either, as China does not accept case law.

122 Benjamin Liebman, 'China's Courts: Restricted Reform' (2007) 191 *The China Quarterly* 620, 637.

123 As will be discussed below, very limited securities-related cases were accepted by the courts until the beginning of the twenty-first century. Clarke, 'Corporate Governance in China' (n 115) 503.

124 *Supreme People's Court Notice on the Temporary Ban on Acceptance of Securities Related Civil Compensation Cases* (21 September 2001). Katharina Pistor and Chenggang Xu, 'Governing Stock Markets in Transition Economies: Lessons from China' (2005) 7 *American Law and Economics Review* 184, 192.

and illegal insider trading cases, the infringed investors were not able to sue the wrongdoers because the court did not accept cases concerning securities at all until 2002. The Supreme People's Court then amended its previous decree to authorise local courts to accept cases of civil compensation caused by false financial disclosure. Nevertheless, the judiciary action still depends on the pre-condition of the administrative action by CSRC – that is, CSRC must first make a penalty decision after initiating an investigation, and the court would then accept the case.[125] Later amendments, especially the revised *Company Law* and *Securities Law* in 2005, mean investor protection has been continuously enhanced and the court can now independently determine whether or not to accept a securities-related case with an expanding judiciary scope; however, investors' fears and desires regarding independent and effective legal protection are self-evident. Few cases are filed. The imbalance between effort and gain may explain this result since a typical case takes approximately two and a half years, and the reward for winning the lawsuit is insubstantial.[126]

In addition to the impact of the court, the legal enforcement mechanism remains problematic at present. Some commentators have rightfully criticised the Chinese legal system as being merely symbolic; it sometimes resembles lip ser-vice rather than something to be genuinely enforced.[127] It is notable that on the one hand, shareholders have extensive rights which make them more powerful than their counterparts in the UK and US, but on the other, there are no corre-sponding remedies or enforcement mechanisms in place. Worse still, enforcement problems may further deteriorate the efficacy of the remedies. Professor La Porta and his co-authors correctly point out that "a strong system of legal enforcement could substitute for weak rules since active and well-functioning courts can step in and rescue investors abused by the management".[128] By the same token, a weak enforcement system could compromise strong rules. If directors' duties are dif-ficult to enforce, or say the breach is difficult to remedy, there is a risk that these duties will regress to a merely educative function. In other words, although share-holders as a whole have extensive powers in China, when their rights are harmed, the remedy mechanism is not satisfactory. There is no guarantee for shareholders to implement their extensive rights in the real business world. In fact, there have been limited cases since the new law came into effect in 2006.[129] An ineffective enforcement system also increases investors' desire for self-protection. It would also be understandable for them to care about their own interests, which might be difficult to rescue when infringed. Partly because of the weak legal protection

---

125 In other words, a precondition of the administrative action is needed prior to courts taking any action. Kang, Shi and Brown (n 36) 21.
126 For more discussions, see Xu *et al.* (n 117) 76–77.
127 Roman Tomasic and Jane Fu, 'Legal Regulation and Corporate Governance in China's Top 100 Listed Companies'(2006) 27 *Company Lawyer* 278, 284.
128 Rafael la Porta *et al.*, 'Law and Finance' (1998) 106 *Journal of Political Economy* 1113, 1140.
129 A recent study of directors' duties shows there were only 40 cases regarding breach of duty of loyalty and 4 cases regarding breach of duty of diligence from 2006 to 2012. Xu *et al.* (n 117) 64.

of investors in China, more attention and efforts are accordingly directed to this area. Whilst there is obviously a long way for China's legal system to go in order to improve its entire legal environment, investor protection and shareholder rights are continually being highlighted.

More importantly, the fact that most important corporate decisions are indeed either decided on or approved by shareholders raises a thornier issue: directors can escape their responsibility for making optimal decisions in good faith. It is difficult to hold directors liable for a decision made by shareholders collectively. Because shareholders in Chinese companies are not only allowed to engage with the corporate management but also have superior managerial power over the board, many serious decisions are made by the shareholders. On the other hand, the board is required to report details of its undertakings to the shareholders' meeting, and in practice directors can submit any issue to the shareholders' meeting. Therefore, the board devolves into an executive branch of the shareholders' meeting by mainly carrying out the latter's decisions, whilst shareholders become the ultimate decision-makers. In other words, directors are able to evade their responsibility for decision-making by asking the general meeting to decide.[130]

In spite of the fact that shareholders as a whole have the right to determine the operational policy and investment plan, they rely on directors of the board to formulate these policies and plans. Similarly, the annual budget and the profit distribution plans of any merger, division, dissolution, liquidation or transformation of the company, among other things, all need directors of the board to *draw them up*, either in law or in practice. In law, these duties are explicitly stipulated as obligations the board should discharge.[131] In practice, when shareholders do not know how to decide business policies, one company law expert who assisted in drafting the law answered: "they can ask the directors (for help)".[132] From this perspective, the shareholders' meeting only plays a rubber-stamping role to a certain extent, in that almost all the important and complicated decisions depend on directors' expertise and advice. In such circumstances, notwithstanding that directors engage with, or substantially influence, decision-making, it would be hard to hold directors liable even if they breach their responsibilities. For instance, directors may intentionally put forward a suggestion which is not in the best interests of the company or simply avoid an optimal decision, since it is up to the shareholders' meeting to ultimately adopt and determine it; the latter may lack the necessary expertise, resources or energy to make an optimal decision, and it may be more difficult to hold directors to account if they only perform an advisory role. Due to the lack of expertise, experience, time, etc., shareholders

---

130 This might be regarded as a delegation by the board of their powers on the particular issue back to the shareholders. See, for example, Paul Davies and Sarah Worthington, *Principles of Modern Company Law* (10th edn Sweet & Maxwell, London 2016) 362.

131 Article 47 of *Company Law 2005*.

132 K L Alex Lau, 'Chinese Limited Liability Companies under the New Company Law' (2006) 36 *Hong Kong Law Journal* 633, 639.

may not discover any irregular suggestion made by directors until the negative consequences arrive. Thus, a potentially large defect exists here.

As discussed at length in the last chapter, the board is ultimately a better decision-maker than the shareholders. Empowering shareholders does not necessarily lead to shareholder wealth maximisation and restraining them may better serve shareholder interests. Indeed, a dependent board may have a negative effect on shareholder interests in the long run, not to mention on the overall welfare of the company. However, the inadequate and unsound enforcement system along with other judicial problems may intensify desires for granting more power to shareholders, which could be seen as an emotional and straightforward reaction.[133] For example, shareholders have extensive powers in the Chinese corporate governance structure, but the ineffective enforcement system makes it difficult to realise some of the shareholders' rights. As changing the enforcement system from the individual investor's aspect is difficult, it is then common for people to ask for more shareholder powers to protect their rights.

Political, economic and other factors

Political determinants can never be ignored when considering corporate governance issues, particularly in China where politics and the "class struggle" have been the priorities for the whole country for such a long time; even now, political construction is still one of the most important government guidelines. Indeed, the main determinant in China's long history is of a political nature. The government to a large extent dominates the progress of corporate evolution and the exercising of shareholder rights. From this perspective, most of the foregoing discussion on historical influence can also be considered political influence. For instance, the government wants to have direct control of industrial enterprises for political reasons (such as maintaining the agrarian-dominated economy or realising its political ideology), therefore merchants, among other non-government investors, find it hard to have a meaningful "say" in decision-making. From another angle, China displays parallels with the concentrated ownership structure of France and Italy, where the politicians who hold state shareholdings have "a natural incentive to favour strong shareholder rights".[134] The state is frequently a dominating shareholder in the largest companies; this means that emphasising shareholder rights and prioritising shareholders' position is an indication of the state's interest.

---

133 This is similar to the emotional appeal of the so-called Enron effect, described by Professor Stout. Lynn Stout, 'The Mythical Benefits of Shareholder Control' (2007) 93 *Virginia Law Review* 789, 806.

134 Kraakman *et al.* (n 59) 84–85. Professors Enriques, Hansmann and Kraakman have further argued that "an interventionist state, concentrated ownership, and shareholder-friendly law may be mutually reinforcing, especially when the state holds large blocks of stock in its own rights". Ibid. 85.

Moreover, even the term "privatisation" continues to be a political taboo in China today. The essence of "corporatisation of SOEs" is to increase private ownership in traditional SOEs – just as there is always a limit to continuously subsidising unprofitable ones. The Chinese government has realised that it is time to accept capital from the private sector in order to avoid unnecessary fiscal burdens. The old Soviet-style dogma has almost been abandoned, replaced by a series of new theoretical innovations created by intelligent and astute politicians to overcome ideological obstacles in the socialist market economy reform following the *Fourteenth CPC National Congress*.[135] The *market* is officially acknowledged to have a significant position in allocating resources and adjusting economic activities, and is therefore expected to play a more active role in the socialist economy. The social status of investors or entrepreneurs is substantially increased compared with the past, and since 2000 even typical "capitalists" have been allowed to join the CPC as members.

The importance of differentiating autonomous corporate governance at the micro-level from government intervention has also been recognised. Essential macro-control by the government will only be carried out when the market does not work. In addition, to attract and thereby utilise private capital to meet the enormous capital requirements for fast and stable development is of vital political significance – for example, maintaining a low unemployment rate by having more thriving corporations. Nowadays, the government in China pays more attention to private property and values market rules, which may have an implicit and subtle impact on encouraging the rise of shareholder primacy.

SWM with sound shareholder protection is conventionally argued to be positively related to corporate value as well.[136] To begin with, it would be more appealing to both domestic and overseas private capital, which is the most desirable at present. Second, and also more importantly, pursuant to the so-called residual claimant theory as proposed by Alchian and Demsetz and developed by neoclassical economists and lawyers, maximising shareholder wealth is seen as equivalent to maximising the wealth of the whole company by virtue of its allocation rule. That shareholders as residual claimants can "reap the marginal dollar"[137] of corporate profits suggests they are entitled only to what is left from the income stream. Maximising shareholder value is therefore equated to enhancing corporate value. Economic efficiency and arguably the potential social wealth maximisation led by SWM simply accords with the government's focus on economic development.[138]

Following on from so-called agency theory, which currently dominates the West, the agency problems or agency costs also largely affect the selection of

135 *Supra* Chapter 4, section 4.1.3.
136 For example, see Marco Pagano and Paolo Volpin, 'The Political Economy of Corporate Governance' (2005) 95 *American Economic Review* 1005–1030.
137 See Chapter 2 footnote 96 and accompanying text.
138 See Chapter 2 footnotes 97–99 and accompanying text.

corporate objective. Apart from agency problems between shareholders and managers, it is not impossible for the controlling shareholder to expropriate the minority shareholders, because the latter group lacks power in corporate governance as well as adequate legal protection. Naturally, the disadvantageous position of minority shareholders is more likely to cause them to hold a short-term view of their corporate involvement. For instance, China's investors hold their stocks for less than 4 months on average whilst US investors usually hold them for about 18 months.[139] This indicates that the only meaningful and valid thing for most minority shareholders is profit maximisation, the faster the better, rather than a long-term development strategy.[140] As the earlier example of *Dasheng Corporation* demonstrated, where shareholders require a high and fixed interest rate on their investment, it is not surprising that non-controlling shareholders nowadays also prefer focusing on profits as the most important way to realise their shareholder rights and interests.[141]

Last but not least, although the ownership structure is not proportional to the level of corporate governance, it will affect the corporate objective. The remaining highly concentrated ownership structures[142] in China, for both historical and political reasons, contributes to the outcome of shareholder primacy as well. Under the concentrated ownership structure, the concentration of either governmental or private ownership means there is a strong likelihood that controlling shareholders will utilise all possible means to accomplish their own best interests, both pecuniary and non-pecuniary.[143] It will be extremely difficult to prevent a model favouring shareholders, principally the majority shareholders, to arise under such a concentrated ownership structure.[144]

---

139 Gongmeng Chen *et al.*, 'Is China's Securities Regulatory Agency a Toothless Tiger? Evidence from Enforcement Actions' (2005) 24 *Journal of Accounting and Public Policy* quoted in Kang, Shi and Brown (n 36) 8. However, even in Western countries, the average time for holding is also dramatically decreasing. Take the US for example, the average holding period in 1960 was eight years while in 2010 it was only four months. William Bratton, 'Hedge Funds and Governance Targets' (2007) 95 *Georgetown Law Review* 1375, 1410. Leo Strine, 'One Fundamental Corporate Governance Question We Face: Can Corporations Be Managed for the Long Term Unless Their Powerful Electorates Also Act and Think Long Term?' (2010) 66 *Business Law* 1, 11.

140 Needless to say the dismissing of stakeholder interests among others.

141 However, shareholders are also stakeholders: they have to breath air, live in the community and buy goods. Thus it is also in their interests when a company not only serves shareholder interests. Moreover, it remains debatable whether economic profits are a retail shareholder's primary focus, as will be discussed below in Chapter 5.

142 The State now still holds the majority of shares after those SOEs transformed into corporate form; as shown by empirical data, 81.6 per cent of companies are directly or indirectly controlled by the state and on average the single largest owner holds 36 per cent of shares among all listed companies at the end of the 2000s. Neng Liang and Michael Useem, 'Corporate Governance in China' in Institute of Directors (ed), *The Handbook of International Corporate Governance* (2nd edn Kogan Page, London 2009) 169.

143 At least from their own perspective, which could include the benefits of leisure or social goals.

144 Though the assessment of concentrated and dispersed ownership is beyond the purpose of this book, it is worth paying some attention to the following argument: a company with

4.4 Concluding remarks

History as well as contemporary empirical research tells us a government-centred model, except under certain specific conditions like wartime, would generally have negative impacts on corporate development over the long term. It is evident from the previous discussion that both economically and politically, government interference should be strictly restrained in order to allow the market and self-governing at the micro-level to perform a more active and decisive role in corporate governance practices and economic activities. The future development of China's economy will depend on the rapid growth of the corporate sector, which in turn relies more on its autonomy and the market, and such a developing trend will be sustainable over a long period with the deepening of domestic reform and globalisation. Shareholders accordingly have a critical position in the modern corporate governance structure in contrast to earlier periods.[145]

The domination of the shareholders' general meeting was also adopted by companies in Western countries in the nineteenth century, where shareholders controlled the company. The shareholder body at that time was also regarded as the supreme organ of the company, and "shareholders could at any time by ordinary resolution give the directors binding instructions as to how they were to exercise their management powers".[146] However, as explained in Chapter 3, shareholder empowerment in the context of modern corporate governance systems creates more harms than benefits, especially from a long-term perspective. The board of directors in modern times is "entrusted with the management of the company, and . . . [is] as independent as possible of the shareholders".[147] As we can see in both the US and UK, even when affected by shareholder empowerment trends, as long as no self-serving behaviour is involved, directors have a wide discretion on how the company should be run.

Nevertheless, in China, in contrast to its own past, shareholders now have extensive powers over corporate affairs, from deciding on business policies to allocation of profits. Shareholders as a whole are regarded as holding the supreme

---

a concentrated ownership structure is more likely to be managed for the best interests of the company since the so-called agency costs such as monitoring and constraining costs are lower and managerial derivation is harder to occur. Large shareholders would more willingly and effectively monitor managers as agents and therefore make them more accountable and limit the divergence of interests between shareholders and managers. For example, see Louis Putterman, 'Ownership and the Nature of the Firm' (1993) 17 *Journal of Comparative Economics* 243, 249.

145 The lesson we can learn from the past is that government interference is generally negative in terms of corporate development. Improving shareholder status is definitely a large step forward for China, which will help further economic development; however, it is doubtful when empowerment exceeds a certain threshold and makes the board of directors too dependent to make unbiased corporate decisions.

146 Davies and Worthington (n 130) 358. However, from the twentieth century, board autonomy had been explicitly recognised. *Supra* Chapter 3 footnotes 50–56 and accompanying text.

147 Kingsley Ong and Colin Baxter, 'A Comparative Study of the Fundamental Elements of Chinese and English Company Law' (1999) 48 *The International and Comparative Law Quarterly* 88, 109.

authority in the company as a result of a mixture of historic, economic, political and judicial factors. Shareholder empowerment is not an effective approach to enhancing shareholder value, as any potential benefits brought about by entrusting shareholder powers might be offset by the negative costs. Especially in China, the already largely limited managerial powers of the board would worsen the situation. Considering the disadvantages of shareholder empowerment, even in the context of SWM, it would be safe to conclude here that shareholders' extensive power is not beneficial to increasing shareholder value, let alone other stakeholders' interests. Therefore, regardless of whether SWM should be the corporate objective, shareholder empowerment is by no means a good approach. A more independent board and its delegated executives with autonomous managerial discretion are necessary for promoting the overall welfare of the company in the long run.

The interests of the company and the shareholders are frequently confused in China's company laws and practice. However, a significant distinction exists between the two. For example, wrongdoings to the company are different from the wrongdoings to the shareholders. If a wrongdoing belongs to the former, shareholders are not allowed to bring a lawsuit unless in the context of a derivative action, and may never recover anything at a personal level. China's company laws also recognise this distinction by adopting the legal person theory.[148] By the same token, corporate interests are not equivalent to shareholder interests.[149] Corporate interests encompass more than mere shareholder interests. The separate corporate personality further suggests that the company as an independent institution should not be confused with its shareholders. Although in most cases shareholder interests could be aligned with those of the company, as shown in Chapter 2 there are increasingly more occasions where shareholder interests are in conflict with, or completely in contrast to, the interests of the company

Furthermore, empowering shareholders or granting shareholders extensive powers is only a means. The end is controversial at the moment, and both SWM and the stakeholder model have certain justifications in China's company law and corporate governance practice.[150] After critical examination, agency theory as the current theoretical foundation also fails to be valid. The agency relationship and residual claimant argument are problematic; so too is the economic justification from the point of view of efficiency.

---

148 Article 3 of *Company Law 2005* states: "a company is a legal person, which has the independent property of a legal person and enjoys the property rights of a legal person. The company shall be liable for its debts to the extent of its entire property".

149 A company is vulnerable to both unsystematic and systematic risks, while shareholders can effectively diversify unsystematic risk; therefore when acting in the interests of shareholders, directors are only required to focus on the systematic risk, and as a result the company will be open to unsystematic risk. See Chapter 2 footnotes 226–227 and accompanying text.

150 For more discussion on the stakeholder factors in Chinese company law, see *infra* Chapter 6.

Thus, there are compelling reasons to look beyond maximising shareholder wealth. Moreover, as a socialist country, stakeholder interests in China are also explicitly emphasised. The emphasis on increasing social return, employee welfare, a high employment rate, social stability, community development and environment protection, among others, is not inconsistent with the essence of stakeholder theory and could be achieved through the stakeholder model.[151] All these indicate that it is time for China to seriously re-review the stakeholder model as the alternative corporate objective.

---

151 There is indeed a dilemma between entrusting shareholders with extensive powers and emphasising the interests of employees and society. As long as shareholders have control over the decision-making process and can easily exert pressure on the board of directors, the interests of stakeholders other than shareholders will hardly receive equal status.

5   Towards the stakeholder model

5.1 An overview

After re-examining shareholder wealth maximisation (SWM) as the corporate objective in Chapter 2, it becomes clear that the shareholder model should not be taken for granted either from an economic or legal perspective. Indeed, the negative externalities and short-termism caused by SWM are detrimental not only to stakeholders but also to the company as a whole. The heterogeneous expectations of different types of shareholder groups could further impair the so-called merit of single-minded measurability of the shareholder model. Moreover, there are in fact no laws requiring directors to only serve shareholder interests. It is then natural to consider that SWM may not be the appropriate corporate objective for large public companies at all. The stakeholder model or stakeholder theory as a theory of the firm is intended to explain and guide corporate behaviour by requiring directors of the company to be accountable to more than just shareholders. It is antithetical to the shareholder model and provides a different angle. It is argued the company should create value for all stakeholders rather than solely for shareholders. In other words, the stakeholder model requests the interests of all corporate stakeholders be taken into account and not be automatically subordinated to shareholders' interests. The main purpose of this chapter is to see whether the stakeholder model can be a more suitable corporate objective.

Companies are not able to succeed or achieve their business goals in the absence of stakeholders' contribution. Other non-shareholding stakeholders' investments such as the credit provided by creditors, the labour and know-how provided by employees, the services and products provided by suppliers and the infrastructure provided by the government, among others, are indispensable. Each stakeholder agrees to contribute their resources, labour or both together with others to pursue the success of the business and realise benefits from it.[1] It is not an overstatement to argue shareholders are not the only resource providers;

---

1 According to Professor Freeman and his co-authors, "business is about putting together a deal so that suppliers, customers, employees, communities, managers, and shareholders all win continuously over time". R Edward Freeman, Andrew Wicks and Bidhan Parmar, 'Stakeholder Theory and "The Corporate Objective Revisited"' (2004) 15 *Organization Science* 364, 365.

various other stakeholders also make their contribution in either pecuniary or non-pecuniary form. Meanwhile, the performance of the company will also affect the welfare of all stakeholders. In the words of Janet Williamson:

> Employees are affected by the wide range of decisions that impact upon their employment with the company; customers are affected by decisions on the price, specifications and standards of products; suppliers are affected by purchasing decisions; creditors are affected by financial procedures; and the local community is affected by recruitment policy and environmental impact.[2]

Similar to shareholders, their investment is also at risk.[3] For example, when a company is badly run or becomes insolvent, creditors may not get back the principal as well as the interest, and employees may be made redundant. They have an interest in the company, or in Professor Freeman's terms, each of these stakeholders has a stake in the company.[4] And these stakeholder groups do not have enough, if any, protection from the incomplete contract by virtue of their unbalanced bargaining power, informational asymmetry, transaction costs and/ or bounded rationality.[5]

Due to the fact that stakeholders receive at least some of the residual gain and undertake some of the residual risks, to require directors to take the interests of all stakeholders into account during decision-making and be accountable to them could be justified. As Professor Blair points out, "if other stakeholders could be shown to share in the residual gains and risks, their interest in being able to exercise some control over corporations would be significantly legitimized".[6] This implies directors' duties are not limited to ensuring returns to shareholders, but extend to those who are interested in, and affected by, the company.[7] Furthermore, in certain situations, as the argument of stakeholder theory goes, directors are even required to possess "a willingness to exhaust the resources of the company" to satisfy stakeholders' interests.[8]

SWM could accordingly be criticised for "using the *prima facie* rights claims of one group – shareholders – to excuse violating the rights of others".[9]

---

2 Janet Williamson, 'The Road to Stakeholding' (1996) 67 *Political Quarterly* 209, 212. More discussion can be found in *supra* Chapter 2, section 2.3.2.

3 Stakeholders also bear residual risks. See Chapter 2 footnotes 108–109 and accompanying text.

4 R Edward Freeman, *Strategic Management: A Stakeholder Approach* (Pitman Publishing, Boston 1984) 25.

5 In particular, during financial difficulties, directors may probably choose excessively risky programmes since shareholders have little to lose in this setting.

6 Margaret Blair, *Ownership and Control: Rethinking Corporate Governance for the Twenty-First Century* (The Brookings Institution, Washington 1995) 231.

7 William Allen, 'Our Schizophrenic Conception of the Business Corporation' (1992) 14 *Cardozo Law Review* 261, 265.

8 Ronald Green, 'Shareholders as Stakeholders: Changing Metaphors of Corporate Governance' (1993) 50 *Washington and Lee Law Review* 1409, 1421.

9 Freeman, Wicks and Parmar (n 1) 365.

Opponents of the shareholder model contend it has an adverse impact on other stakeholders' interests, and argue that shareholders as one group of various corporate constituents have no reason to override other groups' interests. In terms of the stakeholder model, every stakeholder has a right to be treated as an end, not simply a means or an instrument to facilitate the benefit of the shareholder.[10] The often-mentioned reputation, positive relationship with customers and suppliers and motivated employees are thereby not just about fostering the achievement of business goals as in the context of the shareholder model. All stakeholder interests should be considered by directors of the board, even if it means going against shareholders' sectional interests. In essence, to treat stakeholders as an end implies that they are no longer tools for maximising shareholder wealth, even in terms of the so-called long-term perspective; instead, stakeholders' legitimate interests should be seen as an ultimate and intrinsic objective of the company.[11]

In addition, the stakeholder model is beneficial to foster both existing and future contributors' potential, which is subsequently beneficial to advancing aggregate wealth.[12] The internal logic is that the shareholder model would damage the incentives of other stakeholders by virtue of their inferior position compared with shareholders. They may worry about being subordinated by shareholders' interests. Take rank-and-file employees for example. Seeing them as partners rather than as a means would create a more co-operative and productive relationship; it is essential for the company to have well-motivated employees to survive and succeed in this competitive world. Whilst shareholder model advocates insist that maximisation of shareholder wealth would make stakeholders better off, opponents doubt the validity of such an argument and believe it may not necessarily be beneficial to other stakeholders or society as a whole.[13] The lopsided focus on shareholder interests could easily be conducive to negative externalities, such as transferring the costs of the company to stakeholders and retaining the benefits for shareholders.[14]

It should now be plain that the stakeholder model, which attracts increasingly more support, could become a potentially viable substitute to replace SWM as the corporate objective. The rest of this chapter first clarifies the concept of stakeholders and then provides further justification and responses to the main criticisms.

---

10 Thomas Donaldson and Lee Preston, 'The Stakeholder Theory of the Corporation: Concepts, Evidence and Implications' (1995) 20 *Academy of Management Review* 65, 67; Freeman, *Strategic Management* (n 4) 97.

11 R Edward Freeman and Robert Phillips, 'Stakeholder Theory: A Libertarian Defense' (2002) 12 *Business Ethics Quarterly* 331, 333.

12 For example, see Andrew Keay, 'Stakeholder Theory in Corporate Law: Has It Got What It Takes?' (2010) 9 *Richmond Journal of Global Law and Business* 249, 256.

13 E Merrick Dodd, 'For Whom are Corporate Managers Trustees' (1931) 45 *Harvard Law Review* 1145, 1152.

14 Ian Lee, 'Efficiency and Ethics in the Debate about Shareholder Primacy' (2006) 31 *Delaware Journal of Corporate Law* 533, 539. The issue of externalisation in the context of SWM is discussed in Chapter 2, section 2.4.1.

5.2 Concept of the stakeholder

When determining who constitutes a stakeholder, there will be countless answers according to different scholars. For instance, those who "can affect the achievement of an organization's objectives or who is affected by the achievement of an organization's objectives";[15] who "can affect or is affected by a business";[16] who have "explicit contractual claims and implicit claims";[17] who "the corporation is responsible" to;[18] who "have an interest in the actions of an organization and who have the ability to influence it";[19] who "have a legitimate claim on the firm . . . established through the existence of an exchange relationship";[20] who "interact with and give meaning and definition to the corporation";[21] who "can and are making their actual stakes known . . . are or might be influenced by or are or potentially are influencers of, some organization";[22] and who "have, or claim, ownership, rights, or interests in a corporation and its activities"[23] could all be deemed to be stakeholders.[24]

Stakeholders so far have also been classified into categories such as primary vs. secondary; direct vs. indirect; voluntary vs. involuntary; and claimants vs. influencers among many other typologies. In particular, primary stakeholders are those whose continuing participation is essential to the survival of the company as a going concern, whilst secondary stakeholders are those whose participation is not essential but could still affect or be affected by the company.[25] Voluntary stakeholders are those who "bear some form of risk as a result of having invested

15 R Edward Freeman and David Reed, 'Stockholders and Stakeholders: A New Perspective on Corporate Governance' (1983) 25 *California Management Review* 88, 91. Narrowly, stakeholders are those "on which the organization is dependent for its continued survival". Ibid.
16 R Edward Freeman and Daniel Gilbert, 'Managing Stakeholder Relationships' in S Prakash Sethi and Cecilia Falbe (eds), *Business and Society: Dimensions of Conflict and Cooperation* (Lexington Books, Lexington 1987) 397.
17 Bradford Cornell and Alan Shapiro, 'Corporate Stakeholders and Corporate Finance' (1987) 16 *Financial Management* 5, 5–6.
18 Abbass Alkhafaji, *A Stakeholder Approach to Corporate Governance: Managing in A Dynamic Environment* (Quorum Books, Westport 1989) 36.
19 Grant Savage *et al.*, 'Strategies for Assessing and Managing Organizational Stakeholders' (1991) 5 *Academy of Management Executive* 61, 61.
20 Charles Hill and Thomas Jones, 'The Stakeholder-Agency Theory' (1992) 29 *Journal of Management Studies* 131, 133. In their view, each of these groups can be seen as supplying the firm with critical resources (contributions) and in exchange each expects its interests to be satisfied (by inducements).
21 Andrew Wicks, Daniel Gilbert and R Edward Freeman, 'A Feminist Reinterpretation of the Stakeholder Concept' (1994) 4 *Business Ethics Quarterly* 475, 483; Savage *et al.* (n 19) 62–63.
22 Mark Starik, 'Essay by Mark Starik: Reflections on Stakeholder Theory' (1994) 33 *Business and Society* 89, 90.
23 Max Clarkson, 'A Stakeholder Framework for Analyzing and Evaluating Corporate Social Performance' (1995) 20 *Academy of Management Review* 92, 106.
24 These definitions are only a few examples.
25 Clarkson, 'A Stakeholder Framework for Analyzing and Evaluating Corporate Social Performance' (n 23) 106–107.

some form of capital, human or financial, something of value, in a firm" whilst involuntary stakeholders are those who "are placed at risk as a result of a firm's activities".[26] Claimants are those who have legitimate claims who may or may not have the power to influence the company, and influencers are those who have the power to exert influence on the company regardless of whether they have a valid claim against it.[27]

That may explain why the concept of stakeholder is criticised as "blurred" and "relatively vague" in spite of the voluminous academic literature.[28] Professor Freeman and his collaborators also admit the vagueness and ambiguity of the concept.[29] The term itself indicates "many different things to many different people and hence evokes praise or scorn from a wide variety of scholars and practitioners of myriad academic disciplines and backgrounds".[30] Apart from questions as to which other groups should also be included, even for an explicitly defined stakeholder group, indeterminacy is not yet eliminated. For instance, if B provides goods to A and C provides goods to B, then in addition to B, C could also be deemed to be a stakeholder of A according to Freeman's theory, namely the attribute of affecting or being affected, at least indirectly. In a corollary, another party, D, who supplies goods to C, could also be seen as a stakeholder of A. This implies that all the sub-contracting parties could be categorised into stakeholders. Therefore, it would inescapably lead to a more serious problem of relevance.[31]

As Professor Vinten observes, that the term stakeholder is known by more people confirms neither the prevalence of stakeholder theory nor the infallibility of its definition and/or scope.[32] No definition can effectively distinguish stakeholders from non-stakeholders. Worse still, there are many differing subsets of any single stakeholder group, and one could have various capacities at the same time. For example, one could be an employee in a company whilst holding the company's shares, one might live in the community where the company is

---

26 Max Clarkson, 'A Risk Based Model of Stakeholder Theory' in proceedings of the Second Toronto Conference on Stakeholder Theory (Centre of Corporate Social Performance & Ethics University of Toronto, Toronto, May 1994) 5 referred to in Ronald Mitchell, Bradley Agle and Donna Wood, 'Toward a Theory of Stakeholder Identification and Salience: Defining the Principle of Who and What Really Counts' (1997) 22 *Academy of Management Review* 853, 856. Those who have no element of risk are not stakeholders according to Clarkson's classification.

27 John Kaler, 'Morality and Strategy in Stakeholder Identification' (2002) 39 *Journal of Business Ethics* 91, 94–95.

28 Eric Orts and Alan Strudler, 'The Ethical and Environmental Limits of Stakeholder Theory' (2002) 12 *Business Ethics Quarterly* 215, 215.

29 Robert Phillips, R Edward Freeman and Andrew Wicks, 'What Stakeholder Theory Is Not' (2003) 13 *Business Ethics Quarterly* 479, 479–480.

30 Ibid.

31 It is argued that "if the category of stakeholding interests is widened to include those of all potential consumers of the company's products, for example, or to refer to the general interest of society in the sustainability of the environment, there is a danger that the idea of stakeholding will cease to be relevant". Simon Deakin and Alan Hughes, 'Comparative Corporate Governance: An Interdisciplinary Agenda' (1997) 24 *Journal of Law and Society* 1, 4.

32 Gerald Vinten, 'Shareholder Versus Stakeholder – Is There a Governance Dilemma?' (2001) 9 *Corporate Governance: An International Review* 36, 44.

based, and also buy products/services provided by the company. Non-arbitrary criteria do not yet exist.[33] According to the current literature, more than 100 stakeholder groups as well as subgroups exist.[34] The concern of relevance is by no means groundless worry.[35] Further, owing to continuously changing external environment, there is always the possibility of having new stakeholder groups. For example, according to Professor Freeman, if a company changes its business and thereby affects or is affected by a new group of people, then these people could be regarded as stakeholders.[36] Recent financial crises demonstrate that governments could and would back up financial institutions with public funding under various circumstances,[37] effectively making all taxpayers stakeholders of those companies in one way or another.

Definitions of stakeholder can be broad or narrow. Though a broad definition like Freeman's, "any group or individual who can affect or who is affected by", would not miss any actual or latent stakeholders as its door is unambiguously open to almost anyone, a workable stakeholder theory needs to be able to help distinguish stakeholders from non-stakeholders. Narrow definitions of stakeholders are based on the *practical reality* of "limited resources, limited time and attention, and limited patience of managers for dealing with external constraints", whilst broad definitions are based on empirical reality that "companies can indeed be vitally affected by, or they can vitally affect, almost anyone", which is consistent with Professor Freeman's classic definition.[38]

As shown above, a stakeholder can be narrowly defined as those without whose participation a company cannot survive,[39] or who "bear some form of risk as a result of having invested some form of capital, human or financial, something of value, in a firm";[40] under this condition, shareholders, employees, creditors, suppliers, customers, local communities, the environment and the like may all be encompassed. Considering the issue of relevance, the stakeholder concept would be more viable in the real business world from a narrower interpretation.[41]

---

33 Elaine Sternberg, 'The Stakeholder Concept: A Mistaken Doctrine' (1999) 4 *Foundation for Business Responsibilities* 6, 18–19.

34 Yves Fassin, 'The Stakeholder Model Refined' (2009) 84 *Journal of Business Ethics* 113, 120.

35 It is argued that all these problems may arise from the fact that "most work in this field appears to be preoccupied with justifying a stakeholder approach to the firm, rather than the construction of [a] systematic theory to describe more adequately contemporary organizational practices". See Simon Learmount, 'Theorizing Corporate Governance: New Organizational Alternatives' (2002) *ESRC Centre for Business Research, University of Cambridge Working Paper No. 237*.

36 Freeman, *Strategic Management* (n 4) 223.

37 For example, the important role and nature of these financial institutions in the modern economy and society make them too big to fail.

38 Mitchell, Agle and Wood (n 26) 854.

39 Ibid.; Clarkson, 'A Stakeholder Framework for Analyzing and Evaluating Corporate Social Performance' (n 23) 92.

40 Amy Hillman and Gerald Keim, 'Shareholder Value, Stakeholder Management, and Social Issues: What's the Bottom Line?' (2001) 22 *Strategic Management Journal* 125, 126.

41 In fact, there are few controversies on employees, customers, creditors, suppliers, environment and local community as stakeholders.

The ambiguity and vagueness, as Professor Fassin insightfully observes, is to a large extent caused by "the intrinsic flexibility of stakeholder theory".[42] Indeed, the dynamic aspect of stakeholder theory and stakeholder relationships has been acknowledged by many stakeholder theorists.[43] It is true that the same subject may have different capacities under different conditions, which means it may become a stakeholder by acquiring certain attribute(s); at the same time the importance of its claim may vary accordingly.[44] As a result, reliable and systematic sorting criteria are needed to distinguish stakeholders from non-stakeholders, and more importantly to help determine how to treat them.

Professors Mitchell, Agle and Wood propose a useful model that relies on attributes of power, legitimacy and urgency as a sorting system to identify stakeholders.[45] Specifically, if one possesses one, two or all three attributes of "(1) the stakeholder's power to influence the frim,[46] (2) the legitimacy of [the] stakeholder's relationship with the firm,[47] and (3) the urgency of the stakeholder's claim on the firm[48]"; then one can be identified as a stakeholder of that firm. In contrast, if one does not possess any of the above attributes, then one will be regarded as a non-stakeholder.

There are then seven possibilities, pursuant to Mitchell *et al.*'s terminologies: (1) "dormant stakeholders" who only have power; (2) "discretionary stakeholders" who only have legitimacy; (3) "demanding stakeholders" who only have the attribute of urgency; (4) "dominant stakeholders" who have both power and legitimacy; (5) "dependent stakeholders" who have both legitimacy and urgency; (6) "dangerous stakeholders" who have both power and urgency; and (7) "definitive stakeholders" who possess all three attributes.[49] Generally speaking,

---

42 Fassin, 'The Stakeholder Model Refined' (n 34) 117.

43 For example, see Mitchell, Agle and Wood (n 26) 879. In the meantime, the examples of Fortis and General Motors given by Professor Fassin may vividly change the real nature of stakeholder relations. See Yves Fassin, 'A Dynamic Perspective in Freeman's Stakeholder Model' (2010) 96 *Journal of Business Ethics* 39, 44–45.

44 Similarly, an ongoing assessment is necessary as the stakeholders' interests, capability and needs might change under different circumstances.

45 Mitchell, Agle and Wood (n 26) 854.

46 Power is defined as the ability of those who possess it to bring about the outcomes they desire which they would not otherwise have done. A party having power means "it has or can gain access to coercive, utilitarian, or normative means, to impose its will in the relationship". Ibid. 865.

47 Though legitimacy is usually linked with power, in order to advance the argument of stakeholder identification and the question of how to determine the priority when conflicts arise, Mitchell *et al.* acknowledge the German sociologist and philosopher Max Weber's distinction between legitimacy and power, and adopt Professor Mark Suchman's definition and see legitimacy as an independent attribute, namely, "a generalized perception or assumption that the actions of an entity are desirable, proper, or appropriate within some socially constructed system of norms, values, beliefs, and definitions". Ibid. 866. Also see Mark Suchman, 'Managing Legitimacy: Strategic and Institutional Approaches' (1995) 20 *Academy of Management Review* 571, 574.

48 Urgency is defined as being based on "time sensitivity" and "criticality"; in other words, when a relationship or claim is of a time-sensitive nature and important or critical to the stakeholder then such a relationship or claim can be deemed to be urgent. Mitchell, Agle and Wood (n 26) 867.

49 Ibid. 874–878.

the often-mentioned stakeholder groups can be at least classified into one of these definitions, though it might vary from one classification to another under different conditions. For example, employees who could be deemed to possess both power and legitimacy can be classified as "dominant stakeholders", but they may become "definitive stakeholders" by acquiring the attribute of urgency when their claim becomes time-sensitive and critical during a massive redundancy programme or when working conditions materially worsen. All these stakeholder groups deserve the board's attention, though as discussed later, different levels would apply.

The idea of such a sorting system based on several key attributes is helpful, but it may be problematic as it does not identify the "attribute of legitimacy" as a mandatory precondition. The following example, though controversial to some extent, may reveal its key defect. Those who have coercive power to influence the company can be categorised into "dormant stakeholders", but when their claim becomes urgent, they may become "dangerous stakeholders" like terrorists, whose claim is not legitimate. Similarly, it would be unconvincing to require directors of the board to run the company for the interests of its competitors. Competitors have the power to influence the company, but they may not necessarily have the attribute of legitimacy. They may have competing interests against the company as it may lose market share or profit margin if its competitor is run well.[50] It is obvious that competitors or terrorists should not be treated in the same way as stakeholders such as employees or suppliers. Many stakeholder theorists suggest that legitimacy should be the *sine qua non* of the stakeholder concept.[51] In particular, if the stakeholder model requires directors to run the company in all stakeholders' interests, legitimacy should be put forth as the main premise. As argued by Professors Jones and Wicks, there should be a morally acceptable end.[52] Put simply, a group can become a stakeholder only when it adds something to a company either voluntarily or involuntarily.

The sorting system proposed by Professors Mitchell, Agle and Wood may be perfectly acceptable as a managerial strategy, since directors and their delegated managers should undoubtedly consider a group's claim if it has the power to affect the company. However, the groups that do not possess the attribute of legitimacy should not be considered in the same way as those that do. The reason for considering the former is mainly because of their ability to influence the company due to their possession of power – the consideration is also limited to such an ability to affect the company and the real stakeholders – whilst the latter represents those who deserve serious consideration because of their moral legitimacy. It is argued that the justification of considering the groups with

---

50 In other words, competitors would normally hope their rival companies are less successful in order to gain a higher market share. For example, see Donaldson and Preston, 'The Stakeholder Theory of the Corporation' (n 10) 86.

51 Robert Phillips, 'Stakeholder Legitimacy' (2003) 13 *Business Ethics Quarterly* 25, 28.

52 Thomas Jones and Andrew Wicks, 'Convergent Stakeholder Theory' (1999) 24 *Academy of Management Studies* 206, 213.

power to influence the company and its normative stakeholders is based solely on directors' obligations owed to the company and the real stakeholders; consideration should not be extended to advance these groups' interests.[53] The board is only required to run the company for the interests of the real stakeholders.[54] In other words, since groups with power do not necessarily deserve directors' attention, if the influencers' claim is not consistent with the interests of the company and real stakeholders, the directors may even be required to minimise or circumvent their influence.[55] It is therefore worth distinguishing between the influencer and the real stakeholders.[56] This also accords with the principle of narrow interpretation.

A careful balance is needed in each case anyway to identify the specific situation and decide what action should be taken. Favouring one over another occurs on a case-by-case basis depending on different circumstances, and different stakeholder groups may be favoured from time to time. However, in general, no stakeholder group is scheduled to be prioritised or doomed to be sacrificed. For instance, the interests of a stakeholder group which is regarded as not urgent and does not need to be seriously considered on one occasion may have a totally different treatment on another occasion if the interests can be classified as urgent and important. Though all stakeholders' interests matter, this does not mean that all of them need to be equally considered or can be practically protected at the same time. As discussed later, the attribute of urgency could be used as a reference to conduct a trade-off. More urgent interests could in fact be considered first if satisfying all stakeholder interests at the same time is unrealistic. Therefore, the most broadly defined stakeholders, such as sub-suppliers C and D in the earlier example, or those who have a less direct relationship with a given company may normally not materially influence corporate decision-making in practice, since their interests are hard to classify as urgent or important with regard to the company as a whole. That is to say, even though there may be 100 stakeholder groups, only a few will become the real subjects in stakeholder theory and be seriously considered. In other words, those who can only remotely affect, or be affected by, the company are not going to be considered as qualified stakeholders in a workable stakeholder model.

In short, although the potential scope of stakeholders is very wide, it would not significantly compromise the function of the stakeholder model as it is more

53　More discussion can be found in Phillips, 'Stakeholder Legitimacy' (n 51) 31 and 34–35.
54　Nevertheless, it should be noted that to deny a particular group as stakeholders, is not to take everything away from that group which it had been granted before. As Professor Phillips commented, rules such as not breaking promises or contracts without significant cause, not violating basic rights, not egregiously polluting the environment are still valid irrespective of whether that group had stakeholder status. Ibid. 30–31.
55　These influencers without a legitimate claim may cause damages to the company and the real stakeholders. For example, see Freeman, *Strategic Management* (n 4) 53.
56　Sometimes a group may be both a stakeholder and influencer, but some stakeholders may have no power to influence while some influencers have no stake in the company. Donaldson and Preston, 'The Stakeholder Theory of the Corporation' (n 10) 86.

about managing potential conflicts arising from the various divergent interests.[57] It is not impossible to use employees, shareholders, customers, creditors, suppliers, local communities, the environment and the like as substitutes for the term stakeholder as a temporary expedient to encourage opponents puzzled by the definition to change their minds. Running the company for the interests of these common stakeholder groups may solve the potential difficulties of definition, meaning there is no reason to deny the stakeholder model simply based on its definition.[58]

5.3 Justification for stakeholder theory

The question then remains: why should the stakeholder theory be accepted as the substitute? The problems existing in SWM per se may not be enough to justify the stakeholder model becoming a legitimate corporate objective.

As introduced in Chapter I, stakeholder theory can be understood from descriptive, instrumental and normative aspects. It is argued that the descriptive aspect of stakeholder theory describes "past, present and future states of affairs of corporations and their stakeholders", whilst the instrumental aspect establishes "a connection between stakeholder approaches and commonly desired objectives such as profitability".[59] The normative aspect endeavours to "interpret the function of, and offer guidance about, the investor-owned corporation on the basis of some underlying moral or philosophical principles".[60] The justification could also start from these three aspects. In turn, descriptively, stakeholder theory should be able to justify its ability to reflect the reality in practice; instrumentally, it should justify the positive connection between the stakeholder model and corporate performance; and normatively, the fundamental moral or philosophical principles should be appealed to in order to justify its foundation.[61]

5.3.1 Descriptive justification

First of all, it has been stated that the vast majority of directors and their managers "adhere in practice to one of the central tenets of the stakeholder theory,

---

57 Jeff Frooman, 'Stakeholder Influence Strategies' (1999) 24 *Academy of Management Review* 191, 193.
58 With the continuing development of the stakeholder theory, it is optimistic to see that a sounder definition could be established in the future.
59 Donaldson and Preston, 'The Stakeholder Theory of the Corporation' (n 10) 71.
60 Ibid. 72.
61 In the words of Professors Donaldson and Preston: "descriptive justifications attempt to show that the concepts embedded in the theory correspond to observed reality. Instrumental justifications point to evidence of the connection between stakeholder management and corporate performance. Normative justifications appeal to underlying concepts such as individual or group 'rights', 'social contract', or utilitarianism". Ibid. 74. But it should be borne in mind that this book mainly uses such classification to facilitate discussion, and the argument in each category may possibly have implications for another category.

namely, that their role is to satisfy a wider set of stakeholders, not simply the shareowners".[62]

More importantly, as explained in Chapter 2, the laws in both the UK and US never explicitly state that the company should solely be run for the interests of the shareholders; instead, they require directors to discharge their duties in the best interests of the company.[63] The interests of the company can be different from, or even opposed to, those of shareholders. In contrast, both enlightened shareholder value in the UK and the non-shareholder constituency statutes in the US require directors to take stakeholders' interests into account during corporate decision-making. The increased requirement of disclosure of stakeholder-related information further facilitates directors to better consider stakeholder interests, which also provides potential grounds for judicial review.

Unfortunately, the mainstream viewpoint remains SWM. It is not difficult to find that directors are pressured by shareholders and the market to run companies so as to maximise shareholder wealth, even at the expense of other stakeholders. The reasons will not be reiterated here, but the shareholder model, as the main competitor to the stakeholder model, fails to accurately describe the relationship between the shareholder and the company. As previously discussed, shareholders are not the principals of the directors; they are insulated from corporate management. Neither are shareholders the sole residual claimants. Other stakeholders could at least share part of the residual gain and undertake some of the residual risks, as explained in Chapter 2.

It is however acknowledged that the descriptive support for stakeholder theory is of limited importance. Especially when a new model wants to replace an incumbent, the question shifts from what the corporate objective *is* to what the corporate objective *ought to be*. The other justifications are now discussed in turn.

5.3.2 Instrumental justification

The instrumental aspect questions whether there is sufficient empirical evidence to show that the stakeholder model could help optimise corporate performance from the financial perspective.

It has been shown that involving stakeholders such as employees and suppliers in different parts of the company can produce positive results by enhancing the co-operative potential.[64] According to Janice Dean, this entails "the decision to trust, in business as elsewhere centres on interpersonal expectations, the willingness to accept temporary vulnerability and optimism about one's

---

62 Ibid. 75.
63 Neither the US nor UK laws explicitly require public companies to be run for SWM. At the very least, the law does not unequivocally say the objective of the company should be to maximise shareholder wealth. *Supra* Chapter 2, section 2.5.1.
64 The example of Xerox proves that getting suppliers involved in its production process can reduce production costs and improve efficiency. Savage *et al.* (n 19) 66.

partner's behaviour".[65] Such trust could lower the cost of elaborating contracts and reduce agency costs since directors are trusted to behave properly. The following observation by Fox and Lorsch further illustrates this:

> Paying too much attention to what shareholders say they want may actually make things worse for them. There's a growing body of evidence … that the companies that are most successful at maximizing shareholder value over time are those that aim toward goals other than maximizing shareholder value. Employees and customers often know more about and have more of a long-term commitment to a company than shareholders do. Tradition, ethics, and professional standards often do more to constrain behavior than incentives do. The argument here isn't that managers and boards always know best. It's simply that widely dispersed short-term shareholders are unlikely to know better – and a governance system that relies on them to keep corporations on the straight and narrow is doomed to fail.[66]

Though not enough compelling empirical data can yet be found,[67] it is believed that analytical arguments are able to verify the connection between the stakeholder model and the conventional desired outcome.[68] On the one hand, the so-called economic efficiency argument and social wealth maximisation argument maintained by the opponents of the stakeholder model were proved to be untenable in Chapter 2. The company that put more emphasis on profit was usually less profitable.[69] Suffice it to say, the incumbent shareholder model cannot achieve more economic efficiency, let alone the ambitious goal of creating more social wealth and benefiting the economy as a whole. On the other, if the legitimate expectations of the main stakeholders' group have been looked after and satisfied, then shareholders would undoubtedly benefit as well.[70] The value to shareholders could be enhanced as a by-product of successfully implementing

65 Janice Dean, *Directing Public Companies: Company Law and the Stakeholder Society* (Cavendish, London 2001) 107.

66 Justine Fox and Jay Lorsch, 'What Good Are Shareholders?' (2012) 90 *Harvard Business Review* at https://hbr.org/2012/07/what-good-are-shareholders [accessed 1 March 2017].

67 However, there is a growing body of empirical research supporting the positive relationship between corporate performance and serving the interests of non-shareholder stakeholders. For example, see Hoje Jo and Maretno Harjoto, 'The Causal Effect of Corporate Governance on Corporate Social Responsibility' (2012) 106 *Journal of Business Ethics* 53, 55.

68 Donaldson and Preston, 'The Stakeholder Theory of the Corporation' (n 10) 76, 78.

69 For example, ICI and Boeing were more successful as profit-making companies when they "served customers internationally through the responsible application of chemistry" or "ate, breathed and slept the world of aeronautics" than when they tried to "maximise value for our shareholders" or "go into a value based environment". John Kay, *Obliquity: Why Our Goals Are Best Achieved Indirectly* (Profile Books Ltd, London 2010) 27.

70 Clarkson, 'A Stakeholder Framework for Analyzing and Evaluating Corporate Social Performance' (n 23) 106.

the stakeholder model. In contrast, if these primary stakeholders, in Professor Clarkson's terms, become dissatisfied and withdraw their contribution, the company will be seriously damaged, along with the interests of shareholders.[71]

Issue of long-termism

The stakeholder model is at least beneficial for avoiding short-termism. As explained in Chapter 2, when turning SWM into practice, it is not infrequent for directors to focus single-mindedly on short-term results by increasing current revenue and reducing immediate expense, which constitutes a very important reason for the demand for an alternative model. Short-termism is hard to avoid if SWM is the norm. As demonstrated in the foregoing chapters, the pressure from shareholders to pursue immediate profits is almost impossible for directors to resist.[72] Despite the fact that shareholders' powers to remove directors and bring derivative actions against directors are not effective in practice, this simple deterrent along with the potentially robust hostile takeover may still contribute to such pressure. Equity-based compensation further encourages directors to try every means to boost the current share price by tying their remuneration to share prices. If pursuing short-term profits can satisfy shareholders as the sole orthodox beneficiary in the context of SWM and at the same time benefit directors' personal interests, then there is little reason for them to resist the lure of short-termism. As a result, the long-term welfare of the company along with the stakeholders' interests is not infrequently forced to be sacrificed under the shareholder model.

Even the so-called enlightened shareholder value is not helpful, as discussed earlier, since short-term shareholders always have the advantage when competing with long-term shareholders.[73]

Most shareholders, including institutional investors, only focus on immediate values and become increasingly impatient regarding the time frame for earning profits. Shareholders who are not content with the current share price can choose to vote with their feet and thereby cause the share price to shrink if there is a sufficiently large number of such sell-offs. Fear of a reduction in share price as well as a hostile takeover will compel directors to maximise the current share price.

Moreover, when considering the company as a going concern, it exists in perpetuity, meaning that even a long-term strategy from the shareholders' perspective may not fit with the company's long-termism. Sustainable or say endless research and development (hereafter, R&D) is needed in order to excel in this ever-changing world. This is a straightforward matter. For instance, if shareholders with a long-term view adopt a strategy to invest corporate profits in R&D at time T0, it is reasonable to conjecture that they wish to reap the gains after a period of time, say at T1. However, at the time T1, the original innovation, i.e. the outcome

71 Ibid.
72 For example, see Chapter 3 footnotes 125–138 and accompanying text.
73 A brief discussion on ESV can be found in Chapter 2 footnotes 235–238 and accompanying text.

of R&D at T0, may need further development, otherwise at the future time, T2, the outcome of R&D at T0 might be outdated. In order to ensure long-term prosperity, new R&D is required at T1. Similarly, in order to remain competitive at T3, resources should be invested in R&D at T2. Put simply, for the real long-term prosperity of a company, R&D should be continuously focused on if the timeframe is sufficiently long. Certainly, long-termism encompasses more than R&D investment, and all other measures, such as improving customer service or community relationship maintenance, are not "one-offs" either.

This causes a serious problem for long-term shareholders. For them, a period from T0 to T1 or T2 might be sufficiently long; they cannot extend their timeframe indefinitely in practice. So there must be a time in which long-term shareholders want to retrieve all or the majority of the profits rather than continually reinvesting them for the future. But for the company, continuous investment in R&D, among other things, is required for lasting prosperity. That is to say, a long-term shareholder at T0 may become a short-term shareholder at T1 or T2. This is not surprising as most shareholders, or ultimate beneficiaries to be more accurate, are human beings with finite life spans. It would be impractical or unfair to expect a shareholder to have the same timeframe as a company which can exist in perpetuity.

By contrast, the stakeholder model requires a more balanced strategy to be adopted, as explained earlier. There will not be any need to unduly emphasise any stakeholder group's interests, let alone a given group's short-term interests. Thus, directors will no longer be pressured to abandon an investment programme which only has long-term rewards, to cut R&D budgets or to manoeuvre corporate accounting. Short-term manipulations which are solely for maximising current share prices will become worthless if SWM can be replaced. Second, when the stakeholder model can be adopted, incentive mechanisms such as aligning directors' interests with those of the shareholders through equity-based compensation would be simultaneously altered or discarded due to the internal incompatibility between the two models. As long as the corporate objective and accompanying mechanisms can be correctly set, there will be no incentive for directors to pursue aggressive quarterly earnings at the expense of long-term interests, which would further help eliminate the lopsided emphasis on short-termism.

All stakeholders' interests should be taken into consideration;[74] none should be sacrificed simply for another group's current interests. For shareholder interests under the stakeholder model, the original immediate and short-term profits will be replaced by a continuing, sustainable and fair return. Shareholder interests may even be subordinated to the long-term, sustainable development and well-being of the stakeholders as a whole under certain circumstances. As discussed later, a balanced long-term and sustainable approach could be obtained where

74 Sometimes, the influencers may need to be taken into account in order to protect and advance the interests of stakeholders.

conflicts of interest arise.[75] As Leo Strine, the Vice Chancellor of the Delaware Court of Chancery, points out: "the primary goal of corporate law, therefore, is . . . to facilitate the maximum creation of durable societal wealth by all firms".[76]

Regarding the doubt as to whether directors can forego short-termism and shift towards long-termism, the answer is "they can". It is not a psychological question about whether directors would behave altruistically if there were no pressure from shareholders, the market and arguably the law. The criterion is still there, though changed from SWM to the stakeholder model. Directors are merely liberated from the criterion of maximising shareholder wealth, which is the main cause of the *unavoidable* short-termism, but they are continuously demanded to comply with other criteria. Under the stakeholder model, directors are still required to run the company for its best interests in good faith, and self-serving behaviour is still forbidden. Furthermore, if the right incentive mechanism could be gradually set up to sever the association between directors' personal interests and short-term performance, such as quarterly share prices, then it would be optimistic to see directors could be correctly incentivised to restrain short-termism of their own volition.[77]

5.3.3 Normative justification

Modern public companies are no longer private business devices.[78] As Professors Berle and Means note, shareholders in modern public companies which are typically widely held do not bear all the responsibilities and risks that ownership of property normally implies, therefore they should not be given the same legal rights and protections as owners of other types of property.[79] Values other than economic profits are also worth being a normative rule.[80] From a more macro

---

75 *Infra* Chapter 5, section 5.4.1.
76 He continues to write: "when that is done, over time, corporations will generate good returns for patient investors with diversified portfolios". Leo Strine, 'Toward a True Corporate Republic: A Traditionalist Response to Bebchuk's Solution for Improving Corporate America' (2006) 119 *Harvard Law Review* 1759, 1764.
77 Though it is beyond the purpose of this chapter to design such a mechanism, it can be found that in contrast to the original equity-based compensation system, a new incentive system can use other more long-term related criteria to assess the performance of directors and award them accordingly. In fact, it is observed that directors prefer a quiet life and the continuation of operations, which implies that things such as plant closures or job cuts are not consistent with their wishes. For example, see Marianne Bertrand and Sendhil Mullainathan 'Enjoying the Quiet Life – Corporate Governance and Managerial Preference' (2003) 111 *Journal of Political Economy* 1043, 1066–1067.
78 It was observed by Berle and Means in the 1930s, and these kinds of companies had become social institutions. Adolf Berle and Gardiner Means, *The Modern Corporation and Private Property* (Transaction Publishers, New Brunswick 1991, originally published in 1932) 312–313.
79 Ibid. 304–305.
80 Although it is not the purpose of this chapter to carry out a lengthy philosophical ethics/moral debate, it is important to bear in mind that wealth is not an end in itself but only an instrumental value, just like money is not the only thing we care about as individuals: personal health, family and many other things are no less valuable to us. For example, Kent Greenfield, 'New Principles for Corporate Law' (2005) 1 *Hastings Business Law Journal* 87, 96.

viewpoint, values such as fairness and justice also play a very significant role. It is believed that these values are no less important than the value of economic efficiency, but now too much emphasis is put on economic efficiency and the like.[81] Worse, shareholder primacy could become an excuse for conducting immoral behaviour in the pursuit of the largest possible profits. As Professors Freeman, Wicks and Parmar argue, values including ethics should not be separated from doing business.[82]

Not only should shareholders receive fair consideration regardless of their shareholdings, but all other stakeholders should also be fairly treated. All people have intrinsic values, and it is unfair to treat some as a means instead of an end.[83] Stakeholders have value, even in a narrowly focused corporate environment with reference to corporate success. Shareholders are merely one group of stakeholders who contribute financial capital;[84] there is no reason why they should be prioritised.[85] Failure to take other stakeholders' interests into account might even be accused of being a violation of human rights.[86] As the previous chapters show, the well-being of non-shareholding stakeholders and society as a whole cannot be ensured through maximising shareholder profits. If the company only focuses on shareholder interests and ignores the interests of various stakeholders, there is a risk that avoidance of these demands will incur costs for society. Redundant employees and a polluted environment, for example, will become the costs for society in one way or another, which would ultimately become a cost for individual companies. Thus it would be wiser to effectively balance various stakeholders' interests during the decision-making process, even from an economic point of view.

Pure maximisers of utility or profit do not exist in the real world. More importantly, even if one were free to maximise one's own interests, the bottom line is that such freedom cannot harm the interests of others. As a result, fairness and justice should be respected. In particular, the potential risks of externalisation and short-termism, among others, make the lopsided focus on efficiency or profit maximisation more untenable. Nevertheless, shareholder primacists have argued fairness would inescapably lead to substantial legal uncertainty.[87] It is argued that any substitutes of the shareholder model would face the issue of who should be granted priority when conflicts arise. However, as previously discussed, even within the shareholder group different shareholders might have completely different goals owing to their heterogeneous expectations, so any model may confront the so-called uncertainty problem. Moreover, unequivocal

---

81 For example, Jean Tirole, 'Corporate Governance' (2001) 69 *Econometrica* 1, 2.
82 Freeman, Wicks and Parmar (n 1) 365.
83 Kevin Gibson, 'The Moral Basis of Stakeholder Theory' (2000) 26 *Journal of Business Ethics* 245, 248.
84 David Wood, 'Whom Should Business Serve?' (2002) 14 *Australian Journal of Corporate Law* 266, 273.
85 Even in terms of economic efficiency, Chapter 2 has already rebutted the so-called efficiency argument.
86 Phillips, Freeman and Wicks, 'What Stakeholder Theory Is Not' (n 29) 494.
87 For example, see Jeffrey MacIntosh, 'Designing an Efficient Fiduciary Law' (1993) 43 *University of Toronto Law Journal* 425, 459.

and objective algorithms/mathematics are not sufficient as a guide to human life or business.[88] In fact, if directors are able to balance the various needs of different shareholders, it would be incorrect to deny the ability of directors to balance divergent stakeholder interests.[89]

In fact, people prefer fairness in both the final outcome and the process in either a corporate or non-corporate context:

> Not only have people been found to have an interest in the fairness of the final outcomes of a distributive process, but evidence also suggests that people are concerned about the justness of the process of distribution itself. Among the major findings of procedural justice research is that people are more accepting of outcomes when the procedure for distribution is perceived as fair even in situations where the outcome itself is poor.[90]

It is also argued that shareholders seem to "have the least claim to voting membership" whilst other stakeholders "have at least as good a claim as [shareholders]".[91] As former chancellor of Delaware Court of Chancery William Allen writes:

> Contributors of capital (stockholders and bondholders) must be assured a rate of return sufficient to induce them to contribute their capital to the enterprise. But the corporation has other purposes of perhaps equal dignity: the satisfaction of consumer wants, the provision of meaningful employment opportunities, and the making of a contribution to the public life of its communities. Resolving the often conflicting claims of these various corporate constituencies calls for judgment, indeed calls for wisdom, by the board of directors of the corporation. But in this view no single constituency's interest may significantly exclude others from fair consideration by the board.[92]

The indispensable role of stakeholders to both the survival and prosperity of a company has been already fully discussed in Chapter 2; their important role in modern corporate governance is undoubtedly a significant justification for the stakeholder theory. In many cases, wealth is created by technological or organisational innovation, which means the role of employees and other stakeholders'

---

88 Andrew Crane *et al.* (eds), *The Oxford Handbook of Corporate Social Responsibility* (OUP, Oxford 2008) 61.

89 The next section will discuss this point further.

90 Phillips, Freeman and Wicks, 'What Stakeholder Theory Is Not' (n 29) 487 referred to E Allan Lind and Tom Tyler, *The Social Psychology of Procedural Justice* (Plenum, New York 1988). According to Professor Blair, distributive justice is "based on some socially constructed notion of who has contributed what effort or made what sacrifice, who has what need, or who has made what prior agreement about the uses of the assets". Blair, *Ownership and Control* (n 6) 225.

91 R Edward Freeman and William Evan, 'Corporate Governance: A Stakeholder Interpretation' (1990) 19 *Journal of Behavioral Economics* 337, 344.

92 Allen (n 7) 271.

non-pecuniary input is more important than shareholders' input.[93] But in order to avoid reiteration, this subsection mainly focuses on firm-specific investment and internalisation of negative externalities in order to justify their interests' deserving a normative consideration.

Firm-specific investment

Non-shareholding stakeholders not only contribute various types of resources, but also make firm-specific investment. Firm-specific investment is in contrast to generic investment and implies those skills or assets that cannot be redeployed to alternative use without a loss of value. Stakeholders lock themselves into a relationship once they make such firm-specific investment, which largely stems from the fact that withdrawing the specific investment would destroy much of its value.[94] For example, an employee with skills uniquely specialised to a given company "cannot leave without bearing substantial exit costs in the form of the lower rent stream that their skills can earn in the next best application".[95] Firm-specific investment can include pecuniary and non-pecuniary forms such as time, human capital and the like.[96]

Providing that stakeholder interests are subordinated to shareholder interests, stakeholders will not, or at least have less incentive to, make firm-specific investment since the specialised resources could only have their highest value when utilised in a given project.[97] In other words, although productivity and competitiveness largely depend on firm-specific investment by stakeholder groups, it could also expose stakeholders to potential "holdup" due to difficult and costly transferring.[98] Additionally, as discussed in Chapter 2, inadequate contractual protection and the ineffectiveness of external law protection may further deter stakeholders' firm-specific investment, which is essential for the success of companies. The outcome will be devastating if stakeholders are less willing to make such a contribution. Without satisfactory protective mechanisms, employees will then be less likely to develop highly specialised but non-transferable skills and knowledge, which cost extra time and energy, since they know such investments in skills or knowledge are only useful for the given company and could easily be sacrificed for shareholders' interests. Similarly, suppliers will be less willing to invest in specialised machinery for specific products solely demanded by a

---

93 For example, see Blair, *Ownership and Control* (n 6) 245.
94 Oliver Hart, 'An Economist's Perspective on the Theory of the Firm' (1989) 89 *Columbia Law Review* 1757, 1762; Margaret Blair and Lynn Stout, 'Specific Investment: Explaining Anomalies in Corporate Law' (2006) 31 *Journal of Corporation Law* 719, 734.
95 Hill and Jones (n 20) 133.
96 The contribution in research and development is specific, as are the specialised machines provided by suppliers, and the unique knowledge and skills acquired by employees.
97 Blair and Stout 'Specific Investment' (n 94) 723.
98 Martin Gelter, 'The Dark Side of Shareholder Influence: Managerial Autonomy and Stakeholder Orientation in Comparative Corporate Governance' (2009) 50 *Harvard International Law Journal* 129, 130.

particular company. All other stakeholders will have a similar concern and be less likely to make firm-specific investment, which may ultimately cause the company and society to be worse off.

In contrast, thanks to the liquid equity market, shareholders in public companies are comparatively easier to exit. And only shareholders can effectively diversify their investment and accordingly the risks through the modern portfolio strategy. Thus, there are strong grounds to question the rationale for SWM even in terms of promoting corporate prosperity. A more balanced approach must be adopted in order to encourage all stakeholders to make firm-specific contributions.

Only when the board of directors becomes the mediating hierarchy, can fear of other party's shirking or rent-seeking be correspondingly eliminated.[99] In other words, team members are more willing to make specific investment without ex ante worries and fully cooperate with each other. What is more, the board of directors as a *sui generis* hierarchy is perfectly positioned to perform such a job, which can in turn encourage all stakeholders to make their contribution. It is not worth limiting ourselves to the shareholder model, which is neither required by law nor justified by economics.[100] Directors should therefore be required to take various stakeholder interests into account.

Internalisation of negative externalities

One of the most significant weaknesses of SWM is externalisation. Unless the social costs can be fully internalised, a lopsided focus on maximising shareholders' interests will encourage directors to act in a way that increases social costs, since shareholders do not undertake the full social costs of such behaviour. As already demonstrated, shareholders are not the only risk bearer in the company. For example, if stakeholders' investment is highly specialised to the company, then they will inevitably undertake some form of the residual risk associated with it.[101] Shareholders' limited liability also implies that some of their risks have been transferred to other stakeholders such as creditors, employees and the like.

It should now be plain that existing internalisation mechanisms are not able to function effectively in the context of SWM, and negative externalities in the corporate context can only be effectively tackled by changing the norm of SWM

---

99 First, any ex ante sharing rules can inevitably lead to shirking by virtue of the fact that each party has an impulse to free ride on others' efforts. A fixed share is going to be distributed to the party regardless of how hard or well they work. Even if the ultimate output were reduced as a result of any one party/team member shirking, the shirker would only lose a small portion of the diminished surplus while having enjoyed the entire benefits of shirking. On the other hand, any ex post sharing arrangement could give rise to another severe problem – rent-seeking, that is money, time among other resources may be wasted by various parties in order to compete for a bigger slice of the already fixed surplus. Both situations would erode the aggregate wealth, either by sub-optimum efforts beforehand or wasting part of it afterwards. Margaret Blair and Lynn Stout, 'A Team Production Theory of Corporate Law' (1999) 85 *Virginia Law Review* 247, 249.

100 *Supra* Chapter 2, sections 2.5.1 and 2.3.3.

101 Blair, *Ownership and Control* (n 6) 238–239.

into a more balanced criterion.[102] The unbalanced bargaining power, information asymmetry, opportunism and bounded rationality, among others, mean the contract cannot provide adequate protection for stakeholders. Neither do external laws provide an effective mechanism to prevent the risks of externalising the cost onto third parties.[103] Therefore, internal corporate governance and company law should be resorted to.

Were the stakeholder model to replace SWM, directors would be released from the pressure of focusing on shareholder value at the expense of others.[104] The stakeholder model does not require directors to prioritise one group's interest at the expense of other groups' benefits. Unlike SWM, directors under the stakeholder model are not pressured to enhance a certain group's interest by all kinds of means. In other words, enhancing value through transferring costs to, or benefits from, others would be not acceptable since the interests of all stakeholders should be taken into account. None should be sacrificed simply for others' interests.

Though there may be conflicts between various stakeholder interests – implying not all of them would be protected simultaneously[105] – the stakeholder model would never permit or require directors to externalise costs in order to enhance certain stakeholder groups' interests. Even facing an unavoidable situation in which a decision would negatively affect some stakeholders whilst benefiting others (e.g. closing down an obsolete plant and making redundancies) – which seems similar to the scenario where one is becoming better off by making others worse off, it is fundamentally distinct from negative externalisation. Much like a situation in which only some people can be saved from danger, prioritising some stakeholders' interests after careful consideration of individual cases is exactly what is required in order to protect as many of the potentially affected stakeholders' interests as possible.[106] It would be unrealistic to protect all stakeholder interests at the same time, therefore selecting the most urgent stakeholder interests to protect according to a transparent and justifiable criterion, which will be introduced in the following section, may be the best and fairest approach. For example, when faced with the closure of an obsolete plant, both shareholders and employees' interests are involved.[107] If shareholder interests are to be protected after careful balancing according to the above criterion, then closing

---

102 *Supra* Chapter 2, section 2.4.1.
103 See Chapter 2 footnotes 160–164 and accompanying text.
104 The internal logic is similar to the pressure from pursuing short-term profits as these would be released as soon as SWM is replaced.
105 The following section will fully discuss the issue of balancing different stakeholder interests under the stakeholder model. *Infra* Chapter 5, section 5.4.1.
106 Just like the classical 'Trolley Problem', namely whether to switch the trolley to the side track to sacrifice one person in order to save the five people. Judith Thomson, 'The Trolley Problem' (1985) 94 *Yale Law Journal* 1395–1415.
107 Of course, creditors and other stakeholders may also be affected by such a decision, but here, for the sake of simplicity, we just discuss these two groups whose interests are in direct conflict.

down the plant and reducing employee numbers should not be unacceptable. In contrast, if on balance employee interests should be prioritised, then the interests of shareholders could be subsequently subordinated.

Whilst externalisation simply transfers the costs or risks to a third party in order to maximise one's interests, *selective protection* after balanced consideration under the stakeholder model does not maximise any particular stakeholder group's interests, but is the greatest act of protection in the real business world. The guideline under the stakeholder model is not to deliberately prioritise any group's interests in advance. When it is not realistic to protect everyone, then whose interests should be protected can only be answered after careful balancing and case-by-case analysis. Due to the potential conflicts arising from various stakeholders' interests, those who are not chosen to be protected are an unavoidable consequence, but they are not simply a sacrifice for others' wealth maximisation.

Indeed, board directors should be greatly motivated to avoid externalising costs to third parties when all stakeholder interests must be taken into account. Transferring costs from one party to another can only enhance one's interests whilst harming those of others. Moreover, this is not only a zero-sum game, namely whatever is gained by one stakeholder group is lost by another. It could lead to an even worse situation than this, as the unfairly treated stakeholder group may withdraw its firm-specific contributions or become less willing to make further contributions, which in turn will cause the company as a whole to be worse off.

Under circumstances where all stakeholder interests matter, there is no sense in unnecessarily prioritising one at the expense of another. The original externalities will be internalised to the costs. The criteria for corporate welfare should no longer be narrowly defined by the balance sheet, let alone the financial performance of the shares. Externalising by polluting, investing in high-risk projects, reducing employee welfare and the like in order to transfer wealth from stakeholders to shareholders will be largely eliminated, as the directing guideline including incentive mechanisms has been overturned. The externality on stakeholders in the context of the stakeholder model will be directly seen as costs of the corporate operation, and it is therefore the duty of directors to lower such costs. From the perspective of corporate welfare as a whole, any benefits brought by externalisation will be ultimately discounted, and the cost of externality will be taken onto account in the companies' profit function.

In contrast to the Volkswagen scandal discussed in Chapter 1, the Ford Pinto case explicitly shows how stakeholder thinking can internalise negative externalities.[108] Though it would be much more expensive to redesign the Pinto than to compensate injured litigants after a full cost-benefit analysis, Ford decided to adopt the former in order to avoid potential injury and death. Given that SWM is the only focus, it would be difficult to imagine that the board of Ford would be able to resist the pressure for maximising profits. Even though

---

108 For example, see Robin Malloy, *Law and Economics: A Comparative Approach to Theory and Practice* (West Publishing Co., Minnesota 1990) 148–153.

the potential costs of compensation and the like in this case would be lower than the cost of redesign from an economic perspective, the health and life of consumers are of no less importance than shareholders' economic interests. In other words, Ford gave up SWM and internalised the externalisation by prioritising other stakeholders' interests. The later development of Ford Motor Company proved to be a great success as a result of incorporating broad views instead of a single-minded focus on profit maximisation.

As a matter of fact, even shareholder primacists such as Hansmann and Kraakman admit that company law should maximise the welfare of all stakeholders, and thereby the aggregate social welfare.[109] Unfortunately, however, stakeholders' interests cannot be sufficiently protected by contract or external laws as already explained; thus there is no reason to merely maximise shareholder interests as a means of enhancing social welfare. If the stakeholder model is adopted, externalisation problems in the corporate context can be effectively restrained, implying that aggregate social welfare as the widely accepted metric would not be altered but highlighted.

The relationship between the stakeholder approach and corporate performance is also affected by how performance is defined. If only shareholder interests, in particular share prices, are included, then all the benefits to other stakeholders would be unavoidably downgraded. The aggregate societal welfare as a result would also be unfairly treated if only share price or shareholder interests were used as a measurement. As discussed above, corporate interest is not identical to shareholder interest. Even using shareholder interest as a metric, enhancing its value by externalising costs to other stakeholders is by no means sustainable.[110]

No one should be prioritised at the expense of others; the stakeholder model requires directors to take all stakeholder interests into account and thereby encourages internalising all possible costs which were ignored in the past. Values other than economic profits can also be more effectively respected under this alternative rule. As a result, normatively speaking, the stakeholder model is more valid from both the perspective of the individual company's success and the improvement of social welfare.

5.4 Main criticisms and responses

Whilst the stakeholder model encourages all stakeholders to make their contribution, discourage short-termism and reduce negative externalities, it remains true that the approach is not perfect. There are many criticisms against this model from its functional aspects. This section examines these main criticisms and assesses whether they are valid.

---

109 Although in their opinion, such a result is achieved apparently through the approach of SWM. Reinier Kraakman *et al.*, *The Anatomy of Corporate Law: A Comparative and Functional Approach* (3rd edn OUP, Oxford 2017) 22–23.

110 For the problem of short-termism and its potential to cause catastrophic outcomes, see *supra* Chapter 2, section 2.4.

5.4.1 Issue of balance

On the grounds that more than one group's interests are required to be taken into account and diverse interests are frequently in conflict, one principal task for the stakeholder model is to balance competing interests between various stakeholders. The issue of balance is usually criticised as a fatal weakness compared with the shareholder model. This encompasses two issues: first, ascertaining the real interests of each stakeholder, and second, dealing with the conflicting interests pursued by differing stakeholders.

Concerning the first issue, a thorough understanding of the stakeholder's stake is the essential precondition.[111] It would be difficult to discuss the stakeholder model or claim to manage companies for stakeholder interests if information on what stakeholders really want cannot be assessed or obtained. However, to enquire about the real stake or interest is by no means a straightforward task. Since numerous stakeholders will not automatically provide the prepared information, directors should first collect and then analyse all the views of the stakeholders. Though such channels for collecting information are not yet well established, it is not impossible to obtain such information, such as through common sense, past experience, and direct or indirect conversations.[112]

The second question of how to achieve a balance is a difficult one. It raises concerns about how more diverse and heterogeneous interests could affect decision-making. For example, CLRSG had pointed out that adopting a broader objective requires:

> The trade off of interests of members and others (with whom the company is in some aspects in an adversarial bargaining relationship), would dangerously distract management into a political balancing style at the expense of economic growth and international competitiveness.[113]

In terms of the stakeholder model, managing companies for the interests of any single stakeholder group is expressly rejected. Balanced benefits for each stakeholder become the "definitive" objective and the only legitimate objective of

---

111 Freeman, *Strategic Management* (n 4) 64. Prior to this, directors should first identify who are the stakeholders according to the concept of the stakeholder discussed earlier.

112 Some insights can be found in Professor Freeman's discussion on how to understand stakeholders' perceptions, see ibid. 113–114 and 135.

  What is noteworthy is the incongruent preferences of different subsets of each stakeholder group. Different subsets would probably have entirely differing preferences and these subsets of the subset may also possess dissimilar viewpoints. For instance, 'creditor' encompasses financial institutions, individual lenders, trade creditors, suppliers with title retention, corporate tort victims, etc. A big financial institution may prefer a higher interest rate with higher risk, while a comparatively small individual lender may focus more on the safety of their loan.

113 CLRSG, *Modern Company Law for a Competitive Economy: The Strategic Framework* (DTI, London 1999) 44. It is also argued that stakeholders' rent-seeking ability rather than the value of their firm-specific investment would affect the final decision-making.

the company.[114] As such, it seems onerous to justify a situation in which some stakeholders benefit from one specific corporate decision or investment project whereas others do not. Admittedly, in the business world, no decision could possibly benefit everyone.[115] Whereas a decision or project benefits some portion of stakeholders, it might simultaneously damage the interests of others. For instance, taking project X may cause A to be better off but B to be worse off, whilst taking an alternative project Y may generate a completely opposite outcome. In the event that directors are required to be accountable to both A and B who have to be indiscriminately treated as the ends, a managerial deadlock would subsequently arise. Regardless of whether X or Y is adopted in due course, the interests of either A or B would be disregarded and thereby damaged. Even worse, in order to escape the difficulty and potential liability, directors may choose to do nothing. Under such circumstances, the wealth of the company or the overall welfare of society would not be improved.

Conspicuously, in practice, not all interests can be treated as equal in every case. In fact, egalitarianism has been unambiguously given up as a result; a more defensible stakeholder model is instead asserted, i.e. allocating benefits according to each stakeholder's respective contribution.[116] In this way balancing could at least partly depend on the importance of each stakeholder. In the meanwhile, an ex ante solution for deriving a hierarchy of stakeholders is explicitly rejected by stakeholder theorists.[117] The stakeholder model does not endorse any prioritisation of any single stakeholder group on the one hand, and on the other, the model refuses simple egalitarianism. This is reasonable since the importance of stakeholders varies and the extent to which their interests are affected is not identical in different situations. The practical concern is how to decide which group should be prioritised over another when the interests of two or more groups come into conflict and cannot be harmonised. There is no explicit criterion. Pursuant to Reynold, Schultz and Hekman, balancing embraces: "assessing, weighing and addressing the competing claims of those who have a stake in the actions of organization".[118] But there is still no explicit method to ascertain which

---

114 Sternberg (n 33) 16.
115 It should be noted here that even if no parties were explicitly harmed by a particular decision, it does not necessarily mean that each stakeholder group gains or that everyone is happy. It could be that if other decisions were to be adopted, certain groups might gain a much more substantial benefit. But in order to obtain a balanced effect, such a decision might not be adopted in the end. For these stakeholders, it would be hard to declare that they had received a benefit. Indeed, they might lose compared with what they would have originally received if other decisions instead of a balanced plan had been adopted.
116 Phillips, Freeman and Wicks, 'What Stakeholder Theory Is Not' (n 29) 488.
117 Ibid. 496; also see Andrew Keay, 'Moving Towards Stakeholderism? Constituency Statutes, Enlightened Shareholder Value, and All That: Much Ado About Little?' (2011) 22 *European Business Law Review* 1, 7.
118 Scott Reynolds, Frank Schultz and David Hekman, 'Stakeholder Theory and Managerial Decision-making: Constraints and Implications of Balancing Stakeholder Interests' (2006) 64 *Journal of Business Ethics* 285, 286.

group is more important than the other in a company. Just as the question asked by Professors Sundaram and Inkpen, how can directors distinguish important stakeholders from unimportant ones?[119]

This difficulty could be mitigated on a case-by-case basis according to the urgency of the need. Indeed it may be the only viable way to assess the importance of various classes of stakeholder groups. Freeman suggests putting all the stakeholders into a matrix and ranking them.[120] For instance, in a given situation, if one stakeholders' contribution can be costlessly replaced or one's interests only remotely affected by a specific corporate decision, then such stakeholders may have a lower rank in this case and would thereby be less likely to be prioritised. In contrast, if certain stakeholders' contribution is of great significance to the company and a given corporate decision would greatly affect their welfare, then more consideration and attention should be paid to them. So-called stakeholder salience, i.e. the degree to which directors or their delegated managers give priority to competing stakeholder claims, can also be used here to facilitate the argument, and it is correct to contend that such salience is determined by directors who make the final decision.[121] According to the salience theory, a stakeholder group is regarded as low salient if only one attribute exists, moderately salient if two attributes exist and highly salient if three.[122] Put simply, the class of stakeholders with fewer attributes may be less likely to attract the board of directors' attention during their decision-making, and would be weighted as less important than those who possess more attributes.

The classification proffered by Professors Mitchell, Agle and Wood is still enlightening, though as discussed earlier the attribute of legitimacy ought to be the *sine qua non*.[123] It should be re-emphasised that groups with only power but no legitimacy undoubtedly need to be taken into account by the board of directors; however, it is not because of their inherent value but solely based upon their ability to influence the company and its stakeholders either in a positive or a negative way.[124]

It will be necessary to start by distinguishing claimants from influencers. Influencers can be understood as groups possessing power and urgency, whilst claimants can be understood as groups who possess the legitimacy and urgency. Second, groups with only power may be better classified as potential/dormant influencers,

---

119 Anant Sundaram and Andrew Inkpen, 'The Corporate Objective Revisited' (2004) 15 *Organization Science* 350, 352.

120 Freeman, *Strategic Management* (n 4) 112–113. A simple example is that in the case of financial difficulties, dismissing employees can be acceptable in order to protect the interests of shareholders and creditors.

121 Mitchell, Agle and Wood (n 26) 854 and 871.

122 And they are termed latent, expectant and definite stakeholders, respectively. Ibid. 873–874.

123 *Supra* Chapter 5 footnotes 45–52 and accompanying text.

124 In particular, if those influencers' claims are consistent with the interests of the company, e.g. when certain activist groups or media represent injured stakeholders' interest and urge the directors to take this stakeholder group into account, then it should be regarded as a chance to modify suboptimal decisions and further advance stakeholders' interests. If these influencers simply aim to interfere in the smooth running of the business, which would cause significant damage to both company and stakeholders, directors are required to adopt defensive measures to crack these challenges.

since they may not use their power to influence if they do not feel the urgency of the issue. Groups with only legitimacy may be better classified as potential/discretionary claimants since they have no urgent need to claim their stake.

Professor Fassin's classification of "(real) stakeholders", "stakewatchers" and "stakekeepers"[125] is a useful complement to the sorting system above. Stakewatchers and stakekeepers, who do not really have a stake themselves in the company but either "protect the interests of real stakeholders" or "impose external control and regulations on the firm",[126] can be categorised into those who possess power and probably urgency attributes as well. It is noteworthy that stakewatchers such as environmentalists or other special interests groups may use coercive means to protect and advance supposedly legitimate claims.[127] Though all three types should definitely be considered by the board during decision-making, directors only have a positive responsibility to the *real stakeholders* and endeavours to advance their welfare. Taking influencers like stakewatchers or stakekeepers into account is mainly for the interests of real stakeholders by either taking their constructive suggestions or defusing adversarial hold-ups.

Directors may be accustomed to giving lopsided weight to the attribute of power, which is not surprising as these power holders can influence and affect the company directly.[128] By defining power in the context of the corporate governance system, Professor Frooman observes that the level of stakeholder dependence on the company and company dependence on the stakeholder group determines the ability to affect each other.[129] When one is highly dependent on the other, the latter is able to exert significant influence on the former and even threaten to withhold.[130] It can be summarised as "power resides implicitly in the other's dependency".[131] Generally speaking, the more dependent the company, the more powerful the stakeholder.[132] If stakeholders and the company are mutually dependent, it may be more appropriate to define power as a relative term and see which party is more dependent on the other.[133] Directors should know

---

125 Fassin, 'A Dynamic Perspective in Freeman's Stakeholder Model' (n 43) 40.

126 Ibid.

127 According to Fassin, both stakewatchers and stakekeepers can not only harm but also benefit a company. Ibid. And this is indeed consistent with the analysis of influencers discussed earlier. Accordingly, it may be helpful to distinguish supportive groups from non-supportive ones.

128 Power, or say the ability to affect the company, is usually thought to be a central determinant, though it should not be so, as will be discussed later.

129 Frooman (n 57) 196.

130 Ibid.

131 Richard Emerson, 'Power-Dependence Relations' (1962) 27 *American Sociological Review* 31, 32.

132 Savage *et al.* (n 19) 63. The authors point out that power is a function of the company's dependence on the stakeholder, for instance, "the power of a supplier is a function of the firm's dependence on the supplier". And vice versa. Ibid.

133 Frooman (n 57) 196 referred to Edward Lawler and Jeongkoo Yoon, 'Structural Power and Emotional Processes in Negotiation: A Social Exchange Approach' in R Roderick Kramer and David Messick (eds), *Negotiation as A Social Process* (Sage Publications, Thousand Oaks 1995) 143–165. And in this case, if neither party can succeed without the other, it is then less likely that either party would use the strategy of hold up or say blackmail. Instead, a mutually beneficial decision may be easier to adopt.

how to collaborate with the stakeholders who possess the attribute of power. As explained earlier, power can be understood as the other party's dependence; it can either benefit or harm the interests of the company or the legitimate stakeholders. The case of Eastern Airlines exemplifies the attribute of power in the corporate context and how to respond to it.[134] Clearly an airline company relies heavily on pilots, meaning the latter has material power over the former, but during the strike, when Eastern Airlines resorted to a pilot training school for new pilots, the power of (incumbent) pilots reduced as the company's dependence on them was lowered. But power should not become the determinant for trade-off, just as the group with the attribute of power alone cannot become the stakeholder.[135] It is also worth noting that "the stakeholder with the loudest voice is but one stakeholder among many and may even have a marginal stake".[136]

Since the attribute of legitimacy is the premise, balance under the stakeholder model should require directors of the board to prioritise the interests of legitimate stakeholders with the attribute of urgency. This is important because if directors can respond to stakeholders' urgent claims immediately, it is possible to prevent stakeholders from becoming harmful and exerting a negative influence on the company. In contrast, the original potentially beneficial stakeholders who may add value to the company may turn out to be non-supportive if not treated properly.[137] This suggests that stakeholders may deserve more attention as soon as they acquire the attribute of urgency.

As stated above, the specific condition may change from time to time and from case to case, so even the same stakeholder group in the same company may deserve different attention and/or treatment over time. Similar to the identification theory proffered by Professors Mitchell, Agle and Wood, there is no attempt to predict the circumstances in which it is urgent, but such an attribute is captured when it appears;[138] the balance between various stakeholder interests also needs to be determined on a case-by-case basis according to the specific conditions. Many decisive factors are in a variable state, and it would be impossible to forecast the weight of each stakeholder group's claim. Any attempt to establish a universally suitable model of trading off between various stakeholders' interests will fail to capture the essence of stakeholder theory.

134 Savage *et al.* (n 19) 71.
135 Namely, when this group does not process the attribute of legitimacy. *Supra* Chapter 5, section 5.2.
136 Savage *et al.* (n 19) 72.
137 For example, the bankruptcy of Eastern Airline made their business passengers, tour companies and small feeder airlines worse off and they turned out to be non-supportive stakeholders having originally had supportive status. Ibid. 71.
138 Mitchell, Agle and Wood (n 26) 868. Moreover, they have warned that "managers should never forget that stakeholders change in salience, requiring different degrees and types of attention depending on their attributed possession of power, legitimacy, and/or urgency, and that levels of these attributes (and thereby salience) can vary from issue to issue and from time to time". Ibid. 879. The changing nature of stakeholders can also be seen in Fassin, 'A Dynamic Perspective in Freeman's Stakeholder Model' (n 43) 44.

Long-term sustainable development (hereafter, LTSD) is another important criterion that can be used in addition to the criterion of urgency. The LTSD criterion should be based on the best interests of the company at the time the directors make corporate decisions.[139] The ultimate goal is to enhance the interests of the company as a whole and not solely of any one group. The concept of the best interests of the company could include both profits from today's and tomorrow's activities. It could also include "the interwoven interests of its various constituencies, such as shareholders, employees, customers, the local community, and others" according to Steven Wallman, former Commissioner of the US Securities and Exchange Commission.[140]

Although no single theory or approach could provide concrete measures to resolve all problems,[141] when the best interests of the company can be combined with LTSD, a comparatively more objective criterion can then be established to help make the balance much more traceable and acceptable. Long-termism itself is an inherent requirement of the stakeholder model; both intended and unintended short-termism are explicitly abandoned. In the meantime, the interests of any particular stakeholder groups can be marked if it is against the long-term and sustainable interests of the company. If a decision does not accord with such a criterion, then it should normally be rejected or at least not prioritised. Many difficult balance issues arising from competing stakeholder interests can be solved when the LTSD criterion is applied. The interests more closely aligned with LTSD should be prioritised. Redundancy, for example, is generally deemed to be ignoring the interests of affected employees, or even to be transferring interests from employees to shareholders. On the other hand, maintaining employment by keeping an obsolete and unprofitable plant running may decrease the original available money to creditors, aside from the issue of the diminution in shareholder wealth. Thus, the conflict between employees and creditors/shareholders seems irreconcilable and therefore the balance seems difficult to achieve. However, under the LTSD criterion, maintaining employment through keeping the obsolete and unprofitable plant running is apparently unwise. The ultimate outcome of doing this is to impair the interests of all the stakeholders in due course. Thus, the interests of creditors and shareholders in this particular case should be prioritised in order to maintain long-term and sustainable development.

---

139 It doesn't matter whether such a decision becomes suboptimal later on after the appearance of new conditions.

140 Wallman further argues: "[linking] these interests to the corporation's interest resolves much of the tension that would otherwise exist from competing and conflicting constituent demands. For example, employees could demand such high wages that the corporation would not be able to produce a profit; shareholders could demand such high dividends that the corporation could not withstand a downturn in its business". Steven Wallman, 'The Proper Interpretation of Corporate Constituency Statutes and Formulation of Director Duties' (1991) 21 *Stetson Law Review* 163, 170.

141 Phillips, Freeman and Wicks, 'What Stakeholder Theory Is Not' (n 29) 486, refers to Thomas Donaldson and Thomas Dunfee, *Ties That Bind* (Harvard Business School Press, Boston 1999) 262.

Similarly, supposing one company faced a choice of whether to invest money in reducing pollution and, if so, to what extent. On the one hand, installing equipment to alleviate pollution is undoubtedly good for the environment and the health of the local community, but it would adversely affect profitability which, in turn, could impair employment, tax revenues to governments and even cause plant closures. On the other hand, refusing to install sufficient abatement equipment would give rise to an exactly opposite effect. How should directors make a decision? Although the urgency of the demands by different stakeholders is not straightforward, the answer is comparatively easier when applying the LTSD criterion. To prioritise the interests of the environment here fits the criterion of sustainable development. Although keeping the plant running by ignoring the environment could escape penalty or punishment in the short term and bring benefit to the whole company (except affected stakeholders), in the long run such a pattern is doomed to fail and moreover would cause negative externalities to society as a whole.[142]

Last but not least, the heterogeneous expectations of different shareholders further prove that balance is necessary everywhere. Directors must balance long-term interests with short-term profits, the interests of diversified shareholders with undiversified shareholders, and so forth. In fact, people routinely have more than one responsibility,[143] and can normally handle the conflicts well. There is no reason for directors who receive hundreds of thousands of pounds a year in public companies to escape the duty, or perhaps the burden, of balancing interests.

5.4.2 Accountability and monitoring

As directors have to balance various stakeholder interests which are frequently in conflict, there is a growing suspicion that directors may become more unaccountable if the stakeholder model substitutes the shareholder model. For example, Professor Jensen claims, "it would literally leave managers unmonitored and unaccountable in any principled way for their actions with the vast resources under their control".[144] Therefore, this subsection focuses on the issue of accountability of directors in the context of the stakeholder model.

First of all, it should be clarified that the shareholder model also lacks mechanisms against managerial opportunism.[145] The so-called conventional standard to measure and evaluate the behaviour and performance of directors, such as a

---

142 Of course, the attribute of urgency should also be considered during this process, namely first, whether the environment or people's health would be slightly or significantly affected due to the level of pollution; and second, whether shareholder or employees would be slightly or significantly affected as a result of the cost of such an installation.

143 Greenfield, 'New Principles for Corporate Law' (n 80) 103.

144 Michael Jensen, 'Non-rational Behavior, Value Conflicts, Stakeholder Theory, and Firm Behavior' in Bradley Agle *et al.*, 'Dialogue: Toward Superior Stakeholder Theory' (2008) 18 *Business Ethics Quarterly* 153, 168.

145 Phillips, Freeman and Wicks, 'What Stakeholder Theory Is Not' (n 29) 484.

company's share price and dividends in the shareholder model,[146] are not infallible.[147] Under SWM, there is no explicit route to increase shareholder value. As analysed in Chapter 2, different shareholders may have substantially heterogeneous expectations and different companies may be confronted with different situations; it may then not only be impossible but also unnecessary to design a specific guideline.

The normal approach is that as long as self-interests are not involved and no gross negligence occurs, the directors will then not be blamed, at least from a legal perspective. If this works under SWM, it should also work under the stakeholder model. There is no necessity for an accurately measureable guideline for directors to follow. An accurately measurable guideline means a model under which all directors' behaviour could be quantified. In fact, such a guideline is not available in SWM either. This means we should only look at whether directors conduct self-serving behaviour and whether adequate diligence or prudence is in place. Currently, both the business judgement rule in the US and its counterpart in UK case law effectively shield directors' decision-making from the hazard of judging with hindsight. This has already bestowed on directors autonomous and unrestrained power to freely make a decision in good faith.

In the words of Professors Donaldson and Preston, "it is difficult to conceive of managers having greater scope for self-serving behavior than they have already". The current shareholder model has failed to effectively ensure such accountability, and at the same time no undue attention to any single stakeholder group is allowed.[148] In other words, it would be untenable for shareholder primacists to impose a higher standard on the stakeholder model than SWM with regard to accountability and monitoring, and use the inability of incorporating such higher standards to refuse the stakeholder model.

Opponents may argue that it would at least be easier for directors to conceal their self-serving behaviour under the stakeholder model. The typical argument is constructed as follows: "when management's interests coincide with those of shareholders, management could justify its decision by saying that shareholder interests prevailed in this instance, and vice-versa".[149] Similarly, Marcousx also argues that: "all but the most egregious self-serving managerial behaviour will doubtless serve the interests of some stakeholder constituencies and work against the interests of others".[150] Under such circumstances, it becomes arduous to question the accountability of a director's behaviour. They may only be concerned

---

146 For example, see Simon Deakin and Giles Slinger, 'Hostile Takeovers, Corporate Law, and the Theory of the Firm' (1997) 24 *Journal of Law and Society* 124, 127.

147 Indeed, these criteria are the main reason for directors to pursue short-term interests without regard for long-term development. *Supra* Chapter 2, section 2.3.2.

148 Donaldson and Preston, 'The Stakeholder Theory of the Corporation' (n 10) 87.

149 Stephen Bainbridge, 'In Defense of the Shareholder Wealth Maximization Norm: A Reply to Professor Green' (1993) 50 *Washington and Lee Law Review* 1423, 1438.

150 Alexei Marcoux, 'Balancing Act' in Joseph DesJardins and John McCall (eds), *Contemporary Issues in Business Ethics* (4th edn Wadsworth, Belmont 2000) 97.

with their own position and perquisites, and a rational justification could always potentially be established. Inevitably, it is argued, multiple accountabilities may only leave directors to be accountable to no one on the grounds that they could continually find an excuse to benefit themselves. Like the example of closing down a plant, providing that the bonuses and perks are linked to the overall size of the company, then directors could reject the closure of the obsolete plant by referring to the negative effects on employees and the local community. Or, in the event that their compensation is determined by the profitability of the company, directors are able to support the closure with an argument that the benefits of shareholders, creditors and the welfare of the employees overall should be prioritised. It is pessimistically held by shareholder primacists that the wide scope of duties renders the law ineffective, and directors are immune from blame for their self-serving behaviour as they can always claim that their behaviour at least advances one stakeholder group's interests.

However, the sorting system based on salience and the LTSD criterion, as introduced earlier, may largely deter such a situation. Directors cannot choose to prioritise one stakeholder group over another at will, since they are required to meet these explicit criteria.[151] It is a foundation of stakeholder theory to balance competing interests between different stakeholders and to not place undue focus on the interests of any singe stakeholder group.[152] The rule is quite clear: namely, increasing value for all legitimate stakeholders without favouring one group at the expense of others.[153]

It is also argued that non-shareholding stakeholders could be legitimised to exercise some control over companies when they share residual gains and risk.[154] However, this book does not try to argue that stakeholders should be entitled to more power in order to protect or advance their legitimate interests. Although accountability is important, the value of centralised authority should not be underestimated.[155] Chapter 3 has demonstrated that shareholder empowerment does not help to enhance their value under SWM. By the same token, in the context of the stakeholder model, stakeholders' limited powers may not warrant an immediate change. Since the power over the input and output of the company has been ceded to the board of directors, there are reasons to believe that the board of directors, as a mediating hierarchy, could do the job of balancing well. Otherwise there is no point in having such an arrangement in the first place. In addition to the pressure from the competitive management market, reputation and the legal constraints on self-serving, the criteria in the act of balancing could help to alleviate or eliminate worries about managerial opportunism.

151 When faced with an obsolete plant, for instance, and shutting it down fits with long-term sustainable development, then directors must do so.
152 For example, see Donaldson and Preston, 'The Stakeholder Theory of the Corporation' (n 10) 87.
153 Clarkson, 'A Stakeholder Framework for Analyzing and Evaluating Corporate Social Performance' (n 23) 112.
154 Blair, *Ownership and Control* (n 6) 231.
155 *Supra* Chapter 3, section 3.3.2.

5.4.3 Enforceability

Another important functional aspect of the stakeholder model is the mechanism of enforcement, which requires being effective without incurring excessive costs in the one sense and efficacious in deterring *mala fide* actions in another. It is well known that, "a right without a remedy is worthless";[156] however, it seems in the stakeholder model that enforcement is a tricky issue. Under SWM, the mixture of internal governance right, derivative action and market control, among other things, can be used against directors' opportunistic behaviour and shirk. But under the stakeholder model, what can stakeholders do in the event that companies are not managed in their interests or their interests are damaged? It is suggested that stakeholders should be allowed to take derivative actions or bring actions on the grounds of unfair prejudice.[157] This would mean an increasing possibility of a great amount of unmeritorious actions which might be harmful to the company and necessitate a material change to current company law.[158]

Moreover, it is hard to imagine a court in either the UK or the US taking an active role in judging whether directors are running the company for stakeholder interests or which stakeholder group should be prioritised in the event of conflicts. Judges are not business experts and they should not be expected to bear the responsibility for ensuring the implementation of the stakeholder model. Even under the traditional shareholder model, courts are always ready to defer to good-faith business judgement as long as no self-serving is involved.[159]

Admittedly, the stakeholder model does not provide an algorithm for day-to-day management, neither does SWM. In the eyes of shareholder primacists, SWM as a singular objective is easier to monitor and enforce.[160] However, this is not true. First, it would be very difficult, if not impossible, to distinguish whether in the long run benefits are affected by an action that impairs short-term cash flow. Whether a healthy return is generated by genuine good management or merely short-term manipulation is not easy to distinguish, and a corporate decision for long-term benefits may possibly impair immediate profits.[161] Second, neither case law nor statutes require directors to maximise shareholder profits, not to mention short-term economic benefits.[162] Finally, even if directors fail to maximise current shareholder value in practice, directors are generally immune from failure as long as they act in good faith and with reasonable care, skill and diligence, as

---

156 Morey McDaniel, 'Bondholders and Stockholders' (1987) 13 *Journal of Corporate Law* 205, 309.

157 For example, see Dean (n 67) 176–177.

158 Alexander Schall, Lilian Miles and Simon Goulding, 'Promoting an Inclusive Approach on the Part of Directors: The UK and German Positions' (2006) 6 *Journal of Corporate Law Studies* 299, 300.

159 It can be seen in the business judgement rule in the US and a similar common law practice in the UK. *Supra* Chapter 3, sections 3.2.1 and 3.2.2.

160 This means directors' behaviour can be monitored and measured, and it follows that if their behaviour does not comply with this objective then dissenting shareholders may take action against the directors.

161 *Supra* Chapter 2, section 2.4.2.

162 *Supra* Chapter 2, section 2.5.1.

previously discussed. Much like the argument "a legal duty to maximize profits is too hard to monitor",[163] disappointed shareholders who think their interests are not maximised can rarely resort to the law as a remedy, implying that SWM is not legally enforceable as expected. As a result, the absence of a readily workable enforcement mechanism may not be a lethal weakness for the stakeholder model when compared with SWM.

Further, a stakeholder model based on shareholders' selection of directors is criticised as unconvincing, since the directors are thought to owe their position to the shareholders. However, James McConvill aptly observes:

> The assumption that shareholders had the ultimate control over directors due to the power to elect which directors they wanted was a myth, as the board had effective control over proxies and the agenda of general meetings.[164]

Chapter 3 revealed that boards of directors are generally insulated from share-holders' intervention and they can even elect themselves. Directors' independent judgement is not only preserved but also encouraged. Moreover, there are significant practical hurdles for shareholders to remove directors.[165] In the meantime, allowing all major stakeholders to be represented on the board may not make a material change. First, empirical studies show boards comprised of stakeholder representatives do not have a significant impact on improving stakeholder relations or stakeholder performance.[166] And it would not be surprising if stakeholder representatives on the board were only concerned with the interests of the particular stakeholder group(s) they represented, rather than with the overall welfare of the company. Besides, as explained under the criteria of urgency and LTSD, the rank of importance or urgency could vary case by case. Therefore, it makes no sense to empower stakeholders as the case of shareholder empowerment shows.[167]

Frankly, it cannot be denied that the enforcement issue under the stake-holder model is no better than the situation under the shareholder model. Further research is still needed in this field. However, the positive aspects at the moment include the increasing obligation on disclosure, which may further help stakeholders to access information and get a clearer picture. Especially with

163 Einer Elhauge, 'Sacrificing Corporate Profits in the Public Interest' (2005) 80 *New York University Law Review* 733, 739.
164 James McConvill, 'Shareholder Empowerment as an End in Itself: A New Perspective on Allocation of Power in the Modern Corporation' (2007) 33 *Ohio Northern University Law Review* 1013, 1018. Similarly, Professors Blair and Stout state "shareholders in public corporations do not in any realistic sense elect boards. Rather, boards elect themselves". Blair and Stout, 'A Team Production Theory of Corporate Law' (n 99) 311. It is usually the existing board that nominates the following year's board.
165 *Supra* Chapter 3 footnotes 74–77 and accompanying text.
166 Amy Hillman *et al.*, 'Board Composition and Stakeholder Performance: Do Stakeholder Directors Make a Difference?' (2001) 40 *Business and Society* 295, 308–309.
167 However, this by no means prevents stakeholders from taking derivative action on behalf of the company in the future if the best interests of the company are harmed, which might be another very interesting topic worthy of further research.

the advance of communication and transmission technologies, it is easier for unaccountability to be exposed. Second, having employee representatives on the board may more directly ensure the implementation of the stakeholder model. The example of the dual board structure in Germany and some other European countries provides a useful example. In addition, since the best interests of a company cannot be separated from the interests of various stakeholders,[168] it is not impossible to use corporate interests as a proxy in the stakeholder model.[169]

5.5 Concluding remarks

A good company should provide a fair return to its shareholders, deliver quality products and services to consumers, build a good relationship with suppliers, take care of creditors' interests, improve job security and welfare for employees, and contribute to the well-being of the local communities and the prosperity of society. A narrow, shareholder-focused approach is increasingly more difficult to justify as a suitable guide for directors and their delegated managers in a company.

The failure of theoretical bases and other inherent defects of the shareholder model as discussed in Chapter 2 impel us to consider an alternative more suitable model for modern large public companies. The increasingly important role of stakeholders and their indispensable firm-specific investment in the success of a company imply that the stakeholder model could be the substitute. Such a model requires directors to be accountable to more than just shareholders, which could help to internalise negative externalities and release directors and their delegated managers from a lopsided focus on short-term interests.

This chapter also recognises the imperfections of the current stakeholder model, but these imperfections are by no means insurmountable. The attribute of legitimacy and narrow interpretation could help to identify who are the real stakeholders and their stake in the company. Criteria of urgency and long-term sustainable development can be utilised to facilitate the balancing of different stakeholders' interests, though further research is needed to improve the monitoring and enforcement aspects of the stakeholder model. The current problems should not deter the adoption of this model as we can find the issues under the shareholder model are indeed no better, which means, compared with SWM, the absence of a readily workable enforcement mechanism under the stakeholder model should not be the lethal weakness as attacked by shareholder primacists.

---

168 Dean (n 67) 176.

169 Professor Keay has recently proffered a new approach – the entity maximisation and sustainability model, which is based on the idea that the company is a distinct entity and independent from all its investors. Andrew Keay, 'Ascertaining the Corporate Objective: An Entity Maximisation and Sustainability Model' (2008) 71 *Modern Law Review* 663, 671; Andrew Keay, *The Corporate Objective* (Edward Elgar, Cheltenham 2011).

    However, the inherent defects such as overestimating the artificial nature of the entity, an ill-designed maximisation and profit allocation, and a lack of workability would finally give rise to the directors' unaccountability. Thus more research is needed to further clarify these uncertainties.

6 A more suitable corporate objective in China

6.1 An overview

As a socialist country, China should have added reasons to look beyond maximising shareholders' interests. Nevertheless, under the influence of SWM from the West, the economic analysis of company law, through the lens of agency theory in particular, is increasingly well received by Chinese scholars. They argue the management of large public companies dominated by the state does not optimise economic performance and claim company law and corporate governance is mainly designed to reduce agency costs at all levels. For instance, incentive mechanisms such as share options are regarded as the elixir for aligning the interests of directors with those of shareholders.

However, apart from the problems and concerns detailed in Chapter 2, ignoring stakeholders' interests by cutting jobs and the like is not consistent with the general political and social atmosphere. Indeed, profit maximisation is not necessarily the goal of state-owned enterprises (hereafter, SOEs), which account for the majority of China's largest companies. The preference of SOEs, or companies where the state has a say, is normally not to act against stakeholders' interests.[1] Even for non-state-owned companies, it would be difficult not to see the influence of politics and political responsibility, as discussed later.

Along with the problems under the shareholder model, as well as the potential advantage of the stakeholder model, this chapter takes China's unique national situation into account by analysing the lessons from historic experience. It also considers the role of the working class and corporate social and political responsibilities as stakeholding factors.

6.2 Lessons from the past

Chapter 4 identified how historical legacies and current legal, political and economic elements have advanced the shareholder wealth maximisation ideology as

---

1 Baocai Yu, 'What are the Responsibilities of State-Owned Enterprises' *Xinhua* (Beijing 16 November 2006) at http://news.xinhuanet.com/fortune/2006–11/16/content_5338255.htm [accessed 1 March 2017].

the corporate objective and governance norm in China. The mainstream viewpoint held by both authorities and academics at the moment could be classified as shareholder-oriented, which can be seen as a great leap forward from an era that ignored private interests. Although in terms of path dependency theory, "today's road depends on what path was taken before", due to factors such as adaptive costs, complementarities, network externalities and the like,[2] the traditional government-dominated model is too ineffective, and change, even at significant cost, is essential. The extreme inadequacy of private property rights and an over-emphasis on state control in the past intensified the desire and yearning for change. As soon as investors from the private sector were allowed to participate during the late Qing reform period, a game has continually been playing out between the state/government and private shareholders. The state has dominated most of the time, especially after the establishment of PRC, where collectivism prevails over individualism. Hence it may help to understand why the shareholder-centred argument sprang up after the state started loosening its ties. Moreover, the Western mainstream standpoint that SWM is able to lead to economic efficiency and social wealth maximisation also exerts a great impact on shareholder primacy in China.

Progress is usually based on historical experiences and lessons. If we can learn something from the history of corporate evolution in China, then the most significant lesson, at least from the perspective of ownership and control, should be abstention from excessive state interference. There is no need for excessive state or government involvement. In fact, the company can run well or even better by self-governing at the micro level, as long as a good governance system exists.

Over 150 years of corporate evolution in China, governments during different periods have always exerted an active and dominant role. In this regard, history moves in cycles. It went from complete control at the start of the late Qing Dynasty to gradually granting to private investors more self-governing and discretionary powers over management. The next phase entailed a period where the government once again concentrated economic power by nationalising the majority of both industrial and financial firms.[3] The establishment of PRC then followed on from this, where the new government first obtained complete control of the economic sectors and then corporatised all the SOEs. The engagement of private-sector actors gradually became essential for economic success. Nonetheless, it is observed that no matter how effectively the market-oriented economy runs, "the idea that planning is essential for

---

2 Mark Roe, 'Chaos and Evolution in Law and Economics' (1995) 109 *Harvad Law Review* 641, 648; Lucian Bebchuk and Mark Roe, 'A Theory of Path Dependence in Corporate Ownership and Governance' (1999) 52 *Stanford Law Review* 127, 129.

3 It can be estimated that if *Kuomingtang*, the ruling party at the time, had not been defeated by the *Communist Party*, it may finally have adopted policies to divest its interests in corporate sectors, allowing and encouraging private capitals to be involved as has happened in Taiwan, which is still ruled by *Kuomingtang* until 2016.

China's economic development remains in the mind of government officials".[4] In particular, the recent worldwide economic recession led China to undertake a more active macroeconomic stimulus policy to revitalise the domestic economy, suggesting that central planning is still significant in China's economy.

Nevertheless, directing or influencing the economy can be realised in ways other than directly controlling a multitude of large companies. Withdrawing from the traditional SOEs does not necessarily indicate the government would lose control over the national economy. Neither does it mean public interests would be negatively affected if those strategically significant sectors are not in the hands of the government.

Admittedly, it is easier for the government to fulfil its economic, political or social objectives given that the government directly holds a great number of companies which in turn control substantial quantities of economic resources.[5] Yet, policy, legal and economic measures among others can be utilised to achieve the same end instead of controlling the companies and resources directly. For example, economic incentives such as favourable tax policies, direct financial subsidies or loans can motivate privately owned companies to enter into certain fields or engage in certain activities, with essential macroeconomic control only occasionally being implemented. As soon as the government took their hands off the tiller, the market was able to perform its role and effectively allocate resources to meet various demands in most situations. As highlighted in the previous chapter's discussion, history clearly demonstrates the importance of autonomy in the private sector.[6] Concerning the protection of public interests, as the market has its own limits from time to time, it is absolutely feasible for the government to bring in specific rules or laws to regulate it, either by encouraging or restricting certain behaviours. A prominent Chinese economist incisively points out the real problem:

> Some people, particularly the social and political elites, have tremendous interest in maintaining the old system. If those people with vested interests in the old system cannot regard the interest of the entire society as of primary importance, they will use all kinds of excuses, including political ones, to hinder the progress of reform and restructuring.[7]

4 For example, see Gregory Chow, 'Economic Planning in China' (2011) *Princeton University CEPS Working Paper No.219*.

5 For example, it may be argued, as some scholars do, that China's government wants to retain the ownership of its traditional SOEs in order to ask them to fulfill tasks more than simply undertaking wealth maximisation. Donald Clarke, 'Corporate Governance in China: An Overview' (2003) 14 *China Economic Review* 494, 494–495 and 497–499.

6 Also see John Coffee, 'The Rise of Dispersed Ownership: The Roles of Law and the State in the Separation of Ownership and Control' (2011) 111 *Yale Law Journal* 1, 72.

7 Jinglian Wu, 'China's Economic Reform: Past, Present and Future' (2000) 1 *Perspectives* at www.oycf.org/Perspectives2/5_043000/china.htm [accessed 1 November 2012].

This does indeed correspond to the argument put forward by Professors Bebchuk and Roe, who write:

> Existing corporate structures might well have persistence power due to internal rent-seeking, even if they cease to be efficient. Those parties who participate in corporate control under an existing structure might have the incentive and power to impede changes that would reduce their private benefits of control even if the change would be efficient.[8]

Thus giving up direct control of SOEs will not necessarily hurt the national economy or public interests as long as the market system and corresponding regulations are established.[9] The so-called state economic lifelines, excepting industries involving national security, could be served equally well by utilising market mechanisms and macroeconomic control among other measures. Those who will be adversely affected are normally those people with vested interests in the traditional SOE system, because they will lose their rent-seeking ability for private benefits.

SWM or say the shareholder model is, as a result, regarded by people as a huge improvement over the original government-centred model. Although the former looks very different from the latter on first appearance, both in fact have substantial common features. Under the government-centred model, running the *state-owned* companies to comply with the willingness of the government as the "owner" could still be seen as taking care of shareholder interests, because the state (i.e. the government) is the only shareholder.[10] From this perspective, there is no material distinction between the above two models, as the shareholder-centred model is characterised by maximising shareholder interests. If any dissimilarity does exist, then it is that the interests under the government-centred model are not necessarily economic interests, but normally political or

---

8 Bebchuk and Roe (n 2) 130.

9 Another important reason might be to maintain the ruling status. Given that direct control is held by the state, it is beneficial to ensure stability since the government can more easily reallocate or distribute resources, among other things, without having to explain it to the public. In contrast, if the state surrenders such direct control, then it has to rely on laws, rules, economic measures and the like to regulate and guide development, as discussed earlier, all of which call for explicit supporting reasons that can no longer be manipulated through black-box operations since they would be exposed to the whole population. Some earlier approaches and methods may not work under the new circumstances, and the existing government will surely encounter more direct and indirect challenges as a result.

   Besides, as mentioned by Professor Donald Clarke, the embedded *official suspicion* of "accumulations of wealth" or "any organized activity" not controlled or led by the government would result in the reluctance of the Chinese government to further release its control over SOEs. See Clarke, 'Corporate Governance in China' (n 5) 496.

10 Of course, this is different from the models in the feudal period where government dominated without making any investment.

social ones, such as increasing job opportunities, easing employment pressure, improving infrastructure or environmental protection. Nevertheless, the *interests* of shareholders can be anything. Maximising economic interests may not necessarily be what shareholders demand in every company. For instance, in certain companies with an environmental or social focus, putting too much stress on economic profits would thus not accord with shareholders' real demands.

Moreover, conflicts of interest exist in both models. When private investors began to enter into traditional SOEs, the government remained in a dominant position, and the divergence between the non-economic and economic objectives of government and private shareholders could only be ended at the expense of private shareholders. Similarly, today's shareholder-centred model in China would usually focus on the interests of the majority shareholder.[11] But conflicts between majority and minority shareholders have yet to be eliminated. Controlling shareholders are able to pursue private benefits at the expense of minority shareholders by their dominant position and influence.[12]

6.3 Stakeholding factors with Chinese unique characteristics

Protection for legitimate shareholder rights, especially minority shareholder interests, is absolutely essential. However, the importance of shareholder protection does not necessarily imply other stakeholders' interests are not important or should be subordinated. Stakeholders' contributions, as proved, are also essential for a company's survival and success. The foregoing chapter has dealt with the stakeholder theory in some detail. In short, such a theory or model requests that those who hold a legitimate stake in companies should be taken into account and not be automatically subordinated to any other group's interests. The socialist nature further determines that issues more than economic wealth maximisation should be considered. As a socialist state, it is not surprising for China to emphasise the position of stakeholder groups according to the prevailing political ideology. This section explores the other side of China's company law, i.e. that apart from a shareholder-centred inclination, the socialist character can also be identified.

6.3.1 Role of employees

To begin with, employees, a vital stakeholder group in the Western corporate governance system, have an even more superior position in China. According to socialist ideology, the working class is the ruling and leading class in society.[13]

---

11 *Supra* Chapter 4 footnote 102 and accompanying text. It is also interesting to see that the majority shareholder in the largest public companies in China is normally the state.

12 However, this is not to say that a dispersed ownership structure must be better than a concentrated one. The almost unfettered discretionary power of management and the potential managerial lack of accountability under the dispersed ownership pattern are also tricky problems confronting corporate lawyers.

13 Unlike the West, where employee protection is mainly due to their weaker bargaining power, workers in China are deemed to be the masters of the state according to the *Constitution of PRC*.

Consequently, article 17 of *Company Law 2005* specifies employee protection by stating that the company shall protect the lawful rights and interests of its employees, conclude employment contracts with the employees, buy social insurance and strengthen labour protection so as to realise safe production. The following article provides the foundation for labour union activity in companies in order to safeguard the lawful rights and interests of the employees with respect to remuneration, working hours, welfare, insurance, operational safety and health of employees, among others.[14]

More importantly, regarding a decision on restructuring or any important issue related to business operations, or to formulate any important regulation, the company is mandatorily required to solicit the opinions from its labour union, and shall solicit the opinions and proposals from its employees through the employees' representative congress or other channels.[15] This mandatory provision makes employees' opinions of great significance prior to making certain important corporate decisions.

Further, companies in China have a dual board structure consisting of a board of directors (hereafter, BOD) and a board of supervisors (hereafter, BOS).[16] According to articles 52 and 118 of *Company Law 2005*, representatives of employees are required to sit on the BOS in both limited liability companies (hereafter, LLC) and joint stock limited companies (hereafter, JSLC).[17] The ratio of employee representatives shall not be lower than one-third and individual companies could of course set a higher ratio in its company's constitution. In the meantime, the powers of the BOS in the revised law have been substantially strengthened compared with the *Company Law 1993*.[18] It provides

14 Article 18 of *Company Law 2005* provides that the company shall provide necessary conditions for its labour union to carry out activities. The labour union shall, on behalf of the employees, conclude the collective contract with the company with respect to the above mentioned issues.
15 Article 18(3) of *Company Law 2005*.
16 The German dual board structure was adopted by *Company Law 1993* and then inherited by *Company Law 2005*. The functions of one-tier and two-tier boards are not fundamentally different. The supervision role of the independent directors on the management board has, or at least is supposed to have, the effect of reproducing the monitoring function of BOS.
17 The distinction between LLC and JSLC can be found in *supra* Chapter 4 footnotes 55–56 and accompanying text. It is noteworthy that when a LLC is relatively small in scale with small numbers of shareholders, it may have one or two supervisors instead of a BOS, in which case the law does not say whether an employee representative is still required. However, the companies discussed in this book are large public companies as explained in Chapter 1, and for these companies a BOS is normally required.
18 For example, see the powers specified in articles 54 and 55 of *Company Law 2005*. However, it is also worth noting that the BOS in China, unlike its counterpart in Germany, remains largely toothless and has inadequate power to effectively perform their function. First, the majority of the members of the BOS are normally elected by shareholders. Second, members of the BOD are elected by shareholders. The BOS in China cannot appoint or dismiss a director, which is the norm in the German dual-tier board structure; instead, it can only put forward a proposal to remove directors. The BOD in Chinese companies is consequently not accountable to the BOS. As both directors and the majority of supervisors are chosen by shareholders, particularly the controlling or majority shareholders, it is more difficult for them to resist shareholder influence. Third, the BOS has insufficient information and resources. Although the BOS is able to demand a director rectify

a good chance for the BOS to represent the interests of stakeholders. And when a company is established by two or more SOEs or other state-owned investors or is wholly state-owned, the BOD shall comprise employee representatives who shall be elected through the employees' representative congress, the staff and workers' general meeting or in other ways.[19] Of course, the BOD of any other LLC and JSLC may also comprise the representatives of employees of the company concerned.[20]

Putting employees on the board is a large step forward and a long cherished wish for many stakeholder model proponents. Thus it is not an overstatement to say the interests of stakeholders, particularly employees' interests, are heavily weighted by providing a channel for employee participation at the board level, which is generally regarded as an effective way to carry out the stakeholder model in practice.[21] At the very least, the strong emphasis on the interests of employees among other things implies a leaning towards the stakeholder model by policy-makers.

6.3.2 Social and political responsibilities

In addition to the significant role of employees in the corporate governance system, China is the first country explicitly stipulating mandatory social responsibility in their statutes.[22] Article 5 of *Company Law 2005* stipulates: "in its operational activities, a company shall . . . assume social responsibility". Although without any detailed contents and remedies, it is not merely exhortatory or educational. As Colin Hawes explains, this provision along with others under the first chapter of *Company Law 2005* entitled *General Provision* have significant influence on the corporate governance and management of companies in China due to the prevailing political and corporate culture.[23]

Moreover, all centrally controlled corporations (*yang qi*), normally the largest and most important companies controlled by the central government in China, are required to protect the interests of employees and promote a balance between economic returns, social returns and employee interests by the State-owned Assets Supervision and Administration Commission of the State Council, which performs investor's responsibilities, and supervises and manages the state-owned

---

his wrongful act if it damages the company's interests, on the one hand the BOS would find it hard to obtain such information at first as the BOD is not required to report to the BOS. On the other, even if the wrongful act is discovered, there is little the BOS can do. As discussed above, the BOS cannot remove an incompetent director, and there is nothing they can do if a wrongdoer refuses to rectify their behaviour: the best they can do is to make a proposal to the shareholders' meeting.

19 Articles 45 and 68 of *Company Law 2005*.

20 Articles 45 and 109 of *Company Law 2005*.

21 For example, it is generally agreed that employee representatives on the supervisory board under the German dual-board structure will help to deter behaviours that maximise shareholder profits by externalising risks or costs to employees or other stakeholders.

22 Colin Hawes, 'Interpreting the PRC Company Law through the Lens of Chinese Political and Corporate Culture' (2007) 30 *University of New South Wales Law Journal* 813, 820.

23 Ibid. 814.

assets of the enterprises under the supervision of the central government and enhances the management of state-owned assets.[24]

The rationale, as Chinese corporate law scholars argue, is "to prevent companies maximising their interests at the expense of other people and the community".[25] This is not inconsistent with China's socialist ideology. Social responsibility, improving social return in other words, becomes an important foundation of China's corporate governance system. The interests of shareholders and those of employees, creditors, suppliers, customers, local communities and the environment are in parallel. As explained in Chapters 2 and 5, there is a lack of justification for why one should prevail over the other.

Similar to other Chinese statutes, the purpose of the *Company Law 2005* is clearly stated in its first article. As discussed earlier, the lawful rights and interests of shareholders are not the only focus, at least at the statutory level. Along with maintaining the socialist economic order and promoting the development of the socialist market economy, the interests of the company and its creditors among others are the purpose of Chinese company law. This logically leads to the premise that stakeholders should also be included in the corporate objective. And there are sufficient reasons to question the suitability of SWM as the corporate objective in China.

As discussed in Chapter 4, the political deterrent in China's corporate governance system cannot be ignored. The enormous influence of politics and socialist ideology could also help in understanding the corporate objective in China. First of all, the socialist nature of China determines that large public companies, especially state-owned or state-controlled ones have more responsibilities. As reported by Xinhua Agency, China's official state news agency, there are three types of responsibility, including economic, social and political responsibility, and political responsibility is as important as economic responsibility.[26] Large public companies controlled by the state are the foundation of socialism and undertake the obligation of maintaining the socialist economic order.[27] Further, according to article 19 of *Company Law 2005*, an organization of the Chinese Communist Party (hereafter, CPC) shall, according to the *Charter of the CPC*, be established in the company to carry out the activities of the CPC. And the company shall provide the necessary conditions for the CPC's activities. This applies to all companies regardless of size or ownership structure. It should also be borne in mind that "upholding the leadership by the CPC" is one of the "Four Basic Principles" brought forward by the paramount leader Deng Xiaoping.[28] The chairman of the

---

24 Article 10 of *Guiding Opinion on Strengthening the Building of Corporate Culture in Centrally-Controlled Corporations* at www.sasac.gov.cn/gzjg/xcgz/200504190137.htm [accessed 1 March 2017].

25 Baoshu Wang and Hui Huang, 'China's New Company Law and Securities Law: An Overview and Assessment' (2006) 19 *Australian Journal of Corporate Law* 229, 235.

26 It is argued at least for SOEs, that the political responsibility is no less important than the responsibility to increase economic efficiency. Yu (n 1).

27 Ibid.

28 "Four Basic Principles" as an important content was attached to the party's constitution in the *Thirteenth CPC National Congress* in October 1987. "Upholding Party's leadership" along

board or sometimes the general manager as the key person would at the same time often be the secretary of the party of the company, especially where the state has a large stake. Not surprisingly, in addition to a company's political responsibility, directors if they are party members could be required to uphold the CPC's policies and guidelines, which are of course much broader than the narrow focus on shareholders' economic interests.

An empirical study jointly conducted by the World Bank and the China Centre for Economic Research at Peking University found that ensuring social stability and harmony, promoting economic development and national prosperity, increasing job opportunities, easing national employment pressure and protecting the environment among others are recognised by CEOs in both SOEs and non-stated-owned companies as responsibilities of their companies.[29] It is not difficult to find that providing employment opportunities, supporting the public good, protecting the environment etc. could also be seen as political responsibilities, as these objectives correspond to the central government's policy. Companies are expected to effectively back the state to fulfil these tasks. This tells us that although improving corporate profits to increase the tax revenue to the state is critical, other social and political responsibilities mentioned earlier are no less important. SWM is therefore too narrow to cover these wider corporate responsibilities. Even for large companies not controlled by the state, there is great room for social and political responsibilities to function.[30]

6.4 Looking forward: the possibility to adopt a broader objective

Admittedly, *shareholders* do and can play an important role not only in corporate governance but also in the whole Chinese economy. However, the importance of shareholder protection does not necessarily imply other stakeholders' interests are not important or could be subordinated. A company is much more than a simple aggregate of capital provided by shareholders, and it is not able to succeed or achieve business goals in the absence of stakeholders' contributions, as explained in the foregoing chapters. Suffice it to say here, stakeholders' investments, such as the credit provided by creditors, the labour and know-how

with "keeping the socialist road" are regarded as the most important. For example, see Chao Xi, 'Transforming Chinese Enterprises: Ideology, Efficiency and Instrumentalism in the Process of Reform' in John Gillespie and Pip Nicholson (eds) *Asian Socialism and Legal Change: The Dynamics of Vietnamese and Chinese Reform* (The Australian National University and Asia Pacific Press, Canberra 2005) 97. And until now, these four cardinal principles have been treated as the foundations on which to build and develop this country.

29 Shangkun Xu and Rudai Yang, 'Indigenous Characteristics of Chinese Corporate Social Responsibility Conceptual Paradigm' (2010) 93 *Journal of Business Ethics* 321, 330.

30 For example, 53.1 per cent of the non-state-owned companies have now established grass-root Communist Party organisations, which to some extent could verify the importance of the political influence. Xutao Pan *et al.*, 'Half of Non-state-owned Enterprises have Party Organizations' *China Daily* (Beijing 30 Jun 2015) at http://paper.people.com.cn/rmrbhwb/html/2015–06/30/content_1582067.htm [accessed 1 March 2017].

provided by employees, and the services and products provided by suppliers are indispensable and essential to the success of the company.

Fortunately, it is not impossible to modify the current shareholder-centred inclination to a broader objective by including all stakeholders' benefits. First, there is no explicit expression of shareholder wealth maximisation or similar at the statutory level, which implies pursuing stakeholder interests will not meet any insurmountable legal obstacles. In other words, even under the current legislative circumstances, and without any material or sweeping change, adopting a stakeholder model will not clash with present company law legislation. Take the *Code of Corporate Governance for Listed Companies in China*, for example, it explicitly states: a listed company shall respect the legal rights of banks and other creditors, employees, consumers, suppliers, the community and other stakeholders; shall actively cooperate with its stakeholders and jointly advance the company's sustained and healthy development; shall provide the necessary means to ensure the legal rights of stakeholders.[31] Even article 86 of this *Code* mentions SWM; the latter half of the provision also shows concern for stakeholder interests, as it continues:

> While maintaining the listed company's development and maximising the benefits of shareholders, the company shall be concerned with the welfare, environmental protection and public interests of the community in which it resides, and shall pay attention to the company's social responsibility.

Perhaps more importantly, sustainable development has been recognised and included in the former Chinese President Hu Jingtao's *Scientific Outlook on Development*.[32] Making short-term wealth maximisation at the expense of long-term welfare is no longer acceptable. By the same token, maximising shareholder wealth by externalising costs, or say transferring costs to other stakeholders, would be less likely to be tolerated and ways to internalise that externalisation should be explored.

A company is comprised of various stakeholders rather than simply shareholders, and the contribution provided by stakeholders is also, if not more, vital to the survival and success of any company. Along with the socialist nature, it is not impossible for the stakeholder model to be accepted and adopted in China. In addition to the justification and rationale for stakeholder theory as explored in Chapter 5, the deficiencies of SWM, *inter alia* the externalities, short-termism, unfairness and other negative aspects as discussed in Chapter 2, could not be disregarded either. It is then optimistic to declare that the leap from a government-centred model to

---

31 See sections 81 and 82 of this code which was issued by CSRC and former State Economic and Trade Commission (now incorporated into the Ministry of Commerce of PRC) in January 2001, available at www.ecgi.org/codes/documents/code_en.pdf [accessed 1 March 2017].
32 *Scientific Outlook on Development* was raised by Mr Hu as general secretary of the Central Committee of the CPC and Chinese President in the *Eighteenth CPC National Congress* in 2012. It has become one of the guiding socio-economic principles of the CPC as well as the ruling policy in China.

a shareholder-centred model should not be the ultimate destination of corporate evolution in China; the stakeholder model could potentially be adopted in the not too distant future for the benefit of all stakeholders and the company as a whole.

Also noteworthy is that that some scholars put forward a hybrid corporate governance model, based on the convergence between the shareholder model and the stakeholder model.[33] Contrary to the traditional shareholder model which requires the company to be run for shareholder interests exclusively, adherents of the hybrid model are of the view that this model requires stakeholders' legitimate interests to be considered by directors.[34] This means the hybrid model, similar to the enlightened shareholder value (hereafter, ESV) approach discussed in Chapter 2, aims to protect entrenched shareholder interests and other stakeholder interests, although the interests of shareholders remain to be enshrined.[35] Consequently, it is thought that the hybrid model, by mixing the best practice from both shareholder and stakeholder models, could overcome the shortcomings of SWM such as short-termism and negative externalisation whilst preserving the advantages of SWM, including so-called economic efficiency.[36]

However, under such a hybrid model, even though stakeholder interests are required to be taken into account during the corporate decision-making process, the predominance of shareholder primacy is unchanged,[37] which means shareholders' interests will always prevail when there is a clash between shareholder interests and stakeholder interests. This is exactly due to the fact that maximising shareholder wealth, or say the superior status of shareholders, is the essence of these models; both the ESV approach and the hybrid model are merely instruments to achieve the ultimate goal. Although stakeholder interests could be more proactively considered and thereby protected under the hybrid model, as soon as the stakeholder interests come into conflict with shareholder interests, the guideline

---

33 For example, see Jingchen Zhao, 'Modernising Corporate Objective Debate towards a Hybrid Model' (2011) 62 *Northern Ireland Legal Quarterly* 361–390; On Kit Tam, 'Ethical Issues in the Evolution of Corporate Governance in China' (2002) 37 *Journal of Business Ethics* 303–320; Henry Wei Yeung, *Chinese Capitalism in a Global Era: Towards a Hybrid Model* (Routledge, Oxford 2004).

34 Zhao, 'Modernising Corporate Objective Debate towards a Hybrid Model' (n 33) 373 and 379.

35 The difference between the hybrid model and ESV approach is that the former emphasises more the convergence perspective. For example, Professor Zhao argues that a country that has a traditional shareholder model or stakeholder model can look to and adopt the elements from the other model in order to combine best practice from both sides. Ibid. 384.

36 Of course, it should be admitted that both the hybrid model and ESV approach are a step forward from SWM, because at least the importance of stakeholders as well as the their interests are recognized to some extent. Running companies for short-term profits is explicitly denied under these models. Nonetheless, only the stakeholder model can solve the problems in SWM fundamentally. *Supra* Chapter 5, sections 5.3.2 and 5.3.3.

37 Deryn Fisher, 'The Enlightened Shareholder – Leaving Stakeholders in the Dark: Will Section 172(1) of the Companies Act 2006 Make Directors Consider the Impact of their Decisions on Third Parties?' (2009) 20 *International Company and Commercial Law Review* 10, 12. Moreover, it is argued that the increase of socially responsible investment practice, for example, is ultimately for the benefit of shareholders. Shuangge Wen, *Shareholder Primacy and Corporate Governance: Legal Aspects, Practices, and Future Directions* (Routledge, Oxford 2013) 149.

of the so-called hybrid model will be *shareholder primacy*. This shows that protecting stakeholder interests or minimising stakeholder costs is allowed as long as it does not affect maximising shareholder interests. There is no room for SWM or its modified version to allow the interests of shareholders and stakeholders to be assessed and balanced under the same criteria. In other words, any model containing the principle that shareholder interests could unconditionally outweigh other stakeholder interests under all circumstances is still essentially a shareholder-centred model, regardless of how much it seems to other corporate governance models. That is also why the stakeholder model is perhaps the only alternative to overcoming the problems and negative aspects under SWM.[38]

In the context of China, adopting the stakeholder model may help the government to further release control over both state-owned and non-state-owned companies. The foregoing discussion reveals the Chinese government's inevitable focus on social and political causes, and it is not difficult to imagine the government's intervention in companies either directly or indirectly as long as factors other than economic profits are ignored. The history of corporate evolution has already proved that. However, if the stakeholder model can replace SWM as the corporate objective, shareholders' immediate profits will no longer be the first priority. Interests of various stakeholders will be inherently incorporated into the corporate operation, and even so-called political responsibility will be more easily reconciled.

6.5 Enforcing the stakeholder model

Enforcement, as discussed in Chapter 5, is still the Achilles' heel of the stakeholder model. Whilst it is outside the scope of this book to offer a comprehensive enforcement system for the stakeholder model due to space constraints, this section endeavours to provide some preliminary suggestions on how to facilitate the enforcement of this model in China.

To start, shareholders can remove directors from office or bring derivative actions against directors.[39] Similarly, on the grounds that the stakeholder model requires directors to run companies in the interests of all stakeholders, it would be natural to suggest that a stakeholder should be allowed to take legal action against directors if they fail to do so. However, the short-termism and rent-seeking brought about by shareholder empowerment as discussed in Chapter 3 remind us that empowering shareholders is not the optimal way to enhance shareholder value. By the same token, it may also be safe to conclude that empowering stakeholders might not be a good idea to enhance stakeholder value either.

---

38 More importantly, as discussed in detail earlier, stakeholder interests are no longer a means to an end under the stakeholder model.
39 Although it is thought that directors have to pursue maximum shareholder profits under the SWM due to directors' duties being owed to the company and there being a significant difference between shareholder interests and the best interests of the company as explored in Chapter 2, it is in fact difficult for shareholders to rely on legal action to force directors to maximise shareholder wealth. There are also practical hurdles for shareholders to overcome to exercise such rights.

As different shareholders may have different interests,[40] different stakeholders' interests may also be entirely different and competing with one other. If individual stakeholders have a straightforward route to enforcing directors' duties, directors may end up by only prioritising the interests of activists.

Instead, directors should be expected to exercise a central role in the enforcement of the stakeholder model. As repeatedly emphasised in this book, when the pressure of maximising shareholder wealth is withdrawn, the pressure for directors to pursue short-term profits or externalise costs to other stakeholders will be released. The incentive to do so will also naturally disappear if the corresponding remuneration system under SWM is altered. Consequently, the main task left is to ensure directors are not pursuing their own self-interests. Directors' fiduciary duties and duty of care and skill are the legal mechanisms by which to keep them accountable. The counterparts under Chinese *Company Law 2005*, i.e., duties of loyalty and diligence, are therefore key to ensuring directors' professionalism and trustworthiness. As a result, in order to allow directors to play a central role in implementing the stakeholder model and refraining from self-serving behaviour, the most important step is to strengthen existing directors' duties and their implementation.[41]

Before moving to the question of who could enforce such duties, it is necessary to reiterate that in principle, directors' fiduciary duties are owed to the company rather than to its members.[42] Under the current legal framework, only shareholders are able to initiate legal actions against directors. Normally speaking, if directors breach their fiduciary duties or duty of care and skill, it would hurt the interests of the company, which would in turn affect shareholder value. Shareholders may then have the incentive to bring a case against dishonest directors in the name of the company. Nonetheless, as discussed, diversified shareholders may only focus on short-term profits and be reluctant to spend time and effort on individual companies, which means they may choose to leave quietly and move on to the next company. In other words, although it is not impossible to see that shareholders would stand up and take action if directors breach their duties by shirking or pursuing self-interest activities, shareholders may not be incentivised to initiate a lawsuit in order to protect stakeholders.[43] In particular, when shareholders' interests are in conflict with stakeholders' interests, it would

---

40 *Supra* Chapter 2 footnotes 256–259 and accompanying text.
41 As discussed in Chapter 3, it is essential to ensure managerial accountability, otherwise the value of authority, namely the benefits of centralised board decision-making in the corporate context would be gone. Though the topic on how to improve fiduciary duties in China is beyond the scope of this book, it would be important to say that the key is to make existing duties of loyalty and diligence in China more enforceable and that they should serve as a deterrent against directors who dare to pursue self-interests at the expense of their company.
42 *Supra* Chapter 2 footnotes 231–233 and accompanying text.
43 It is argued that shareholders are allowed to sue derivatively not just to protect shareholders, but to protect the interests of all the members of the coalition that comprises the firm. Margaret Blair and Lynn Stout, 'A Team Production Theory of Corporate Law' (1999) 85 *Virginia Law Review* 247, 293.

not be practical to expect shareholders to initiate an action simply because those stakeholders' interests have been invaded by the directors.[44]

Whilst earlier paragraphs have already discussed that it is not a workable way to empower various stakeholders and allow them to take direct legal actions in general, one possibility is to rely on derivative actions in a restricted way. Contrary to the unfairly prejudicial action which focuses on personal grievance and redress, derivative action is argued to be a mechanism for *corporate-regarding behaviour* and achieving collective outcomes.[45] Therefore, various stakeholders with different emphases may not use the tool of derivative action to fulfil purely personal goals, but rather for corporate concerns. Although a more elaborate derivative action system should be set up to filter out potentially malicious legal actions, allowing stakeholders to initiate derivative actions against directors who breach their fiduciary duties might be a viable route to solve this dilemma.[46] After all, as long as sufficient deterrents can be established, it would be optimistic to see directors abide by their fiduciary duties, *inter alia*, and refrain from self-serving behaviour.

Moreover, the Chinese dual board structure could provide some additional safeguards. The BOS is able to enforce the directors' duties and take action against directors who breach their duties.[47] Nonetheless, currently the supervisory power of the BOS is quite soft. For example, unlike the German model in which members of the BOS have the power to appoint and dismiss members of the BOD, the BOS in China can only bring forward proposals on the removal.[48] Therefore, the BOS and its members should have more real power in practice in order to effectively monitor the BOD, and ensure the directors' accountability to serve the best interests of the company. Given that directors are not pressured to maximise shareholder profits and at the same time a supervisory board monitors directors' self-serving behaviour, directors are more likely to run companies for all stakeholder interests if SWM can be replaced by the stakeholder model.[49]

Employee representatives sitting on the board help to avoid a lopsided focus on shareholder wealth maximisation as well. Employees are one of the most

---

44 Indeed, shareholders may even benefit from directors' actions in invading stakeholders' rights, for example when directors externalise costs to stakeholders to boost shareholder profits.

45 Stephen Bottomley, *The Constitutional Corporation: Rethinking Corporate Governance* (Routledge, Oxford 2016) 166–167.

46 A constructive proposal can be borrowed from Professor Andrew Keay's argument on enforcement of his entity model. See Andrew Keay, *The Corporate Objective* (Edward Elgar, Cheltenham 2011) 254–274.

47 According to articles 54 and 152 of *Chinese Company Law 2005* (now articles 53 and 151 in *Company law 2013*), the BOS is able to file actions against directors who violate the law or breach their duties.

48 More discussion can be found in Donald Clarke, 'Lost in Translation? Corporate Transplant in China' (2006) *George Washington University Law School Public Law and Legal Theory Working Paper No.213* available at http://ssrn.com/abstract=913784 [accessed 1 March 2017] 7–8.

49 Of course, as argued in Chapter 2, the current incentive mechanism in the form of share options and conventional value judgement standards should also be transformed accordingly in order to give directors the correct incentive to run companies for the long run and not only in shareholders' interests.

important stakeholder groups in the company, and having their voice heard at board level results in a greatly improved and more balanced decision-making process. Also, these representatives are able to effectively drive the BOS to take action against directors who pursue self-interests. Nevertheless, the main weakness of employee representatives is that their concerns tend to be limited to employees' interests.[50] The principle under the stakeholder model is that all stakeholder interests should be considered and balanced during the decision-making process, but it is by no means necessary for all stakeholder groups to be represented on the board. In fact, empirical studies show that stakeholder representation on the board has no direct relation with stakeholder performance.[51] However, considering that the current mainstream remains with SWM, it is essential to have different voices at board level to avoid shareholder wealth maximisation. Therefore, having employee representatives at the moment has more benefits than disadvantages, especially in correcting the lopsided focus on shareholder value. In other words, the board composition and requirement for employee representatives in China currently is helpful in altering the corporate objective from SWM to the stakeholder model.[52] As a consequence, the detailed procedures of how to elect employee representatives to the BOS should be clarified,[53] and their corresponding rights to supervise directors should be enhanced and protected.

Increasing the obligation on disclosure is also helpful in implementing the stakeholder model. Take UK company law for example: directors of a company are required to produce strategic reports by disclosing issues regarding stakeholder interests, such as information relating to environmental matters and

50 That is also a major reason why Professor Greenfield's suggestion to have all important stakeholder groups represented on the board would not be workable. For example, see Kent Greenfield, 'Reclaiming Corporate Law in a New Gilded Age' (2008) 2 *Harvard Law and Policy Review* 1, 24. If the stakeholder directors only focus on the interests of the groups they represent, then the corporate decision-making process will end in chaos.

51 For example, see Amy Hillman, Gerald Keim and Rebecca Luce, 'Board Composition and Stakeholder Performance: Do Stakeholder Directors Make a Difference?' (2001) 40 *Business and Society* 295, 308–309.

52 However, it should be very careful when considering the effect of employee representatives. Returning to the Volkswagen case as discussed in Chapters 1 and 2, Volkswagen as a large German public company also has employee representatives siting on the supervisory board, but the emission scandal which was mainly driven by mania for profits still happened on their watch. One possible explanation is that employees or their representatives may think that increasing profits (or say saving redesign costs) can be shared at least indirectly with shareholders via bonuses and similar. This means that when shareholders' interests are not in conflict with employees' interests, it becomes difficult to expect employees to monitor corporate decisions of maximising shareholder wealth at the expense of stakeholders other than employees. As in this case, when directors chose to externalise costs to customers and the environment, employee representatives did not object. So employees, like shareholders, cannot be trustees of other stakeholders either; the solution is to replace the ideology of SWM by eliminating both the pressure and the incentive to maximise shareholder wealth. Employees and other stakeholders can then play a role in monitoring directors' self-serving behaviour to ensure the enforcement of the stakeholder model.

53 Though it is not impossible for employee representatives to be elected onto the BOD, there is no mandatory requirement for a company to do so unless it is established by two or more SOEs or is wholly state-owned. See *supra* footnote 19 and accompanying text.

employee issues.[54] On the one hand, the enhanced disclosure could help directors to acknowledge their responsibilities and encourage them to proactively consider stakeholder interests. On the other, if the information can be made more transparent or more easily accessible, directors themselves will be less likely to run a company in an unbalanced, reckless or self-serving manner.[55] Though difficulties may exist in providing the qualitative information, the inability of quantitative information to reflect intangible contributions and nonfinancial performance determines that such an enhanced disclosure is essential and a viable way to improve the traditional reporting system.[56] China definitely has long way to go to improve its quantitative and qualitative disclosure levels, which may also potentially expand the grounds for a judicial review of directors' decision-making.

We should bear in mind that changing the ideology of SWM is much more difficult than proving it is untenable. As we already know, "cultural change does not come easy".[57] Consequently, it is by no means easy for directors to suddenly change the tenet from managing companies solely for shareholders' interests to managing companies for the benefit of all stakeholders. One possible solution is through educating future corporate directors and managers. This might include modifying or updating the syllabi of law schools and business schools alike, and including a framework that is broader than simply shareholders' financial returns being the ultimate objective of the company.[58] This may be a potential way to challenge the deep-seated viewpoint of SWM and help our business leaders of the future to understand how to manage under the stakeholder model, though it would be a slow, gradual and incremental process. However, there is still a lot China can do now to directly or indirectly help the employment of the stakeholder model in China.[59]

---

54 According to Section 414C of the *Companies Act 2006*, further information about social, community and human rights issues among others should be disclosed in the case of a listed company. *Supra* Chapter 2 footnotes 249–251 and accompanying text.

55 Furthermore, the media and others could also help to expose directors' lack of accountability.

56 It is also worth noting that the conventional corporate accounting practice, i.e. only the value provided to shareholders counts towards corporate value, should be amended as well. In the context of the stakeholder model, value to other stakeholders should also be included rather than being regarded as expenditure or a cost to the company.

57 David Milman, 'Ascertaining Shareholder Wishes in UK Company Law in the 21st Century' (2010) 280 *Company Law Newsletter* 1, 5.

58 In other words, if we stop instilling our students with traditional SWM, but instead teach them about stakeholder theory and how to effectively deal with various stakeholders, when they grow up and become corporate directors and managers, it is hopeful that they will have a broader view and not treat stakeholders as a means to an end.

59 Further research in this area is still urgently needed. For example, on the grounds that the best interests of a company cannot be separated from the interests of various stakeholders, it is not impossible to use corporate interests as a proxy to realise the stakeholder model. *Supra* Chapter 5 footnote 169 and accompanying text. The value of centralised authority and the aim of avoiding sea changes to the current legal framework at this stage should also be fully considered.

Conclusion

This book contributes to the recurring theme of the corporate objective by critically re-examining conventional shareholder wealth maximisation (SWM) and the stakeholder theory in the Anglo-American sphere. More importantly, due to the significance of China on the global business stage, the book has also thoroughly discussed the objective of companies in China and endeavoured to offer some constructive suggestions on this topic, one that has been largely ignored by domestic Chinese scholars so far.

The objective of Chinese companies is largely influenced by the Anglo-American shareholder model. Although shareholder rights and private property rights were once despised, nowadays shareholders in China have extensive powers and increasingly improved status. Compared with shareholder rights in the UK and US, Chinese company law grants shareholders far more managerial powers and enables them to actively participate in corporate management. It is generally agreed by both academics and policy-makers in China that the company should serve shareholders' interests. Apart from the Western influence, this book also discusses other main reasons behind it: both complicated historical factors and current legal/political/economic factors drive the focus on shareholders' roles and powers, making them the centre of corporate governance.

Admittedly, the willingness to improve shareholder status in the corporate governance system and give them a greater say are positive steps for corporate development in China, especially when considering the evolution of corporate form and shareholder rights in its past. However, bearing in mind the conclusion from the re-examination of SWM, China should not take SWM as a corporate objective for granted.

Focus is then placed on the stakeholder theory as the alternative corporate objective. The book has justified the stakeholder model from descriptive, instrumental and normative aspects. First, increasingly more laws and best practice rules urge directors to take stakeholder interests into account, and indeed, the stakeholder relationship is a better explanation for modern large public companies. Instrumentally, due to a company's survival and success depending on the investment from various stakeholders, it is encouraging that if all stakeholders – including shareholders – are fairly well looked after, they may be more willing to "go the extra mile"; seeing them as a partnership rather than as a means would create a more co-operative and productive relationship. Normatively, the modern public company is no longer a private business, so even aside from a strictly moral perspective, a broader concern should be adopted. All people have intrinsic value. In the corporate context, all stakeholders make firm-specific investment and valuable contribution; their financial or non-financial investment is no less important to the success of the company. Non-shareholding stakeholders can also become residual claimants and residual risk-takers. Therefore, it would be unfair to give shareholders too much privilege as they are merely one group of stakeholders who contribute financial capital.

By the same token, it could be said that SWM is descriptively incorrect as its theoretical basis is not valid and no law requires such a sole focus on maximising shareholder wealth. Instrumentally, SWM is unsuitable given the failure of its economic efficiency argument. It is also normatively unsuitable as other stakeholders' investment is no less important and economic profits are not the only value. The problems of short-termism and negative externalisation under SWM can only possibly be dealt with if the stakeholder model replaces SWM as the corporate objective.

This book is also fully aware of the criticisms against the stakeholder model, and admits the model is not yet perfect. However, these problems are not unsolvable. The real stakeholder groups can be identified by utilising the attribute of legitimacy as a filtering system and the narrow interpretation of the stakeholder concept. This book has introduced the criteria of urgency and long-term sustainable development (LTSD) during the decision-making process to assist with balancing the various stakeholders' interests when there is a conflict. The capabilities of directors who are used to balancing heterogeneous shareholder interests should not be underestimated either; balancing different or competing stakeholder interests is by no means insurmountable. Third, regarding the issue of monitoring and enforceability, though there is no straightforward solution, it should not impede the final adoption of the stakeholder model, since directors and delegated managers under the stakeholder model could not have a greater scope for self-serving behaviour than at present. Further research is essential in this area to establish a more robust enforcement system. But suffice it to say, there is no necessity to grant stakeholders more power, even if the stakeholder model were to be adopted. The lesson from shareholder empowerment as a means to SWM could apply to the stakeholder model.

The inability to reconcile the stakeholder model with SWM does not mean shareholder interests and stakeholder interests cannot be harmonised. When utilising a long-term perspective and giving up a lopsided focus on one group's immediate interests, externalisation of costs or risks solely for short-term profit maximisation would be much easier to overcome. After all, shareholders are by themselves an important stakeholder group. So if improving all stakeholders' interests becomes the corporate objective, the economic interests of shareholders are also required to be well looked after. The distinction is that no one's interests could supersede others unconditionally; a case-by-case assessment using the criteria of urgency and LTSD should be adopted to balance the various interests in conflict during decision-making.

Returning to China, due to its unique history and the Western influence, the current mainstream viewpoint can be identified as being supportive of SWM as the corporate objective. From the perspective of corporate governance development, it is fair to argue that acknowledging and adopting a shareholder-centred model in China at the moment could be seen as significant progress from the previous bureaucratic control and state intervention. However, as shown above, SWM is not the appropriate corporate objective. Whilst the stakeholder model is not perfect, and further research and improvement remain essential, it is by far a more tenable corporate objective from both legal and economic aspects.

Moreover, as a socialist country in which values other than economic profit account for more weight, there are even more grounds for China to look beyond maximising shareholder wealth and to adopt the stakeholder model. In particular, the master status of the working class, companies' social and political responsibilities, and the sustainable development requirement determine that prioritising shareholders above all other stakeholders is not appropriate, whereas a broader objective is a better fit. The current legal framework also provides opportunities for accommodating the stakeholder model without any sea change. Further, the two-tier board structure with employee representatives sitting on the supervisory board makes it easier for stakeholders like employees to participate and, to some extent, ensure the implementation of the stakeholder model. Though further research in the field of enforcement is still required, the stakeholder model is in general more suitable than SWM as the corporate objective for companies in China.

The lesson from shareholder empowerment as a means to shareholder wealth maximisation shows that extensive shareholder power would go against shareholder value even in the context of SWM. As a result, it is worth restraining shareholder empowerment in order to overcome the potential pressure from activists to excessively pursue short-term profits or special interests. Although it is necessary to continue to improve directors' managerial accountability, ensuring independence on the board is not in conflict with this. In particular, considering the benefits of centralised authority, there are strong reasons to build a more independent board system in China. By the same token, empowering stakeholders is not essential to the stakeholder model. The board of directors should be expected to exercise a critical role to run the company for the interests of all legitimate stakeholders and balance various stakeholder interests.

On top of that, it will also be encouraging to consider that were a stakeholder model to be adopted and effectively implemented in China, there would be fewer grounds for government intervention which is generally considered detrimental to corporate governance. The state's political and social goals can be effectively incorporated into the stakeholder model, as social wealth maximisation represented by the aggregate of various corporate stakeholders is not inconsistent with the essence of the stakeholder model.

Index

guan ban 112–13, 138
guan du shang ban 113–14, 138, 140
guan shang he ban 113–14, 138, 140

Halsbury LC, Lord 37n43
Hamilton, Gary 116
Handy, Charles 5n22, 18n93
Hansmann, Henry 8, 45n90, 46n93, 173
Hart, Oliver 38, 60n158
Hawes, Colin 192
health and safety law 59n155
hedge funds 5, 51, 53, 74n230, 78–9,
    83, 105, 134n95
Hekman, David 175
heterogenous expectations of
    shareholders 52–3, 77–80, 100, 105,
    180, 181, 190, 198, 203
high trading frequency 11, 103–4
Hill, Charles 155n20
Hill, Jennifer 82n2
Hobbes, Thomas 98
holding periods 11, 78–9, 81, 103,
    148n139
hold-up 108, 169
homogeneity of shareholder interests
    52–3
honest mistake 88
Horwitz, Morton 36n28
hostile takeovers 66, 67, 79, 108, 124,
    164
Hu, Henry 3
Hughes, Alan 156n31
Hu Jingtao 195
human capital: firm-specific investment
    169; high-tech/ knowledge-
    based companies based on 12n52;
    proprietary justification 40;
    stakeholder theory 15–16, 17n83, 156
human rights 20, 77, 167
Hutchinson, Harry 92
hybrid corporate governance models
    196–7

idiosyncratic risk 73, 81, 134
imperfect markets 66
incentives 48–51, 67–8, 166, 199n49
incomplete contracts 19, 60, 153
incorporation 32, 35
independent legal personality of
    company: and agency theory 10;
    artificial person 73; China 133;
    contractarian theory 45; legal and

beneficial owner of its property 37;
    modern proprietary justification 39;
    and shareholder dividends 48; and
    SWM 32–3, 34–6; in UK 73
indirect externalisation 62–3
individualised products 24, 66
inequality gaps 25
influencers 155-6, 160, 165n74, 176-7
informational asymmetry: accountability
    versus authority 102; agency theory
    43; balancing conflicting interests
    174–80; and centralised decision-
    making 99–100, 104; in China 24;
    contractarian theory 41;
    non-shareholder stakeholders 12;
    short-term versus long-termism 69
infrastructure development 49
Inkpen, Andrew 57n144, 63, 176
input owners 40–1
insolvency: Chinese 119n31; effect
    on non-shareholder stakeholders
    19; effects on stakeholders 153;
    externalisation 58; insolvency law 48;
    and residual claims theory 48; and
    SWM 12, 17
institutional investors 11, 69, 100-5, 164
institutional shareholders 65-6, 80, 97,
    102-3, 164
insurance companies 103–4
interest payments 20–1, 31, 139
internal regulation 61
interpersonal networks, as sources of
    capital 116
intershareholder opportunism 105, 110
investment banks 103–4
involuntary stakeholders 156
IPOs (Initial Public Offerings) 70,
    108n158, 109
Ireland, Paddy 15, 36–7, 73, 134
irrationality 20

Japan 114
Jensen, Michael 1n2, 7n29, 9n43, 40,
    41–2, 59, 78n255, 180
job cuts 25, 58, 137, 179
Johnston, Andrew 82n1
joint stock limited companies (JSLC)
    125–6, 191–2
Jones, Thomas 20, 155n20, 159
judiciary 77, 93, 143, 183
jurisdictional limitations 61n166
justice 19, 54n130, 167, 168

For Product Safety Concerns and Information please contact our EU
representative GPSR@taylorandfrancis.com
Taylor & Francis Verlag GmbH, Kaufingerstraße 24, 80331 München, Germany

www.ingramcontent.com/pod-product-compliance
Ingram Content Group UK Ltd.
Pitfield, Milton Keynes, MK11 3LW, UK
UKHW020958180425
457613UK00019B/741